Routledge Explorations in Development Studies

This Development Studies series features innovative and original research at the regional and global scale. It promotes interdisciplinary scholarly works drawing on a wide spectrum of subject areas, in particular politics, health, economics, rural and urban studies, sociology, environment, anthropology, and conflict studies.

Topics of particular interest are globalization; emerging powers; children and youth; cities; education; media and communication; technology development; and climate change.

In terms of theory and method, rather than basing itself on any orthodoxy, the series draws broadly on the tool kit of the social sciences in general, emphasizing comparison, the analysis of the structure and processes, and the application of qualitative and quantitative methods.

Structural Transformation and Sustainable Development in the Global South
An Integrated Approach
Seung Jin Baek

Caribbean Regional Integration
A Critical Development Approach
Patsy Lewis

Leadership and Organisational Culture in Development
Challenging Exceptionalism
Violeta Schubert

New Leadership of Civil Society Organisations
Community Development and Engagement
Edited by Ibrahim Natil

European Civil Society and International Development Aid
Organisational Incentives and NGO Advocacy
Balázs Szent-Iványi

For more information about this series, please visit: www.routledge.com/Routledge-Explorations-in-Development-Studies/book-series/REDS

European Civil Society and International Development Aid

This book explains how and why European non-governmental development organisations (NGDOs) engage in advocacy towards the European Union (EU).

It analyses the heterogenous structure of the sector, with examples ranging from large multinational networks to essentially single person NGDOs. The book provides a detailed map of the topics which have featured in NGDO advocacy since 2006, arguing that NGDOs have generally been reactive in their advocacy towards the EU. The author explains how they have contested a number of policy issues on the agendas of the EU institutions, especially around the diversion of aid to manage migration and leverage private sector investments. Furthermore, some NGDOs have used the COVID-19 pandemic as an opportunity to re-package their pre-existing policy demands. Based on an analytical framework focused around three variables, namely moral vision, funding concerns, and the need to build/maintain a 'good' reputation, the book explains these advocacy choices, and argues that much of NGDO advocacy seems to be consistent with funding motivations. The author highlights the importance of moral vision and reputational concerns in moderating how far NGDOs will go with funding-driven advocacy, arguing that motivations need to be looked at in their complexity, and within the specific policy context.

Drawing on a range of quantitative and qualitative data sets to provide a rich and varied picture of the advocacy work of European development NGOs, *European Civil Society and International Development Aid* is a key reference for researchers and practitioners working in the field.

Balázs Szent-Iványi is a Reader in Politics and International Relations at Aston University, Birmingham, UK, and also holds an Associate Professor position at Corvinus University Budapest, Hungary. His research focuses on the political economy of foreign aid, with an emphasis on how foreign aid policy decisions are made in donor countries and the EU. His most recent research has been published in journals such as *Third World Quarterly*, *International Relations*, *Development Policy Review*, the *European Journal of Development Research*, *International Migration*, and *Democratization*.

European Civil Society and International Development Aid

Organisational Incentives and NGO Advocacy

Balázs Szent-Iványi

Routledge
Taylor & Francis Group
LONDON AND NEW YORK

First published 2023
by Routledge
4 Park Square, Milton Park, Abingdon, Oxon OX14 4RN

and by Routledge
605 Third Avenue, New York, NY 10158

Routledge is an imprint of the Taylor & Francis Group, an informa business

British Library Cataloguing-in-Publication Data
A catalogue record for this book is available from the British Library

Library of Congress Cataloging-in-Publication Data
A catalog record has been requested for this book

ISBN: 978-1-003-01755-4 (hbk)
ISBN: 978-1-032-36569-5 (pbk)
ISBN: 978-0-367-86187-2 (ebk)

DOI: 10.4324/9780367861872

Typeset in Goudy
by Taylor & Francis Books

To Gyöngyi, Áron, and Benedek

Contents

Illustrations

Figures

Tables

Acknowledgements

I am indebted to various excellent academic colleagues with whom I have worked and published in the past years on topics related to non-governmental organisations: Simon Lightfoot, Patrycja Rozbicka, Krisztina Szabó, András Tétényi, and Péteris F. Timofejevs. Many colleagues have commented on the manuscript of this book, as well as on previous journal articles on this topic; I am especially grateful to Tamás Barczikay, Sarah Delputte, Mark Furness, Niels Keijzer, Nadia Molenaers, Jan Orbie, Beáta Paragi, and Davide Vampa. In the past decade, I have had the pleasure to meet and interview a number of dedicated people working at different development NGOs. The interviews and the more informal conversations with them have greatly contributed to the book, and I appreciate that they have devoted their time to speak with me. I would also like to thank the editorial team at Routledge, Rosie Anderson and Helena Hurd, for guiding me throughout the writing process and being so tolerant about my constant delays to submission deadlines. Last but certainly not least, I am grateful for the support I have received over the years and especially while researching and writing this book from by family: Gyöngyi, Áron, and Benedek, as well as my parents. As usual, any remaining errors are mine.

Acronyms and abbreviations

ACP	African, Caribbean and Pacific countries
ADRA	Adventist Development and Relief Agency
APRODEV	Association of World Council of Churches Related Development Organisations in Europe
CARE	Cooperative for Assistance and Relief Everywhere
CIDSE	Coopération Internationale pour le Développement et la Solidarité (French for International Cooperation for Development and Solidarity)
CSO	Civil Society Organisation
CLONG	Comité de Liaison des Organisation Non Gouvernementales (French for NGO Liaison Committee)
CONCORD	European Confederation of Relief and Development NGOs
OECD DAC	OECD Development Assistance Committee
DEAR	Development Education and Awareness Raising
DFI	Development Finance Institution
DfID	Department for International Development (UK)
DG ECHO	Directorate-General for European Civil Protection and Humanitarian Aid Operations (European Commission)
EC	European Commission
EDF	European Development Fund
EEC	European Economic Community
EFSD	European Fund for Sustainable Development
EP	European Parliament
EU	European Union
EURODAD	European Network on Debt and Development
EUTFA	European Union Emergency Trust Fund for Africa
FDI	Foreign Direct Investment
FORS	Czech Development Cooperation Forum
FTS	Financial Transparency System
GAP	Gender Action Plan
HAND	Hungarian Association of NGOs for Development and Humanitarian Aid
IATI	International Aid Transparency Initiative

IMF	International Monetary Fund
LAPAS	Latvian Platform for Development Cooperation
LDCs	Least Developed Countries
MDGs	Millennium Development Goals
MFF	Multiannual Financial Framework
NDICI	Neighbourhood, Development and International Cooperation Instrument
NGDO	Non-Governmental Development Organisation
NGO	Non-Governmental Organisation
ODA	Official Development Assistance
OECD	Organisation for Economic Cooperation and Development
PC(S)D	Policy Coherence For (Sustainable) Development
PFD	Policy Forum on Development
SDGs	Sustainable Development Goals
STC	Save the Children
TAN	Transnational Advocacy Network
TOSSD	Total Official Support for Sustainable Development
UN	United Nations
WWF	World Wide Fund for Nature

1 Introduction

Non-governmental organisations in international development

The importance of non-governmental organisations (NGOs) in international development cooperation has increased significantly since the 1980s. In the past four decades, non-governmental development organisations (NGDOs, or development NGOs) have become officially recognised policymaking and project implementing partners for developed aid donor countries and international organisations. With the increasing weakness and even disintegration of the state in many developing countries, NGDOs have widened their participation in the delivery of a number of public services, mainly in the fields of education and health. The number of active international NGOs has increased from around 10,000 in 1980 to 37,500 in 2018 (Werker and Ahmed 2008: 75; Brass et al. 2018: 136). Their increasing importance is also reflected in the funding they receive from official aid donors: in 1980, direct official contributions to NGDOs amounted to a mere $47.6 million (about 0.2% of all development aid that year), while by 2017 this had risen to more than $3.7 billion (or 2.5% of all aid; OECD 2019a). These numbers however do not reflect the true extent of NGDO participation in development aid, as they do not include measures of the role they play as contractors implementing donor-funded development projects. Indeed, according to the OECD (2019b), a further $17 billion were channelled through NGDOs this way in 2017. In case of the World Bank, NGDOs or other civil society groups were involved in about 90% of its projects in 2018, compared to around 20% two decades earlier (Brass et al. 2018: 136).

In line with their increasing importance, the academic literature examining NGOs in international development cooperation has also expanded considerably since the 1990s. A key theme in this literature has focused on evaluating whether NGDOs truly live up to the claims their proponents make about them (Banks et al. 2015). The 'usual' pro-NGDO narrative argues that these organisations possess a number of advantages when compared to official actors in the international development system: they are more flexible, can react rapidly, are more likely to target the poor and work directly with them, and they also understand the actual needs of the poor

DOI: 10.4324/9780367861872-1

and marginalised better than others (Werker and Ahmed 2008). NGDOs can thus collect the voices of the poor, and channel these into policymaking processes. Furthermore, they have lower overhead costs and have dedicated people working for them, who are driven by moral vision and a genuine desire to do good. All these characteristics mean that NGDOs may be more effective and efficient than official donors in supporting poverty reduction, and can even work in contexts which officials donors may perceive as risky, making the 'impossible possible by doing what governments cannot or will not' (Simmons 1998). NGDOs work directly with their beneficiaries, which means they can circumvent national governments in developing countries, allowing them to support the poor even in cases where national governing institutions are weak. More broadly, the growing role of civil society in international relations supports the emergence of a more open, transparent, and norms-based global society, which in turn supports democratisation and democratic consolidation in developing countries (Keck and Sikkink 1998). NGOs have the ability to shape, monitor, and enforce policy commitments by governments and international organisations (Mathews 1997), thereby changing power relations between states and society. NGOs have been at the heart of many transnational advocacy networks and campaigns, and have had transformative effects in a number of policy areas, including women's rights, the policies of multilateral development banks (Keck and Sikkink 1998; Park 2005), banning landmines (Price 1998) or forgiving the debts of poor countries (Busby 2007).

This positive narrative, which sees NGOs/NGDOs as the 'magic bullet' (Edwards and Hulme 1995) that can solve many of the ills of developing countries, has however come under increasing scrutiny. As noted by Fisher (1997), many contributions to the early pro-NGO literature lacked actual empirical evidence beyond anecdotes, and many were ideologically driven. While some early papers, even though generally supportive of civil society and NGDOs, where not uncritical (Bratton 1989; Fowler 1991), the counter-narrative gained strength in the late 1990s, focusing on how dependence on official funding distorts the incentives and performance of NGDOs (Edwards and Hulme 1996; Cooley and Ron 2002). NGDOs, as players in the multi-billion dollar 'aid business', have strong interests in ensuring that they are able to access funding, which causes them to prioritise grant seeking at the expense of their activities on the ground (Cooley and Ron 2002). With the growth in NGDO numbers, obtaining funding has become highly competitive, and the need to gain contracts from donors has turned many Northern NGDOs into professionalised grant-seeking machines (Banks et al. 2015). In order to get funding, NGDOs need to align their work with donor priorities, thus compromising their neutrality (Carbone and Lister 2006). To build a good reputation and track record of success, they may become more risk averse and engage in 'easy wins' instead of truly tackling forms of deep deprivation and poverty (Fruttero and Gauri 2005). Due to their need to please donors, NGDOs may become more detached from their actual beneficiaries, and place more emphasis on aligning with donor priorities than the interests of the poor. Indeed, some of the largest Northern NGDOs subcontract most of their implementation work to local partners. In essence, they work similarly to aid agencies, and have lost much of their direct contact with the poor (Agg 2006). Furthermore, the rise of NGOs in development cooperation seems to have provoked a backlash from some developing country governments, who view foreign NGOs as threats to their rule. Anti-NGO legislation, making their access to funding and daily activities more difficult, has increasingly become common in developing countries (Carothers 2006; Gill 2017).

A key message from the literature is that good intentions do not automatically result in good outcomes (Bloodgood 2011). NGDOs may be driven by normative motivations and a desire to do good, but they also face organisational imperatives: they need to ensure their access to funding and thus survival, which, in turn, may require them to engage in practices which are at odds with what their normative motivations would dictate (Hill et al. 2013). Which set of motivations prevails, and how NGDOs actually behave is an empirical question, and a significant amount of research has been devoted to exploring this. Much of this research has focused on examining how the operational, i.e. project related work of NGDOs in developing countries is impacted by funding concerns. One way of looking at this has been the examination of NGDO aid allocation patterns: are moral concerns reflected in where development NGOs work, or do they follow the interests of the donors who fund them? In other words, are NGDOs more likely to work in poorer, less well governed countries, with lower levels of human development, or is their aid allocation affected by the geopolitical, strategic, and economic considerations which the literature generally agrees drive the allocation of official aid (see e.g. Hoeffler and Outram 2011)? The results are mixed, but there is none the less significant evidence of NGDOs bowing to donor pressure, at least in terms of which countries they work in. For example, there does not seem to be any difference between the patterns of official US aid allocation and the aid allocation of US-funded NGDOs, and indeed US NGDOs seem to mimic official aid allocation (Keck 2015). Nunnenkamp et al. (2009) found similar results for Swiss NGDOs, and Dreher et al. (2012) argued that German NGDOs also follow the state, and actually tend to avoid difficult situations. Koch et al. (2007) found that NGDOs tend to cluster in the same recipient countries as official donors do, reinforcing the 'aid darling/aid orphan' divide. While there are some findings in the literature to the contrary, i.e. arguing that NGDO aid allocation is impacted by moral concerns (Nancy and Yontcheva 2006; Dreher et al. 2012), these seem less prevalent.

Going beyond aid allocation between countries, a number of contributions to the literature have examined the activities on NGDOs within specific developing countries, focusing on whether their actual impacts live up to the expectations derived from the moral visions they profess. The impact of NGDOs on education, health, or governance in developing countries has especially been scrutinised in detail (see e.g. Duflo and Kremer 2005; Brass et al. 2018). While it is difficult to generalise from individual case studies, the impact of NGDO development projects seems mixed, although probably leaning more towards the positive side (Brass et al. 2018). NGDOs provide services which lead to changes in behaviour, and engage in advocacy with the goal of empowering the poor or changing government policies and performance (Salehin 2018). Relatively few of these works however ask the question explicitly of how reliance on donor funding distorts the effectiveness of NGDO projects, although related criticisms of NGDOs do come up often, such as a lack of engagement with the grassroots level, problems of legitimacy, and how their focus on service provision takes their attention away from political activism (Rahman 2006). However, the papers which do look more explicitly into the impact of funding concerns on NGDO behaviour, raise substantial issues. Cooley and Ron (2002) for example documented how the need to renew contracts with donors had led NGDOs to turn a blind eye towards the misuse of aid by the final beneficiaries. Fruttero and Gauri (2005) showed that NGDOs may focus on visible measures such as expanding their coverage, which may be at odds with tackling entrenched forms of poverty. Competition for funding forces NGDOs to align with donor priorities (Epstein and Gang 2006), although some NGDOs make significant efforts to fight back and assert their autonomy (Elbers and Arts 2011).

The literature has mainly focused on how donor dependence and organisational imperatives impact the development work of NGDOs 'on the ground'. Implementing projects and programmes in developing countries is not the only activity of NGDOs, however. NGDOs also work in development education and awareness raising (DEAR) in donor countries; have important roles in holding official donors to account in terms of the quality and quantity of their foreign aid; and engage in advocacy and lobbying to shape the official development policies of these countries. Dependence on donor funding may, on the one hand, make NGDOs more reluctant to confront the donors and 'speak the truth to power'. On the other hand, donor dependence may change the nature of NGDO advocacy, making them act in a more rent-seeking way and lobby for policy change which is favourable for their own access to funding. However, questions related to how exactly dependence on donor funding impacts development NGO advocacy have only marginally been addressed in the literature (see e.g. Bloodgood 2011; Bloodgood and Tremblay-Boire 2017), and with a strong focus on US organisations.

The relative neglect of this topic in the case of development NGOs is all the more surprising given that it does feature in the broader literature on NGOs. It is well documented, for example, how international human rights NGOs face dilemmas between funding concerns and advocacy (Hill et al. 2013), or how groups engaged in domestic social service delivery in the US change the content of their advocacy when dependent on government contracts (Mosley 2012). How the tensions between the content, style and degree of advocacy and the need to access resources from donors plays out specifically in case of development NGOs is relatively under-researched.

Aims and overview of the argument

The aim of this book is to contribute to filling this gap in the literature, by focusing on the advocacy work of European NGDOs. Specifically, the book is structured around five key objectives. First, it aims to map the European development NGO community and its advocacy behaviour. Second, it analyses the contents of European development NGO advocacy, focusing on identifying what topics, norms, and practices NGDOs are particularly vocal on in their advocacy, and which are the ones they neglect. Third, the book examines the funding of European NGDOs, with a view to establishing patterns in terms of funding structures and EU-wide trends and differences. The fourth aim is to analyse if, and how various motivations to engage in advocacy, including concerns on accessing funding, distort the advocacy behaviour of European NGDOs, in particular towards the development cooperation policies of the EU, managed by the European Commission (EC). The final aim is to examine NGDO advocacy during the COVID-19 pandemic, and analyse how various motivations of NGDOs shaped this advocacy.

The book is structured around these five aims: each of them is dealt with in a separate chapter. Following a presentation of the book's overarching theoretical framework in Chapter 2, Chapters 3 to 5 present the analysis on the first three objectives respectively. The fourth objective is discussed in Chapter 6, followed by a detailed case study in Chapter 7.Chapter 8 deals with the final objective, NGDO advocacy during the COVID-19 pandemic. To give a sense of the book's methods, arguments, and main findings, the remainder of this section provides an overview of each chapter.

Following this Introduction, Chapter 2 provides a theoretical framing for understanding how development NGOs engage in advocacy towards donors, and how various sets of motivations may influence these activities. The chapter builds on the literature on international NGO advocacy, but adapts it to the specific case of NGDOs. As opposed to other NGOs, such as human rights groups, which have possibly been the most important subjects of the international NGO advocacy literature (see e.g. Hafner-Burton 2008; Hendrix and Wong 2013; Murdie and Davis 2012; Hill et al. 2013), development NGOs have a number of unique characteristics. Most importantly, they are not only engaged in advocacy, but often also serve as contractors for the same organisations and governments whose policies they seek to change through advocacy. The theoretical framework therefore needs to account for the different incentives NGDOs face, and provide insights into the determinants of which incentive becomes dominant under which conditions, and how this affects advocacy.

The theoretical framework groups the incentives of development NGOs into three broad categories: moral, organisational/financial, and reputational. Moral incentives are clearly important drivers for NGDOs, especially on the level of staff. There is abundant evidence in the literature that most of the people working for these organisations are driven by a genuine desire to do, what they perceive as, 'good' (Werker and Ahmed 2008). These moral drivers are almost always reflected in the mission statements of the organisations as well. Organisational incentives, most importantly the need to secure funding from individual grassroots donations, grants and contracts from donors and other sources, as well as attracting volunteers and professional staff, may however complicate how development NGOs act in reality, and can compromise the moral drivers. Reputational incentives, which refer to the image NGDOs wish to promote of themselves, can moderate the impact of financial incentives. Reputational incentives are not always easy to separate from moral incentives, and indeed a good part of an NGDO's reputation comes from whether it lives up to its moral commitments. But there are other sources of good reputation as well: doing effective development work, for example, can also establish an NGDO as a good and reliable partner for official donors.

A number of factors will determine whether moral, organisational, or reputational incentives prevail as drivers of advocacy. These include the exact funding structure of specific development NGOs, organisational size, as well as characteristics of the specifics policy issue, such as its degree of politicisation. The conflict between the different sets of incentives determines the issues NGDOs include in their advocacy, and what policy changes they call for. For example, if organisational interests prevail, development NGOs may be less keen on calling for policy change which, while beneficial for the global poor, may harm their own access to funding. Untying aid from donor country exports is usually cited as an example of this problem: while it is almost universally accepted that tied aid is not as valuable for recipient countries as untied aid, Northern development NGOs benefit if their home country's aid is tied, as it results in lower competition (Carbone 2006). These and other conflicts of interest may incentivise development NGOs to dampen their criticism of donor policies, or refrain from certain forms of advocacy altogether. NGDO advocacy may become more insider, and groups may eschew visible forms of advocacy such as initiating mass campaigns. Chapter 2 elaborates these possibilities in detail in order to arrive at a concise yet relevant theoretical framework for the book, which informs the analysis of all five of the book's main objectives.

Chapter 3 focuses on addressing the first objective of the book, mapping the European development NGO community and making some general observations around its advocacy behaviour. First, it provides an overview of the sector's recent history. There have been some historical accounts of the European NGDO sector (see Carbone 2006; Hurt 2006), but more recent developments, especially since the creation of the European Confederation of Relief and Development NGOs (CONCORD) as a single advocacy body for the sector towards the EU in 2003, have received little attention.

Second, and building on this historical overview, Chapter 3 introduces the actors in the European development NGO sector, and provides a picture of the sector's population's ecology. Studies focusing on population ecology have been common in the interest group literature (see e.g. Nownes 2004), but there is little understanding of the European development NGO sector's structure. The chapter therefore looks into how organisations in this sector can be grouped, what hierarchy is present, how they link together, and how the sector engages in advocacy. The main data sources for mapping the sector include the European Transparency Register, a database of all lobby organisation registered with the EU, the list of CONCORD's members, and those of member state level development NGO associations (often called platforms). The mapping exercise reveals that European development NGOs are a highly heterogeneous group, ranging from large, professionalised, transnational networks which have larger development aid budgets than many official donor countries do, all the way to 'citizen's initiatives' (Pollet et al. 2014), which are basically single-person NGOs. Clearly, a vast section of these organisations does not engage in direct advocacy, especially not on the EU level, thus it is vital to understand which are the organisations that actually do.

A third aspect of Chapter 3 is to provide a mapping of the sector's engagement in advocacy in terms of approaches and techniques. The literatures on interest groups, NGOs, and social movements all study advocacy strategies, tools and repertoires of action extensively (see e.g. Della Porta and Diani 2006; Tarrow 2011; Rozbicka and Szent-Iványi 2020), and the chapter provides a mapping of the techniques most frequently used by the NGDO sector. Generally, development NGOs seem to use insider tactics, such as taking part in meetings and consultations, submitting written responses, or issuing professional publications based on facts and research. However, there is evidence of shifts, at certain times, to more outsider tactics aimed at mobilizing public opinion, such as during the 2015 European refugee crisis (see also Rozbicka and Szent-Iványi 2020).

Chapter 4 proceeds to examine the *contents* of development NGO advocacy along the lines of the book's second objective. This chapter maps the main issues which have entered the advocacy of the European development NGO community between 2006 and 2018. To determine what main issues development NGOs have put on their advocacy agenda, the chapter uses qualitative text analysis, looking at the publications of CONCORD, and as a case study of an individual NGDO, research by Oxfam. In the case of CONCORD, the chapter first examines its flagship annual AidWatch Reports between 2006 and 2018, to identify the main themes and topics. This exercise provides a detailed list of topics NGDOs promote in their advocacy. Furthermore, given the fact that the mapping covers 12 years, it allows the identification of when a specific topic entered advocacy, and how the relative emphasis NGDOs placed on it varied through time. Comparing this dynamic advocacy topic map with the issues on the EU's development policy agenda makes it possible to judge how proactive NGDOs have been in their advocacy. In other words, does NGDO advocacy mainly react to policy proposals which the EU institutions are already debating, or do NGDOs act in a more proactive manner and push for the inclusion of new topics which are not on the policy agenda? Similar topic mappings are also carried out in the chapter for a number of further publications by CONCORD, going beyond the AidWatch Reports, and for advocacy publications by Oxfam.

The analysis shows evidence of both reactive and proactive advocacy: development NGOs have come up with some creative ideas and solutions, which they have advocated for heavily, most notably, the concept of 'genuine' aid, which calls on EU member states to change their reporting of official development assistance (ODA) to only include expenditure which actually leaves the donor country. Calling on donors to stop inflating their aid figures with debt relief, refugee costs, or tied aid has been a perennial feature of CONCORD's advocacy since 2006. Another example of proactive advocacy includes calls for ensuring that climate finance provided by donors is additional to existing development aid commitments. NGDOs have developed rather detailed technical guidelines on how donors should measure and report their aid for climate change mitigation and adaptation, with the aim of ensuring that existing development aid commitments are not simply 'repackaged' by donors as climate aid.

In many other areas however, development NGO advocacy seems to have been much more reactive. There is clear evidence that NGDO advocacy follows the topics which are emphasised by the EC. For example, after the EC published a policy document entitled Agenda for Change in 2011 (European Commission 2011), which (among other topics) proposed using EU aid to leverage development resources from the private sector, NGDO advocacy quickly reoriented its focus to the problems of relying on the for-profit private sector in development. NGDOs were similarly reactive during the 2015 European refugee crisis: they heavily criticised the EU's shift towards using aid to reduce migration flows, and emphasised the positive contributions migration from developing to developed countries has for poverty reduction.

Chapter 5 analyses the funding of European development NGOs, which is the third objective of the book. Organisations can receive income from official grants (both from member states, the EC, and other multilateral donors), grassroots donations, grants from private philanthropic foundations (although these are less common in Europe than they are in the United States), and can even have their own (commercial) income, such as through charity stores. The EU provides a multilevel funding environment for development NGOs, and they can engage in 'venue-shopping' to ensure an optimal funding mix (Sanchez Salgado 2017). There are variations between how member states fund their NGDO communities, leading to different funding mixes. France, for example, has a relatively weak national NGDO funding system, which forces these organisations to seek funding on the EU level. In federal countries like Belgium, the regional level can also provide significant funding for development NGOs (Molenaers et al. 2014).

Given the size and heterogeneity of the European development NGO sector identified in Chapter 3, it is difficult to establish clear sector-wide patterns in funding which would take into account all forms of funding for all types of organisations. The chapter adopts two key methods. First, it uses the EU's Financial Transparency System to assess patterns of EU-level NGDO funding. This online database includes details of all contracts and grants awarded by the EU institutions, including those to NGDOs funded under the EU's development policy. This dataset allows the identification of the largest beneficiary NGDOs of EU funding. By looking at the home countries of NGDOs winning EU development funding, the dataset also provides a glimpse into the relative strengths and weaknesses of the national level development NGO sectors. While some research on NGOs has already made use of this and similar EU transparency databases (see e.g. Nancy and Yontcheva 2006; Mahoney and Beckstrand 2011; Sanchez Salgado 2014; Szent-Iványi 2014), none has specifically focused on determining similar key characteristics of the beneficiaries of the EU's development funding.

Going beyond EU funding and examining the national, regional, and grassroots funding sources of development NGOs poses a number of challenges. There is no single comparable EU-wide database where information on national level funding would be available, and wide disparities in terms of transparency across member states make the construction of any such dataset prohibitive. Similarly, there are no registers on levels of grassroots funding received by NGOs. In order to overcome these problems, the second data collection approach looks into the financial accounts of selected NGDOs. Most of the larger groups and networks are highly transparent and provide detailed breakdowns of their funding sources. The chapter analyses the accounts of the 20 largest recipients of EU funding. While this approach does not allow generalisation for the entire European development NGO community, it does allow the analysis of the balance between various forms of official funding and private donations for the NGDOs which are most likely to be active in advocacy.

On the one hand, the findings from these two approaches confirm some well-known details from the literature, for example how Western European NGDOs are much more successful in winning funding than Eastern ones (cf. Szent-Iványi 2014). On the other hand, some interesting new findings emerge. At least for the largest development NGOs, EU funding is not a major source of revenues. These organisations have highly diversified and resilient funding streams. This diversity of funding streams implies that Western NGDOs need to satisfy multiple constituencies, sometimes with conflicting preferences, in order to ensure their access to funding. Some smaller NGDOs however, especially ones from the Eastern member states, are highly dependent on official funding, especially from their home country governments.

Chapters 6 and 7 identify links between development NGO motivations and advocacy behaviour, addressing the fourth objective of the book on how these motivations may distort advocacy towards the EU.

Chapter 6 uses the theoretical framework from Chapter 2 to analyse the drivers behind six of the main themes in development NGO advocacy, identified in Chapter 4: increasing aid volumes, aid effectiveness, aid allocation, managing migration, climate aid, and private sector aid. The chapter discusses how policy changes proposed by the EU or called for by NGDOs in these six themes would impact NGDO access to funding, and also how they relate to NGDO moral visions and how politicised they are. The advocacy topic map presented in Chapter 4 provides much of the data for this analysis, which is further complemented by 31 qualitative interviews carried out between 2012 and 2017 with NGDO officials in Brussels (working at CONCORD and other networks) and various member state capitals (mainly from national NGDO platforms). The interviews focused on a number of topics related to NGDO advocacy, and contain a significant degree of information on the process of how NGDOs decide which topics they place on their advocacy. This allows teasing out stronger cause-effect arguments between the contents of NGDO advocacy and their motivations.

A key finding is that a significant part of development NGO advocacy behaviour is consistent with the funding hypothesis: a number of policy changes which NGDOs call for, including increasing the amount of aid, would enhance their own access to funding. Significant parts of their advocacy are very clearly driven by organisational interests, such as calls for their own greater involvement in policy making, or advocacy specifically focused on the terms and conditions of EU and member state grant funding. It is also telling that advocacy on topics which might have a negative impact on NGDO access to funding is much weaker: for example, while NGDOs have championed topics like aid effectiveness, they have been rather selective in which specific aspects of this broad concept they address. NGDOs put heavy emphasis on increasing the transparency of aid, but talk less about aid effectiveness norms like budget support or the division of labour among donors, which may harm their access to funding.

While the interviews provide some evidence of the impact of funding concerns on advocacy, it is also clear that NGDOs need to balance these with their moral vision and reputational concerns, the latter may be especially important if a topic is highly politicised. Politicisation matters strongly, and generally, as expected, greater politicisation leads to more morally-driven advocacy. This is especially visible in the case of using aid to manage migration: the topic was highly politicised in Europe following the 2015 migration crisis, and NGDO advocacy was very much aligned with moral vision. The analysis shows that NGDO motivations need to be looked at in the policy context. They also need to be considered jointly, as they will have different interplays in each context. The chapter concludes that while funding concerns are undoubtedly present, it would be a strong exaggeration to say that this is the only, or even the most important driver of NGDO advocacy. The empirical analysis confirms theoretical expectations on the multiple incentives NGDOs face, and also provides evidence of organisational imperatives which actually ensure that they behave in ways which are consistent with their declared normative priorities.

Chapter 7 takes the arguments in Chapter 6 further, and examines how NGDOs have engaged with the European Union Emergency Trust Fund for Africa (EUTFA). The fund was set up in 2015, with the goal of supporting the EU's migration management policies towards Africa, aiming to address the root causes of migration. It provides an example of a funding instrument where NGDO moral motivations clash with funding considerations. NGDOs have put forward positive views about migration and have been vocal about protecting the rights and well-being of refugees, however, the EUTFA also provided them with new opportunities for accessing funding. The chapter maps NGDO advocacy specifically towards the EUTFA, and finds that they have vocally rejected using aid to manage migration and have pointed out a number of flaws in the EUTFA. Despite this however, there has been significant NGDO participation in implementing actions from the EUTFA, meaning that they benefitted from it financially. This seems to imply a contradiction: while NGDOs 'talk the talk, they do not walk the walk'. However, the chapter argues that this contradiction is smaller than it may first appear. Following a quantitative analysis of the determinants of NGDO participation in EUTFA projects using Probit regression analysis, the chapter finds that NGDOs were actually highly selective in terms of the types of EUTFA projects they participated in. The range of projects funded under the EUTFA was actually very broad, and included hard security type border management support, interventions which promoted the return and readmission of migrants, funding for supporting livelihoods in home countries, as well as ones aimed at addressing the needs of refugees. NGDOs have steered away from the types of projects that were not compatible with their moral vision, and have mainly engaged with ones aimed at protecting and empowering refugees, and supporting resilience in home country communities. They did not engage with border management type projects, or ones which aimed at promoting and enhancing the return and readmission of migrants.

Clearly, a fully principled approach would have been for NGDOs to boycott the EUTFA entirely, but this is perhaps an unrealistic expectation given the competitive funding environment they are in. Instead, they have been selective in the types of projects they participate in, and have used advocacy to signal their concerns and moral positions towards their stakeholders. This approach allowed them to project a reputation as morally driven actors, while also benefitting from EUTFA funding.

The final aim of this book is to examine NGDO advocacy towards the EU during the COVID-19 pandemic, which is addressed in Chapter 8. The pandemic has created a new humanitarian emergency in the countries of the Global South, and has also threatened to reverse decades of development gains. Chapter 8 first examines the ways through which the pandemic has hit developing countries, focusing on three channels: (1) the health effects, (2) the effects of local lockdowns and other measures to slow the spread of the virus, and (3) the impacts of decisions made in the developed world, including lockdown measures, but also purchases of equipment, treatments and vaccines. It is important to get a sense of these effects, as policy responses to supporting the lives and livelihoods of people, especially the poor, need to be tailored to these. The chapter therefore discusses the 'ideal' policy responses, focusing on recommendations from various academics and think tanks. Most importantly, cash and food transfers to the poor have been identified as a key measure to support the poor, and other suggested policy responses include increasing healthcare aid and ensuring access to equipment and vaccines, support for education for the most vulnerable, and actions related to debt.

Chapter 8 compares NGDO advocacy to this ideal set of policies, and asks whether NGDO advocacy has focused on promoting these, or whether it reflects other NGDO priorities or motivations, building on the theoretical framework from Chapter 2. Using similar qualitative text analysis as in Chapter 4, the chapter analyses advocacy publications from CONCORD, Oxfam, and also Save the Children (STC). CONCORD's COVID-19 advocacy included a wide range of topics, some of which related directly to the pandemic and were very closely linked to the issues that needed urgent donor attention identified above. Other advocacy topics however were are much broader, with only more tenuous links to the pandemic: CONCORD used the pandemic to call for broad systemic change to create a more equitable and sustainable world. While Oxfam's advocacy was similarly broad, that of STC was much more focused on the pandemic, and specifically on supporting the education and rights of children during these difficult times.

Explaining these patterns, the broad messages of Oxfam and CONCORD were aligned with their moral visions, which can be traced back, in case of Oxfam, to a broad mandate and set of activities, and in case of CONCORD, to its nature as an umbrella group which needed to put forward common denominator positions that all of its members aligned with. STC's moral vision was focused more narrowly, on (vulnerable) children, which allowed for more focused advocacy messages. The extremely high politicisation of the COVID-19 pandemic has given incentives for organisations to package their pre-existing advocacy messages into their COVID-related advocacy. Oxfam, which was less dependent on official and EU funding for its programmes than STC seemed to have been keener to do this, while STC may have been more cautious not to include messages and demands that are less compatible with the EU's world view, and thus jeopardise its potential access to funds.

The final, concluding chapter summarises the main and findings of the book along the five objectives and reflects on these. The most important overarching conclusion is a call for a much more nuanced conceptualisation of development NGOs in the development studies literature. NGOs are driven by a complex set of motivations, and while NGO advocacy is definitely influenced by funding concerns, there are limits as to how far these organisations can go with this. The need to ensure credibility weighs heavily, and ensures that by and large, European development NGOs can indeed be seen as representatives of Southern interests. The concluding chapter also discusses two areas for future research in light of the findings: the effectiveness of NGDO advocacy, and what more grassroots funding would mean for advocacy.

Relevance and contributions

The book makes three important contributions. First, it expands the literature on development NGOs by providing a more systematic account of the links between the motivations that drive these organisations and their advocacy behaviour, with a focus on European groups. While there have been some contributions looking into the links between NGO funding and advocacy in general (see Mosley 2012; Hill et al. 2013), as well as the impact of development NGOs on policy outcomes in developing countries, there has been relatively little work on the advocacy of Northern development NGOs towards the EU and their own national governments. Exploring this topic, using mainly qualitative methods, provides a detailed understanding of what European NGDOs lobby for, how, and why.

Second, given how the book puts a strong emphasis on the advocacy of NGDOs towards the EU institutions, it provides contributions to the literature on EU development policy. While this literature has not neglected European NGDOs, it has tended to centre heavily on the EU institutions and member states when analysing how policy decisions are made and implemented. Contributions to this literature have examined how non-state actors influence specific aspects of EU development policy (see e.g. Holden 2019 on the links between trade and development), and the book adds to this literature by providing a detailed account of the advocacy carried out by development NGOs between 2006 and 2018 (and even beyond, with focus on the EUFTA and the COVID-19 pandemic).

Third, the book also contributes to the literature on interest groups. Interestingly, there have been relatively few contributions in the development studies literature which would have conceptualised NGOs as a form of interest group (see Bloodgood 2011 and Rozbicka and Szent-Iványi 2020 for notable exceptions). There are some good reasons for this: the moral motivations of NGDOs clearly set them apart from other types of interest groups, most of which exist to promote the interests of their members. However, development NGOs have organisational interests towards the development policies of donors, and there is evidence that they take these into consideration, at least to some degree, in their lobbying activities. Therefore, the book represents a call towards the interest group literature to integrate NGOs more strongly into their analysis of lobbying.

NGDOs: What organisations does this book cover?

Some clarifications are in order about the exact type of organisations this book focuses on. The book's focus is on Northern, especially European, non-governmental development organisations (NGDO or development NGO). The EU places relatively little restrictions on how it defines NGOs/NGDOs, and there is no formal EU-level definition (European Court of Auditors 2018). According to the World Bank's admittedly broad definition, NGDOs are 'private organisations that pursue activities to relieve suffering, promote the interests of the poor, protect the environment, provide basic social services or undertake community development' (World Bank 1995: 7). This definition basically includes everything from local community-based organisations run entirely by volunteers in Southern countries to large, professionalised transnational networks with origins in Northern countries, which have larger aid budgets than many official donor countries (World Vision, for example, had revenues of 2.2 billion dollars in 2017, larger than the total aid budgets of countries like Finland or Austria – see KPMG 2018).

Beyond size and their countries of origin, NGDOs also differ in terms of their activities. Some are highly specialised and focus on a single specific development challenge, while others have very broad activities addressing many aspects of poverty. Some only engage in grassroots development work in the Global South, while others may do advocacy, research, or development education in Northern countries, and some may cover all of these roles. Some large transnational NGDOs are specialised in raising funds, and subcontract most of the actual implementation work to local partners. Some NGDOs, such as community-based organisations, exist to benefit their members, while other groups provide services such as healthcare and education to specific segments of the population (Werker and Ahmed 2008: 74). A number of NGDOs are closely affiliated with churches or have religious roots.

Many contributions in the literature have tended to bundle these different organisations together when talking about NGDOs, which is a highly questionable practice given this wide diversity in origins, size, and activities. In this book, a number of limitations are made in order to narrow the focus of the organisations under study. First, the analysis only focuses on Northern NGOs which are headquartered in, or raise a significant portion of their funding in, European Union member states. There has been a significant amount of literature focusing on NGOs based in the United States (see e.g. Büthe et al. 2012), but the behaviour of European NGDOs remains comparatively understudied. While Southern NGDOs would also be a valuable field of study, the book does not deal with these organisations directly. Second, the focus in the book is on NGDOs active in the field of international development aid, i.e. foreign aid aimed at the long term promotion of sustainable poverty reduction and structural change in developing countries. Little emphasis is put on NGOs engaged in humanitarian assistance, which aim at the immediate alleviation of human suffering caused by natural or man-made crises and catastrophes. While development assistance and humanitarian aid are conceptually very different, in practice, clearly separating the two poses analytical challenges. The boundary between the two forms of aid is not always clear, and many NGDOs, especially the largest ones, engage in both. However, the separation is possible when looking at NGDO advocacy, as groups usually make clear distinctions between the two in their advocacy. Third, in terms of size, the book concentrates on two sets of actors: large NGDO networks, and advocacy associations (platforms) created by NGDOs. Large NGDOs matter not only because of their size, but also because they usually engage in the full range of NGDO activities, including both fundraising and advocacy. Transnational networks like Oxfam, ActionAid, Caritas Internationalis, or Save the Children, discussed more in Chapter 3, engage in significant and often highly visible advocacy towards national governments and international organisations, and are active on the EU level. Development NGOs also create associations specifically for advocacy purposes, which allow smaller NGDOs who may not have the capacities to engage in advocacy directly, to gain a voice. From among these, the book focuses mainly on the EU-wide 'platform of platforms', CONCORD, but also touches on member state level platforms. However, it does not analyse the advocacy activities of small NGOs directly.

Finally, a further caveat on what this book does not aim to do is in order: it does not look at the impacts and effectiveness of development NGO advocacy. NGOs engage in advocacy to achieve policy change, and their degree of success in this is definitely an issue which warrants research (see Chapter 9). However, it is beyond the scope of this book. The book aims to provide an understanding of *why* and *how* development NGOs engage in advocacy: what motivations and incentives drive these choices, and what these tell us about how development NGOs makes decisions. It is crucial to understand the drivers of NGDO advocacy first, as impacts and effectiveness need to be evaluated in light of these motivations.

References

Agg, C. (2006). Winners or Losers? NGOs in the Current Aid Paradigm. *Development* 49 (2): 15–21. https://doi.org/10.1057/palgrave.development.1100252.

Banks, N., Hulme, D., & Edwards, M. (2015). NGOs, States, and Donors Revisited: Still too Close for Comfort? *World Development* 66: 707–718. https://doi.org/10.1016/j.worlddev.2014.09.028.

Bloodgood, E. (2011). The Interest Group Analogy: International Non-governmental Advocacy Organisations in International Politics. *Review of International Studies* 37 (1): 93–120. https://doi.org/10.1017/S0260210510001051.

Bloodgood, E. & Tremblay-Boire, J. (2017). Does Government Funding Depoliticize Non-governmental Organizations? Examining Evidence from Europe. *European Political Science Review* 9 (3): 401–424. https://doi.org/10.1017/S1755773915000430.

Brass, J. N., Longhofer, W., Robinson R. S. & Schnable, A. (2018). NGOs and International Development: A Review of Thirty-five Years of Scholarship. *World Development* 112: 136–149. https://doi.org/10.1016/j.worlddev.2018.07.016.

Bratton, M. (1989). The Politics of Government-NGO Relations in Africa. *World Development* 17 (4): 569–587. https://doi.org/10.1016/0305-750X(89)90263-5.

Busby, J. W. (2007). Bono Made Jesse Helms Cry: Jubilee 2000, Debt Relief, and Moral Action in International Politics. *International Studies Quarterly* 51 (2): 247–275. https://doi.org/10.1111/j.1468-2478.2007.00451.x.

Büthe, T., Major, S. & Souza, A. (2012). The Politics of Private Foreign Aid: Humanitarian Principles, Economic Development Objectives, and Organizational Interests in NGO Private Aid Allocation. *International Organization* 66 (4): 571–607. https://doi:10.1017/S0020818312000252.

Carbone, M. & Lister, M. (2006). Introduction. Integrating Gender and Civil Society into European Union Development Policy. In: Lister, M. & Carbone, M. (eds) *New Pathways in International Development. Gender and Civil Society in EU Policy*. Aldershot: Ashgate, pp. 1–14.

Carbone, M. (2006). European NGOs in EU Development Policy: Between Frustration and Resistance. In: Lister, M. & Carbone, M. (eds) *New Pathways in International Development. Gender and Civil Society in EU Policy*. Aldershot: Ashgate, pp. 197–210.

Carothers, T. (2006). The Backlash Against Democracy Promotion. *Foreign Affairs* 85 (2): 55–68. https://doi.org/10.2307/20031911.

Cooley, A. & Ron, J. (2002). The NGO Scramble: Organizational Insecurity and the Political Economy of Transnational Action. *International Security* 27 (1): 5–39.

Della Porta, D. & Diani, M. (2006). *Social Movements: An Introduction*. Malden, MA: Blackwell.

Dreher, A., Nunnenkamp, P., Thiel, S. & Thiele, R. (2012). Aid Allocation by German NGOs: Does the Degree of Official Financing Matter? *The World Economy* 35 (11): 1448–1472. https://doi.org/10.1111/j.1467-9701.2012.01455.x.

Duflo, E. & Kremer, M. (2005). *Use of Randomization in the Evaluation of Development Effectiveness*. In: Pitman, G. K., Feinstein, O. N. & Ingram, G. K. (eds) *Evaluating Development Effectiveness*. New Brunswick: Transaction Publishers.

Edwards, M. & Hulme, D., eds (1995). *Beyond the Magic Bullet: NGO Performance and Accountability in the Post Cold-War World*. London: Earthscan.

Edwards, M. & Hulme, D. (1996). Too Close for Comfort? The Impact of Official Aid on Nongovernmental Organizations. *World Development* 6: 961–973. https://doi.org/10.1016/0305-750X(96)00019-8.

Elbers, W. & Arts, B. (2011). Keeping Body and Soul Together: Southern NGOs' Strategic Responses to Donor Constraints. *International Review of Administrative Sciences* 77 (4): 713–732. https://doi.org/10.1177/0020852311419388.

Epstein, G. S. & Gang, I. N. (2006). Contests, NGOs, and Decentralizing Aid. *Review of Development Economics* 10 (2): 285–296. https://doi.org/10.1111/j.1467-9361.2006.00318.x.

European Commission (2011). Increasing the Impact of EU Development Policy: An Agenda for Change. COM(2011) 637 final. Brussels: European Commission.

European Court of Auditors (2018) Transparency of EU Funds Implemented by NGOs: More Effort Needed. Special Report 35. https://www.eca.europa.eu/Lists/ECADocuments/SR18_35/SR_NGO_FUNDING_EN.pdf, accessed 13/01/2020.

Fisher, W. F. (1997). Doing Good? The Politics and Antipolitics of NGO Practices. *Annual Review of Anthropology* 26: 439–464. https://doi.org/10.1146/annurev.anthro.26.1.439.

Fowler, A. (1991). The Role of NGOs in Changing State-Society Relations: Perspectives from Eastern and Southern Africa. *Development Policy Review* 9 (1): 53–84. https://doi.org/10.1111/j.1467-7679.1991.tb00175.x.

Fruttero, A. & Gauri, V. (2005). The Strategic Choices of NGOs: Location Decisions in Rural Bangladesh. *The Journal of Development Studies* 41 (5): 759–787. https://doi.org/10.1080/00220380500145289.

Gill, T. M. (2017). Unpacking the World Cultural Toolkit in Socialist Venezuela: National Sovereignty, Human Rights and Anti-NGO Legislation. *Third World Quarterly* 38 (3): 621–635. https://doi.org/10.1080/01436597.2016.1199259.

Hafner-Burton, E. (2008). Sticks and stones: Naming and Shaming the Human Rights Enforcement Problem. *International Organization* 62 (4): 689–716. https://doi.org/10.1017/S0020818308080247.

Hendrix, C. & Wong, W. (2013). When is the Pen Truly Mighty? Regime Type and the Efficacy of Naming and Shaming in Curbing Human Rights Abuses. *British Journal of Political Science* 43 (3): 651–672. https://doi.org/10.1017/S0007123412000488.

Hill, D. W., Moore, W. H. & Mukherjee, B. (2013). Information Politics Versus Organizational Incentives: When are Amnesty International's "Naming and Shaming" Reports Biased? *International Studies Quarterly* 57 (2): 219–232. https://doi.org/10.1111/isqu.12022.

Hoeffler, A. & Outram, V. (2011). Need, Merit, or Self-interest? What Determines the Allocation of Aid? *Review of Development Economics* 15 (2): 237–250. https://doi.org/10.1111/j.1467-9361.2011.00605.x.

Holden, P. (2019). Finding Common Ground? European Union and European Civil Society Framing of the Role of Trade in the Sustainable Development Goals. *JCMS: Journal of Common Market Studies* 57 (5). 956–976, https://doi.org/10.1111/jcms.12862.

Hurt, S. R. (2006). Civil Society and European Union Development Policy. In: Lister, M. & Carbone, M. (eds) *New Pathways in International Development. Gender and Civil Society in EU Policy*. Aldershot: Ashgate, pp. 110–122.

Keck, M. E. & Sikkink, K. (1998). *Activists beyond Borders: Advocacy Networks in International Politics*. Ithaca: Cornell University Press.

Keck, M. (2015). Comparing the Determinants of US-funded NGO Aid Versus US Official Development Aid. *Voluntas: International Journal of Voluntary and Nonprofit Organizations* 26 (4): 1314–1336. https://doi.org/10.1007/s11266-014-9464-z.

Koch, D.-J., Dreher, A., Nunnenkamp, P. & Thiele, R. (2009). Keeping a Low profile: What Determines the Allocation of Aid by Non-governmental Organizations? *World Development* 37 (5): 902–918. https://doi.org/10.1016/j.worlddev.2008.09.004.

KPMG (2018). World Vision International and Consolidated Affiliates. Consolidated Financial Statements, September 30, 2017 and 2016. https://www.wvi.org/sites/default/files/Consolidated%20Financial%20Statements%202017%2C%202016.pdf.

Mahoney, C. & Beckstrand, M. J. (2011). Following the Money: European Union Funding of Civil Society Organizations. *JCMS: Journal of Common Market Studies* 49 (6): 1339–1361. https://doi.org/10.1111/j.1468-5965.2011.02197.x.

Mathews, J. T. (1997). Power Shift. *Foreign Affairs* 76 (1): 50–66.

Molenaers, N., Jacobs, B. & Dellepiane, S. (2014). NGOs and Aid Fragmentation: The Belgian Case. *Voluntas* 25 (2): 378–404. https://doi.org/10.1007/s11266-012-9342-5.

Mosley, J. E. (2012): Keeping the Lights On: How Government Funding Concerns Drive the Advocacy Agendas of Nonprofit Homeless Service Providers. *Journal of Public Administration Research and Theory* 22 (4): 841–866. https://doi.org/10.1093/jopart/mus003.

Murdie, A. M. & Davis, D. R. (2012): Shaming and Blaming. Using Events Data to Assess the Impact of Human Rights INGOs. *International Studies Quarterly* 56 (1): 1–16. https://doi.org/10.1111/j.1468-2478.2011.00694.x.

Nancy, G. & Yontcheva, B. (2006). Does NGO Aid go to the Poor? Empirical Evidence from Europe. IMF Working Paper WP/06/39.

Nownes, A. (2004). The Population Ecology of Interest Group Formation: Mobilizing for Gay and Lesbian Rights in the United States, 1950–98. *British Journal of Political Science* 34 (1): 49–67. https://doi.org/10.1017/S0007123403000346.

Nunnenkamp, P., Weingarth, J. & Weisser, J. (2009). Is NGO Aid Not So Different After All? Comparing the Allocation of Swiss Aid by Private and Official Donors. *European Journal of Political Economy* 25 (4): 422–438. https://doi.org/10.1016/j.ejpoleco.2009.01.001.

OECD (2019a). Total flows by donor (ODA+OOF+Private) [DAC1]. OECD.stat, https://stats.oecd.org/Index.aspx?datasetcode=TABLE1#.

OECD (2019b). *Aid for Civil Society Organisations. Statistics Based on DAC Members' Reporting to the Creditor Reporting System Database (CRS), 2016–2017*. Paris: OECD.

Park, S. (2005). How Transnational Environmental Advocacy Networks Socialize International Financial Institutions: A Case Study of the International Finance Corporation. *Global Environmental Politics* 5 (4): 95–119. https://doi.org/10.1162/152638005774785480.

Pollet, I., Habraken, R., Schulpen, L. & Huyse, H. (2014). *The Accidental Aid Worker: A Mapping of Citizen Initiatives for Global Solidarity in Europe*. Leuven: KU Leuven HIVA.

Price, R. (1998). Reversing the Gun Sights: Transnational Civil Society Targets Land Mines. *International Organization* 52 (3): 613–644. doi:10.1162/002081898550671.

Rahman, S. (2006). Development, Democracy and the NGO Sector: Theory and Evidence from Bangladesh. *Journal of Developing Societies* 22 (4): 451–473. https://doi.org/10.1177/0169796X06072650.

Rozbicka, P. and Szent-Iványi, B. (2020). European Development NGOs and the Diversion of Aid: Contestation, Fence-sitting, or Adaptation? *Development Policy Review* 38 (2): 161–179. https://doi.org/10.1111/dpr.12417.

Salehin, M. M. (2018). *Islamic NGOs in Bangladesh: Development, Piety and Neoliberal Governmentality*. London: Routledge.

Sanchez Salgado, R. (2014). Rebalancing EU Interest Representation? Associative Democracy and EU Funding of Civil Society Organizations. *JCMS Journal of Common Market Studies* 52 (2): 337–353. https://doi.org/10.1111/jcms.12092.

Sanchez Salgado, R. (2017). Europeanization of Civil Society Organizations in Times of Crisis? Exploring the Evolution Grant-seeking Strategies in the EU Multi-level System. *European Politics and Society* 18 (4): 511–528. https://doi.org/10.1080/23745118.2017.1286283.

Simmons, P. J. (1998). Learning to Live with NGOs. *Foreign Policy* 112: 82–96. https://doi.org/1149037.

Szent-Iványi, B. (2014). The EU's Support for Democratic Governance in the Eastern Neighbourhood: The Role of New Member State Transition Experience. *Europe-Asia Studies* 66 (7): 1102–1121. https://doi.org/10.1080/09668136.2014.927646.

Tarrow, S. (2011). *Power in Movement. Social Movements and Contentious Politics* (Third Edition). Cambridge: Cambridge University Press.

Werker, E. & Ahmed, F. Z. (2008). What Do Nongovernmental Organizations Do? *Journal of Economic Perspectives* 22 (2): 73–92. https://doi.org/10.1257/jep.22.2.73.

World Bank (1995). *Working with NGOs. A Practical Guide to Operational Collaboration between the World Bank and Non-Governmental Organizations*. Washington D.C.: World Bank.

2 The drivers of development NGO advocacy

Moral, reputational, and organisational concerns[1]

Introduction

The goal of this chapter is to provide a theoretical framing for understanding NGDO advocacy and the factors which may influence these activities. NGDOs face different sets of incentives which shape the forms and contents of the advocacy they engage in. The chapter groups these into three broad categories: moral, reputational and organisational incentives. While most development NGOs have been created for moral reasons and tend to attract staff who share these visions, NGDOs are also organisations which need to ensure their access to funding, expertise, and other resources in order to maintain their operations. These organisational incentives can 'contaminate' and derail advocacy based on moral vision. For example, development NGOs may be less keen on calling for policy change, which while beneficial for the global poor, may harm their own access to funding. However, NGDOs also face important incentives in terms of maintaining their reputations. Reputational pressures mean that they need to be at least *seen* as living up to their moral commitments and altruistic vision. These reputational concerns may therefore moderate the degree to which organisational incentives can actually dominate advocacy at the expense of moral vision. Using moral, organisational and reputational incentives, the chapter develops a framework which can be used to analyse NGDO advocacy and explain why these groups promote certain topics while putting relatively lower emphasis on others.

International NGO advocacy

The advocacy and campaigning work of international NGOs has been at the forefront of the scholarship dealing with these groups, mainly asking questions regarding how effective civil society is in initiating or catalysing policy, political, and even societal change, especially in developing countries (Keck and Sikkink 1998; Hafner-Burton 2008; Hendrix and Wong 2013; Murdie and Davis 2012). The impact of NGO advocacy has been a highly salient issue in the field of human rights, where a key question has focused on the

DOI: 10.4324/9780367861872-2

role of NGOs in pushing governments to reduce human rights violations and other abuses (Hafner-Burton 2008; DeMerritt 2012). Albeit to a lesser degree, the literature has also started to ask other questions around the strategies human rights and other NGOs pursue in their advocacy, and what these reveal about their motivations for advocacy. Murdie and Urpelainen (2015) for example examined how international environmental NGOs select their targets for advocacy, and argued that they are more active in countries where domestic opportunity structures are weak. Hill et al. (2013) asked whether international human rights NGOs have incentives to exaggerate claims of government abuse in their advocacy reports in order to raise their own profile in the media. However, they find only limited evidence for this in the case of Amnesty International. McPherson (2016) analysed the strategies of Mexican human rights NGOs for increasing their credibility and getting their information into the news.

While the literature on human rights groups is quite extensive, there has been relatively little work on the advocacy strategies and their determinants in case of development NGOs, although some contributions have addressed the topic indirectly (see for example Jones 2017) and more recently, directly (Rozbicka and Szent-Iványi 2020; Szent-Iványi and Timofejevs 2021).

NGDOs differ from human rights groups on a fundamental issue. Human rights NGOs are advocacy and campaign-focused organisations, and much of their other activities, such as research or developing relationships with local NGOs, are designed to serve this focus. They collect information either directly or through local partners and the media on rights abuses, analyse and compile this, and use it to put pressure on governments, international organisations, or other actors such as multinational companies, mainly through the use of publicity and 'shaming'. Advocacy by NGDOs can have similar naming and shaming elements, such as examining whether donor governments live up to the promises or vaguer moral commitments they have made on issues like aid volumes, aid effectiveness, or other policies impacting developing countries, and publicising non-compliance. However, the difference between human rights and development NGOs is that advocacy is not the main activity of the latter. All of the large development (and humanitarian) NGOs which engage in advocacy are primarily focused on doing development and relief work in Southern countries, in the forms of providing urgent humanitarian assistance as well as funding and implementing more long-term development projects. They often do this work as contractors or grantees of official donors (states and multilateral organisations), as well as other funding agencies. In fact, historically, their advocacy work grew out of their development work, as NGDOs gradually realised that fundamental change for communities in Southern countries can only come through wider political and societal transformation, both locally and internationally (see e.g. Korten 1990).

Development NGO advocacy is often, although not exclusively, aimed towards the very same governments and agencies they receive funding from.

This implies a potential conflict of interest for NGDOs, which human rights groups do not face, or face only to a much lesser degree. Development NGOs seek to promote the interests of their beneficiaries, i.e. the poor in the Global South, towards rich country governments and international organisations, which can involve being at times highly critical of their actions and policies. At the same time however, they also seek funding from these same governments and organisations, which raises questions about how critical and vocal they will actually be towards them. In other words, do concerns associated with funding outweigh the moral missions of development NGOs?

The impact of the need to secure funding on NGDO activities has long been recognised in the literature (see e.g. Edwards and Hulme 1996), but it has rarely been given systematic theoretical treatment, especially with a view on its impacts on advocacy. Classic contributions, such as the work by Edwards and Hulme (1995, 1996) or Cooley and Ron (2002) have tended to promote an overly negative view of development NGOs and portray them as heavily biased by their funding concerns, to a degree that their original missions become secondary. However, reality is rarely so simple. The world of NGDOs is highly complex and diverse (Gourevitch and Lake 2012), as the analysis focusing on their European population in Chapter 3 will demonstrate. Motivations for an organisation, especially if it is large and engaged in a wide variety of activities, are also complex. The following sections of this chapter provide a theoretical framework for understanding how the various motivations NGDOs face interact with each other and what impact they ultimately have on the advocacy of these groups, while also acknowledging diversity.

Determinants of development NGO advocacy

When deciding if, how, and when to engage in advocacy on specific policy issues related to development policy, NGDOs face three broad sets of incentives. They need to consider how it relates to their *moral missions*, how it links to their *organisational priorities*, especially in terms of funding, and how their advocacy activity will impact their *reputation*. This section examines these three incentives in turn, and their potential impact on advocacy choices.

Moral incentives

The literature on development NGOs has traditionally tended to assume that altruistic, moral incentives drive these organisations (Keck and Sikkink 1998; West 2001; de Jong 2011). Two arguments are often made to support this: first, almost all NGDOs strongly and visibly proclaim moral goals; second, the people who work for development NGOs tend to be altruistic individuals with genuine commitments to helping others.

In terms of proclaimed goals, most NGDOs were founded based on a moral vision to help those suffering, often in reaction to violent and traumatic historical events. The first humanitarian NGOs, such as the Red Cross, were created after the increasingly bloody conflicts of the second half of the 19th century to protect the victims of war. Save the Children was founded in the aftermath of the First World War, with the intention of supporting children experiencing famine in Germany, Austria-Hungary, and Russia (Save the Children 2019). Oxfam was created in 1942 to alleviate starvation in axis-occupied Greece (Oxfam 2021a). CARE was established in 1945 to provide food aid to Europeans following the Second World War. The creation of all these and many other organisations was clearly driven by the moral desire of people to help others in need and reduce their suffering. In many cases, there was a strong element of Christian faith, especially the teachings of the New Testament, on the need to care for the poor and the oppressed. This moral vision to helping those in need is reflected in the missions, goals, and values publicly stated by most development NGOs, which frequently emphasise saving lives, fighting poverty, tackling vulnerability, helping the most deprived and marginalised, achieving social justice, promoting human transformation, fighting for equality between men and women, and empowering the vulnerable (see for example CARE International 2020; World Vision 2021; Oxfam 2021b).

When it comes to development NGO workers, de Jong (2011: 21) argues that the popular (idealised) conception of NGDOs is that they are composed of 'people who work out of a sense of duty to create social justice, unmotivated by profit or politics'. Whether paid aid professionals or volunteers, NGDO workers are seen to be driven by intrinsic motivations linked to altruism and a morally driven desire to help others. The strength of moral motivations is shown by the fact that NGO workers are willing to make sacrifices for their activism: there is considerable evidence that salaries are lower in the non-profit sector than in case of comparable employment in the for-profit sector, or even public administration (Werker and Ahmed 2008; Serra et al. 2011; Fechter 2014). Also, working for a development NGO usually involves lower degrees of job security and frequent travel, not to mention the psychological strains that the job can create, and the potential health and safety risks associated with working in developing country contexts (Hindman and Fechter 2011). Many NGDO workers see themselves as activists working for a better world, for whom material rewards are secondary (Yarrow 2008).

Individuals with moral motivations are more likely to join organisations whose mission aligns with their own, and this, in turn, increases the effectiveness of the organisation in pursuing its moral mission (Serneels et al. 2010; Serra et al. 2011). This leads to a self-reinforcing process which continuously reconstructs and maintains moral vision in NGDOs as a driver of their activities.

This understanding of NGDOs, focusing on their moral motivations, paints them as 'knights in shining armour' (Bloodgood 2011), who sacrifice themselves to champion the interests of the poor in the Global South. Morally driven Northern development NGOs are expected to act as voices of the South; their advocacy should focus on representing the best interests of the people, communities, and organisations of the developing countries they work in, or globally. In this sense, Northern development NGOs are seen as mediators or conduits of the interests of the Southern poor towards policy makers in the North, and altruism should imply that their advocacy is not tainted by any interests which are not fully aligned with those of their Southern constituents.

Morally driven NGDO advocacy campaigns will therefore call for policies which are beneficial for the poor, even if they have little public support or outright hurt the interests of people or certain groups in the North (Szent-Iványi and Timofejevs 2021). They will campaign for the alleviation of global poverty, a reduction in immediate suffering, empowering the poor and respecting their rights. Specifically in the field of development aid, they will advocate for aid that is 'pro-poor', or in other words targeted at areas and sectors which have strong and direct impacts on the daily lives of the poor, most commonly in health, education, sanitation or rural development. Targeting marginalised groups, such as women or children and calling for their empowerment will also be a key part of advocacy. Moral incentives should also have an impact on the development work of NGDOs: the aid projects they implement should aim to use scarce resources to achieve maximum impact on the welfare of the poor (Unerman and O'Dwyer 2010), focusing on sectors where they can make meaningful differences. Their moral dedication allows them to work more flexibly and at lower cost than other (governmental) aid agencies (Werker and Ahmed 2008).

Organisational incentives

Academics have become increasingly pessimistic about this 'saintly' view of NGDOs driven purely by moral incentives (Brass 2012; Brass et al. 2018). Starting from the 'people' side, more critical contributions in the literature have pointed out that conceptualising NGDO workers as being driven by altruism is highly simplistic (De Jong 2011; Hindman and Fechter 2011; Okabe et al. 2019). Individuals are seldom driven by a single motivation. While it is reasonable to expect that people driven by intrinsic moral and altruistic motivations will be more likely to self-select into development NGO careers, they may have a number of other motivations as well, and even people with little altruism may find work at NGDOs. Hindman and Fechter (2011) document that due to the changing nature of development work, aid workers increasingly need to consider career logics in their choices. Subcontracting, short-term consultancies, project-based contracts and an increasing audit-culture and bureaucratisation have become the norm for development agencies, including Northern NGDOs, and these require a significant degree of personal fluidity. Workers at development NGOs not only need to take issues like benefit packages and work-life balance into account, but also need to look at the kinds of actions which would be most likely to help them get their next contract. When ‘contracts for a new project are being negotiated, agencies are looking for the engineer with the most successful track record, not the one who cares the most’ (Hindman and Fechter 2011: 7). The literature on international volunteering has similar conclusions, arguing that similarly to paid NGDO workers, volunteers are also driven by a mix of incentives, many of which can be seen as egoistic, including a quest for personal self-fulfilment and growth, the need to experience something new, or opportunities to improve future employability (Tiessen 2012; Okabe et al. 2019).

In these organisational contexts, development workers and volunteers have to constantly negotiate choices between altruism and their more selfish motivations and potentially prejudiced feelings (Vaux 2001). While most contributions in the literature agree that altruism is an important driver and the majority of development NGO workers genuinely care about the people and communities they work with (Hindman and Fechter 2011), altruism, on the personal level, has its limits which need to be taken into consideration. Furthermore, if NGDO workers are not fully driven by moral motivations, it makes sense to question the degree of moral incentives the organisations as a whole have as well.

Development NGOs are organisations. Larger NGDOs especially are highly professionalised organisations employing thousands of people around the world. To achieve the moral goals set out in their mission statements, NGDOs need to ensure their own survival through access to resources (Bloodgood 2011). Indeed, given the long-term nature of NGDO missions, these operations need to be sustained over long periods of time. NGDOs therefore ideally need sustainable and predictable flows of resources to allow long term planning, which is generally seen as essential for impactful development work.

Staff and people are one aspect of the ongoing costs NGDOs face. NGDOs need to ensure that they have the right people working for them, many of whom need to be highly skilled professionals, with expertise in project management, fundraising, finance, advocacy, communication, etc., not to mention softer skills including inter-cultural awareness or team-working (Hindman and Fechter 2011). Professionals from backgrounds in sectors like engineering, healthcare, education, or agriculture are also essential to project planning and implementation. While professionals who end up working for NGDOs may be highly committed and morally driven, and as discussed above may settle for lower salaries than in other sectors, NGDOs still have to compete for talent, and need to make efforts to retain their employees by offering competitive material compensation, including benefits, and secure employment. NGDOs also face a number of costs associated with staff, including overheads such as office space or IT equipment.

Beyond permanent staff, many NGDOs also work with volunteers, who can complement their capacities, especially in terms of grassroots fundraising or project implementation. While volunteers are generally unpaid (and in some cases they even need to cover their own work-related expenses), working with them is not costless for a development NGO: organising their work can take up the time of paid staff, and volunteers require training. Volunteers used for door-to-door canvassing-type fundraising, or as sales clerks in charity shops may require relatively little training, but sending volunteers to developing countries can incur higher costs. Some NGDOs rely heavily on the voluntary work of highly trained professionals to carry out their work: for example, Médecins Sans Frontières relies on voluntary, short-term trips by doctors and other health professional to achieve its goal of providing healthcare services to the poor (Lasker 2016).

A second aspect of the costs NGDOs face links to their operations. Implementing development projects and doing advocacy require significant amounts of funding, which usually make up the bulk of development NGO expenditures and are the main vehicles for achieving moral missions. Depending on the kind of development work NGDOs engage in, development projects can have high costs, and most organisations will argue that the demand for their work is potentially unlimited. Providing funding to local partners in developing countries, carrying out physical investments, or even projects which involve more intangible transfers of knowledge all have costs. Advocacy towards policymakers and donors also has costs: NGDOs need to be close to government bodies or multilateral agencies to ensure regular interactions and develop contacts with decision makers, journalists and other opinion formers. This requires funding for offices (potentially in expensive international cities like Brussels or Geneva), travel, participation in conferences, online and offline communication materials, etc.

The two groups of expenditure for NGDOs, staff and operations-related expenses, are of course linked: staff are very often funded from project budgets, which means that significant numbers of workers at these organisations are employed on a fixed term basis. Running the organisation and finding the resources to cover these costs, thus ensuring the NGDO's survival and continued ability to work towards its moral mission, is therefore a key incentive. In turn, maximising revenues will be a key concern for NGDOs, and these revenues will generally come from four main sources. Traditionally, and in-line with the long-standing notion of NGOs being embedded in (civil) society, and indeed being manifestations of societal activism, development NGOs have raised most of their incomes from small-scale *individual/grassroots donations*. As each donation is usually small, organisations will need to collect many of them, which can be a relatively expensive and labour-intensive task: it may require advertising in the traditional or online media, other visible campaigns, or engaging in street or door-to-door canvassing with volunteers. Despite being difficult to collect, income gained from grassroots donations can be highly valuable to NGDOs, because it usually comes with few strings attached. Of course groups need to be transparent on how they use these resources and communicate this to their donors (see the discussion on reputation below for more details), but other than that, they are free to use the resources however they see fit, provided it fits their communicated mission and objectives.

The second source of revenue comes from NGDOs working as *project implementers for official donors*. Donors and recipient governments are usually required to publish procurement calls for supplies, works, or services when implementing development projects. The exact eligibility rules for these will differ between donors, and many of these contracts, due to the nature of what is required, are not suited for development NGOs (such as building transport or energy infrastructure). But, NGDOs can have competitive advantages over businesses for specific types of contracts, especially ones which require service delivery to the poor, in areas like healthcare or education. Their not-for-profit nature, theoretically at least, means that NGDOs can offer lower prices than private businesses can. In the case of implementation contracts, NGDOs need to make choices on what to bid for, and decide whether a specific procurement call aligns with their expertise and moral vision or not.

The third source of income, *grants from official donors*, or other funders like philanthropic foundations, while conceptually different than implementing contracts for donors, raises similar dilemmas for NGDOs in terms of fit with expertise and moral vision. As opposed to working as project implementers for donors, grants usually allow NGDOs to submit bids for projects that they themselves develop. Official grants often require co-financing from NGDOs, and there are stipulations that the groups cannot make any profits from the funding. Not all government grants however are for specific projects: some governments offer longer term block grants and framework agreements to selected NGDOs, or grants to cover operating expenditures (Pratt et al. 2006).

Finally, NGDOs may also engage in *commercial activities* to raise funds. Most commonly, this takes the form of charity shops, where the organisation sells donated second-hand items, such as clothes, books, household items, furniture, etc. Such shops are extremely common in countries like the UK or Germany, and are used by a wide variety of NGOs, not just those working in development. These shops are also seen as a way of increasing name recognition, as they are usually present in town and city centres. They can thus support grassroots fundraising as well. However, due to the significant start-up costs associated with these shops, they are usually not an option for smaller groups.

To ensure financial resilience, most development NGOs, and especially the larger ones, will rely on a mix of all four income sources (see Chapter 5) and will employ professionals specialised in the various forms of fundraising: raising resources from the general population requires very different expertise than writing funding bids to official donors. Ensuring access to funding, especially renewing implementation contracts and getting grants from donors, is perhaps the most important organisational incentive faced by NGDOs (Cooley and Ron 2002; Mosley 2012). In fact, it has become even more important in the past few decades: the funding landscape is generally seen to have shifted towards greater competition since the 1990s, partially due to the growing number of NGDOs (see Chapter 3), but also due to donors shifting some of their rules on eligibility for funding. For example, in terms of nationality, untying aid from domestic procurement has been a general trend in the past decades, with the view of increasing the effectiveness of aid in terms of its developmental impacts in recipient countries. As discussed later in this book (Chapters 6 and 7), access to aid resources has also been increasingly opened up to private for-profit businesses, and due to the appearance of new purposes for aid, most notably combating climate change, new NGOs, such as ones focused on environmental protection, are also increasingly competing for aid resources.

The incentive to access funding in an increasingly competitive environment can have a number of impacts on NGDO behaviour, and has received some attention in the literature. Resource dependency theory argues that the funding sources of NGOs have a large influence on their behaviour (Molenaers et al. 2014). As agued by Amagoh (2015), the 'inherent danger for NGOs who depend on specific donors lies in the fact that the NGOs may become more like the bodies from which they attract funding, rather than the societies whose interests they intend to represent' (see also Sakue-Collins 2021 for a more radical critique). How funding concerns impact the development work of NGDOs has been well documented: there is evidence that in order to ensure access to contracts and grants, NGDOs will shift their activities to projects which are less innovative and ambitious in scope, with more readily observable outputs; they will tend to follow donors instead of going to more neglected areas; they will shift their priorities to reflect those of the donors; they will have incentives to professionalise and work along standard aid effectiveness criteria; they will be more likely to cover up failure; and their ties with local beneficiaries will weaken (see, for example: Cooley and Ron 2002; Fruttero and Gauri 2005; Banks et al. 2015; Keck 2015; Paragi 2021; although see also Davis 2019 who makes a contrary argument). Most of the literature has focused on the operational work of NGDOs, and less so on their advocacy. However, some clear theoretical ideas emerge, which give reasonable predictions as to how NGDO advocacy behaviour may be diverted from moral vision by organisational, and especially funding concerns.

First, NGDOs may place a greater focus in their advocacy on promoting policies which have a positive impact on their own funding, as opposed to policies which benefit the Southern poor. Funding-driven advocacy may focus on the conditions and criteria of the way the government provides funding to NGDOs, and how much it provides – the emphasis will therefore be on negotiating access to resources for NGDOs (Mosley 2012). This may or may not align with the interests of the poor: more aid may be beneficial for development, but as the literature has shown, aid is usually thought to have diminishing marginal returns, and above a certain 'optimal' level it does more harm than good in the recipient country (McGillivray et al. 2006).

Furthermore, not all agree that channelling more aid through NGDOs is always what is needed to reduce poverty, regardless of the country context. NGDOs may also limit advocacy on policy issues which support the poor, but may potentially harm their own access to funding. Untying aid from donor country exports is usually cited as an example of this problem: while it is almost universally accepted that tied aid is not as valuable for recipient countries as untied aid, Northern development NGOs benefit if their home country's aid is tied, as it results in lower competition for resources (Carbone 2006). A large majority of NGOs within the EU Member States may have opposed reforms which enhance aid effectiveness, as it reduces their own access to aid contracts (Carbone 2014).

Second, NGDOs may alter their positions and advocacy priorities to better align with donor priorities. They may aim to maintain a good relationship with donors and not be too critical about policies, as such criticism may have a negative impact on the relationship and jeopardise funding. There is evidence that donors may favour groups which have similar priorities as they do (Mahoney and Beckstrand 2011; Sanchez Salgado 2014), and NGOs may change their own approach in the expectation that this would increase their chances of success. The disciplining effect of official funding may also lead to NGOs decreasing their political activity, making them more apolitical and less participatory organisations (Sanchez Salgado 2010) which spend less on lobbying and advocacy (Bloodgood and Tremblay-Boire 2017). For example, Paragi (2021) has shown how NGDOs in the West Bank and Gaza are pressured into changing their political positions on Israel to increase their chances of winning funding from Western donors. Similar pressures can also apply to grassroots donations: NGDOs may shift their positions to better align with public opinion, or focus on topics which are more likely to generate public sympathy.

Third, NGOs may change the tools and strategies they use in their advocacy. If their aim is to maintain good relations with donors, they will not only refrain from criticism in the substance of their advocacy, but also be less confrontational in the tools they use. Advocacy may therefore shift towards a greater usage of insider or more direct tactics, involving meetings and direct contacts with policy makers and aid agencies, as opposed to outsider/indirect tactics, which aim to mobilise public opinion for change by highlighting and publicising problematic performance by official policies. This later approach often involves 'naming and shaming' (Szent-Iványi and Timofejevs 2021, but see also Hill et al. 2013), and by bringing negative publicity to the donor, it can lead to confrontation. NGDOs seeking funding may want to avoid any such confrontation.

In summary, NGDO advocacy driven by organisational incentives is likely to focus on promoting access to funding by calling for more aid levels and greater amounts channelled specifically through NGDOs. It may neglect issues on aid effectiveness, especially ones which may hurt NGDOs, such as untying aid. NGDOs will also be less critical of donors, and make lower use of confrontational tactics like naming and shaming. The third variable in the framework, reputation, helps provide insights on whether moral, or organisations incentives dominate NGDO advocacy. Or, to put it another way, reputational motivations explain how NGDOs make choices between morally and organisationally driven advocacy, and find an 'optimal' mix between the two.

Reputational incentives

Development NGOs have strong incentives to maintain a 'good' reputation of themselves, or ensure that they 'look good' (Jones 2017; Mitchell and Stroup 2017). Reputation matters, because it influences how other actors in international development, including policy makers, donors, other NGOs, or beneficiaries perceive and interact with the groups. It thus ultimately has an impact on how well NGDOs are able to do their jobs, including fulfilling their moral missions and accessing the financial means for doing so.

These different audiences will have different understandings of what a 'good' reputation for an NGDO will mean (Gourevitch and Lake 2012). Official donors are more likely to fund NGDOs who are 'professionalised', and have a reputation and track record of effective and efficient project implementation and service provision (Paragi 2021). Grassroots donors usually provide donations due to moral reasons, to organisations they see as credibly championing these in practice. Other NGDOs will be more willing to work with groups which they perceive as like-minded. In terms of advocacy, policy makers and journalists will be more likely to engage with, and take information into account provided by NGDOs which have a reputation for being accurate and credible (Bloodgood 2011; McPherson 2016). Given the focus on advocacy behaviour, the role of NGO reputation towards policy makers is explore in more detail below, looking the broader world of NGOs beyond NGDOs as well.

The literatures on interest groups and human rights NGOs agree that these groups have a key function in channelling information to policy makers (Keck 1998; Bloodgood 2011; Hill et al. 2013), which is one of the most important tools of NGO advocacy. When strategically framed to fit the advocacy goals of NGOs, information can be used to convince decision makers about specific policy choices. Policy makers have reasons to value the information NGOs provide, as they may not otherwise have access to it. Information on how current policies affect constituents or various other stakeholders, the policy preferences and interests of those represented by NGOs, or specific trends and developments in their sectors, are all issues where NGOs can have an informational advantage over policy makers. NGOs can also collect information from their partner organisations abroad. Hill et al. (2013) for example show how organisations like Amnesty International rely on local partners in less democratic countries to provide detailed, on the ground information about daily politics and other developments, which can include different perspectives than what policy makers can access through their country's embassies or the media. Furthermore, while policy makers have access to vast amounts of information, it is cognitively impossible for them to process this. NGOs, due to their specialisation (in at times rather narrow fields), can poses a much greater degree of expertise in a specific policy issue than policy makers, and can present information in a clear and systematic form, making it easier to digest (McGann and Johnstone 2006).

While policy makers may find the information provided by NGOs useful, they will also be aware of the fact that these groups have incentives to distort information, or report only the information that fits their framing of the policy issues (Bloodgood 2011). Indeed, as discussed above, NGOs are at least partially driven by moral missions, which may not necessarily align with the political goals a government may aim to achieve. NGOs have incentives to use information strategically to support their narratives, and decision makers will take this potential bias into consideration when using the information (Bloodgood 2011). They will be more likely to use information which comes from sources seen as reputable or credible, or, in other words, from NGOs which they accept to generally make 'truthful' statements (Gourevitch and Lake 2012). Similar relationships exist between NGOs and the media. Journalists value the 'information subsidy' which credible NGOs can provide: i.e., information coming from an NGO which is seen as reputable by journalists will require fewer additional verification, and thus lead to more rapid publication and lower costs for news outlets (Gandy 1982; McPherson 2016).

Therefore, if NGOs, development NGOs included, want to have influence over policy processes either directly by providing information to policy makers, or indirectly through the media, they need to make efforts to maintain and actively shape their reputations. Reputation can come from several sources, and perhaps the most important source for NGDOs is their moral mission. As discussed above, NGDOs proclaim altruistic and virtuous goals in their mission statements in terms of saving lives, helping the poor, educating children, or empowering women. Clearly communicated moral vision can create a reputation of being selfless and dedicated to a cause, and thus send signals that the information provided is not biased by self-interest.

As argued by Gourevitch and Lake (2012) however, being virtuous, while an important source of reputation and credibility, does not guarantee it. People may have moral lapses, and as NGDOs grow and become large organisations, other interests may also emerge. Highly publicised scandals associated with NGDOs reinforce this point, and can harm the reputation of the entire community (Gibelman and Gelman 2004; Scurlock et al. 2020). Furthermore, it is difficult, or close to impossible to verify whether NGDOs actually live up to the claims they make about their goals in practice (Edwards and Hulme 1996). Often, there are few alternative sources of information available on NGDO actions other than what the groups themselves report. Claims of how many children they have vaccinated or how many schools they have built are difficult and costly to verify independently. NGDOs therefore have incentives to take measures to ensure that their claims of being morally driven are actually believed by policy makers, donors, and other audiences. They must actively build their reputation and send credible signals about their behaviour to their various constituencies (Amagoh 2015; Keating and Thrandardottir 2017).

A number of suggestions have been put forward on what measures NGDOS can use to build their reputations (see, for example, Gourevitch and Lake 2012; Amagoh 2015). Below, the focus in only on the ones which are relevant from an advocacy perspective.

First, at the very minimum, NGDOs need to ensure that their most observable actions are consistent with their moral missions. Their advocacy-related publications, press releases, websites, social media, and other public documents need to be aligned with what they proclaim to believe in. This is especially important, as rich country citizens are most likely to hear about NGDOs through their advocacy, fundraising campaigns (Davis 2019), and not their actual development work. In their public advocacy, they need to unequivocally stand up for what they believe in, even if this risks antagonising donors or policy makers. Their criticism of government policies needs to be well argued and underpinned by research to be credible, and these arguments need to be consistently aligned with their moral positions on improving the livelihoods and rights of the Southern poor. This becomes especially important when an issue they campaign on becomes highly politicised, or in other words is a salient part of public political debates with potentially polarised opinions (Zürn 2014: 50; Hackenesch et al. 2021). This makes their entire advocacy more visible, and potentially increases public attention to, and scrutiny of NGDO positions, making the need to stick to their moral positions even greater.

Second, when engaging with policy makers and the media, NGDOs need to focus on building a track record of providing information which is later proven accurate by other sources. They can send signals about the efforts they put into the research that underpins their advocacy, such as by providing public information about their research capacities, or including sections into their publications which explain the methodology they used to gather and analyse data. This can also improve credibility by collecting and reporting all information, not just what might be of interest to the media; or, as McPherson (2016) terms it, NGDOs should avoid 'selling out' to news outlets.

Third, development NGOs need to be transparent about their funding and governance, and also be careful on who they accept funding from. As McGann and Johnstone (2006) argue, the proliferation of NGOs since the early 1990s, and various scandals associated with some being used as seemingly neutral fronts to promote corporate, or foreign political interests, have placed additional pressure on 'real' NGOs to demonstrate credibility. Transparency regarding funding is therefore especially important to demonstrate that the given group is not just a front for political interests, but is genuinely guided by moral motivations. Donations from (certain) corporations or foreign governments can harm an NGDO's reputation, as these raise the question of whether funding came with strings attached (McGann and Johnstone 2006), or whether NGDOs changed their behaviour on their own accord to align with funder priorities. Actors representing political or corporate interests most at odds with NGDO positions, such as state actors from countries with repressive regimes, or companies with reputations for unsustainable or unethical practices (such as oil companies, or those associated with exploitative labour practices), are obviously ones to avoid. However, the finances of NGDOs are usually less visible to the public than their advocacy. While transparency in funding sources is necessary for improving reputation and trust towards donors (Amagoh 2015), groups can often 'be creative' with exactly how much information they publish (see Chapter 5). Nonetheless, accepting money from controversial funders should be a red line for NGDOs.

Fourth, while the impact of their actual development projects may be difficult to observe, NGDOs can put in place a number of mechanisms which can be seen as associated with effective development work. Transparency about funding and budgets helps with this as well, and so does providing information on how they work, where they work, and how they select projects and beneficiary communities. Developing internal guidelines and procedures for their development work and routinely carrying out and publishing independent impact analysis of their work also support building a reputation for effective development cooperation. Adopting autonomous governance mechanisms, such as independent boards with reputable members to provide oversight above their work is also a common option. Scandals, most commonly associated with corruption and financial mismanagement (Gibelman and Gelman 2004; see also the discussion on CLONG in Chapter 3), can harm an NGO's reputation, and thus its ability to engage in effective advocacy. They therefore need to ensure that they have internal processes which can identify wrongdoing. Owning up to mistakes is usually better than attempts to cover them up, as shown by the scandal around the sexual misconduct of Oxfam staff in Haiti in 2010–2011 (BBC 2019). The changes NGDOs can make to send signals about their work generally fall under the broad category of professionalisation. Through professionalisation, NGDOs can increase their reputations towards policy makers and donors by showing that they function in similar ways as official development agencies do, and are thus effective partners.

Fifth, NGDOs can create networks and communities of shared values. Participation in networks can signal that the group accepts the standards of the sector, and that other NGDOs acknowledge this. Signing up to these sector-wide standards and codes of conduct on transparency or operations can thus improve reputation, although these usually have few verification or enforcement mechanisms, so actual compliance is not guaranteed (McGann and Johnstone 2006). Carrying out collaborative development projects or advocacy with other groups (perhaps ones which already have a strong reputation of being credible) can also send important signals to policy makers. Furthermore, participation in networks also allows development

NGOs to share their practices and learn from each other. Meetings and working together with other groups are often more important as signals of credibility than the actual impact they achieve (Gourevitch and Lake 2012).

These five measures to increase reputation push NGDOs to act according to their moral incentives and practice what they preach, but they also go beyond these and drive them to become more professional, transparent, and collaborative. The final section of this chapter brings together moral, organisational, and reputational incentives into a coherent analytical framework to explain NGDO advocacy behaviour.

The analytical framework

The three groups of incentives and their expected impacts on development NGO advocacy are summarised in Table 2.1.

The relationships between the three groups of incentives are complex, and they clearly show that development NGDOs have conflicting interests when

Table 2.1. Development NGO incentives and their expected impacts on advocacy

	Moral	*Organisational*	*Reputational*
Source	NGDOs are created to achieve moral missions and attract workers who are perceived as altruistic.	In order to ensure their survival and achieve their moral missions, NGDOs need to access to funding.	To be effective in advocacy, NGDOs need to be perceived by their stakeholders as professional, credible, and morally-driven agents.
Impact on advocacy	Advocacy is aligned with proclaimed moral visions. • A focus on the interests of the Southern poor. • Promotion of pro-poor policies which have an immediate and sustainable impact on livelihoods (in sectors like education, health, sanitation, rural development, etc) • Empowering the poor	Advocacy focused on ensuring or improving access to funding for the group itself. • More aid and more of it channelled through NGDOs • Less emphasis on aid effectiveness • Less confrontational advocacy towards donors • Stronger alignment with donor goals • More low-key and insider advocacy	Advocacy aligned with moral vision, especially in politicised policy areas. Signals beyond advocacy • Provision of accurate and unbiased information • Transparency on funding and positions on issues • Professionalised operations, processes and governance • Collaboration with other NGOs

Source: author.

it comes to their advocacy. The interactions between the three groups however in specific policy areas, should be able to provide explanations on the type of advocacy NGDOs actually engage in. Which incentives prevail and what shape advocacy will take depends on conscious decision making carried out by the specific NGDO for a specific issue. This section provides a simple model for understanding how these decisions are made.

The starting point for the model acknowledges that Northern development NGOs are altruistic and their moral motivations matter. Most contributions in the literature agree that at their core, NGDOs are indeed morally driven actors, although others have tended to downplay this (see the discussion earlier in the chapter). Moral motivations are perhaps strongest in terms of explaining why an NGO is created and what mission it sets for its operational work and advocacy.[2] However, the everyday operations of the group, as well as its potential growth, may bring in further incentives which the organisation needs to conform to in order to ensure its ability to access funding and ultimately its survival. Organisational incentives can divert resources and focus from the organisation's primary (moral) goals (Lasker 2016). NGDO leaders and workers may see these as 'necessary' compromises to achieve the 'greater good', i.e. sustain the positive work they do, as laid out in their moral mission.

Organisational and financial incentives dictate advocacy which is different from, and at times at odds with what would flow from moral missions. So, how does the NGDO find the balance in its advocacy between moral and organisational incentives? The model uses reputational incentives as playing this balancing role. While reputational incentives can also divert attention from moral missions, they can incentivise NGDOs to not stray too far from these stated missions as well. For advocacy to remain credible, and thus effective, NGDOs need to ensure that they maintain a reputation of being morally driven actors. The literature on human rights NGOs offers similar conclusions. The need for credibility provides a strong incentive for the largest transnational groups, like Amnesty International or Human Rights Watch to provide unbiased and unexaggerated information about human rights abuses (Hill et al. 2013), and can outweigh the organisational incentives in terms of the extra media coverage and donations that exaggeration might bring. Based on this analogy, the argument is that while development NGOs will have strong temptations to allow organisational incentives to impact their advocacy, these tendencies will be tempered by their need to maintain their reputation to ensure that their advocacy work is actually listened to. In other words, reputational incentives will provide an extrinsic motivation for NGDOs to act along their intrinsic moral incentives.

Reputational concerns will therefore lead to an optimal balance of moral and organisational incentives in advocacy. The question then is where exactly this balance emerges, and which incentives are more dominant in this optimal situation. The model argues that this will depend on two groups of factors: those related to the characteristics of the specific NGDO in question, and those related to the specific issue/policy area on which the NGDO is carrying out advocacy.

Looking first at NGDO characteristics, Chapter 3 shows that European development NGOs come in a wide variety of shapes and sizes. These and other characteristics matter for how these groups will engage in advocacy. Size is an especially important variable: the literature generally perceives larger NGOs to be more heavily professionalised and thus more strongly driven by organisational concerns (Gourevitch and Lake 2012). Smaller NGDOs would often have actively involved founders who are very much driven by moral vision, and there is potentially a high price for them to pay if they lose credibility due to not adhering to their vision. Larger NGOs on the other hand have more professional staff and will, in general, put greater effort into sending signals about their credibility via transparent finances and annual reports, or independent boards. Organisational incentives may matter more for these groups due to their larger bureaucracies, significant ongoing expenses, and more complex operations. A second key variable is funding structure, which, while not independent from size, is a conceptually different issue. The different types of funding NGDOs have access to mean different things for advocacy. Grassroots funding incentivises NGDOs to build a reputation of sticking to their moral mission. People who donate to NGDOs are likely to agree with the mission of the organisation and will expect advocacy in line with it. Advocacy which is more driven by organisational concerns may risk alienating these donors. Large degrees of reliance on grassroots funding will therefore increase the importance of reputation as a morally driven actor. A strong reliance on funding from official donors on the other hand, whether it is project implementation contracts or grants, will incentivise NGDOs to develop good relations with the donor, and also shift their advocacy in ways that focus on maintaining access to funding. While reputation will still matter, it will matter mainly towards the official donor and less towards the public, which generally means that the NGDO's reputation in terms of moral mission will be less important than its reputation as an effective and efficient project implementer.

The second group of factors includes the characteristics of the policy issue at hand. It is reasonable to expect that development NGOs will have different incentives for different topics, and will make case-by-case choices on their advocacy positions. In some issues, NGDOs may take on a more moral stance, where in others their position will be more driven by organisational concerns. Maintaining reputation may be less important in some cases than others. In some cases, NGDOs can adopt a position driven by organisational incentives without much harm to their reputation, while this may not be possible for other topics. In a previous paper, we identified three factors related to the policy issue which can have an impact on development NGO advocacy: (1) the degree of politicisation around the issue; (2) the impact of the policy (and potential policy change) on NGDO funding; and (3) how the policy relates to NGDOs' moral positions (Rozbicka and Szent-Iványi 2020).

The first variable, politicisation, has already been mentioned as a factor which may increase the public and political visibility of NGDO advocacy and thus the importance of maintaining a good reputation. Hackenesch et al. (2021) provide a detailed definition and discussion of what politicisation entails, specifically in the case of international development policy. They identify three dimensions of the concept: increasing salience, the polarisation of opinion, and the expansion of actors and audiences involved in the policy issue. Salience focuses on the public and political attention devoted to the issue, and what importance actors place on it. Polarisation refers to the degree of conflict and the presence of differing positions and viewpoints on the issue. Finally, more politicised issues will generally have a wider range of actors involved in policy debates. Hackenesch et al. (2021) argue that development policy has traditionally been an 'elite affair' with low degrees of politicisation, however, this has changed recently with increasing opposition and greater numbers of actors. Furthermore, issues within development policy have differing levels of politicisation: some issues are much more highly politicised than others: for example, there are strong public and political debates in countries like the UK or the Netherlands on how much aid the country should give, or who they should give it to. Other issues however do not enter politics at all, and are mostly seen as expert-level, technical issues which draw very little public interest. For example, the effectiveness of aid is generally seen as such a technical issue (see Chapter 6). Advocacy on a policy issue which is more politicised means that the NGDO's position becomes more visible, not just to policy makers, but also other NGDOs and the general public. In these cases, the NGDO needs to be more careful with the messages it sends, especially in terms of their potential impact on reputation. Greater politicisation of a policy issue therefore means that reputational concerns will weigh more heavily, and NGDOs need to be careful to keep organisational interests in check. Lower degrees of politicisation on the other hand are often associated with less visible advocacy, directed towards expert staff at donor agencies. This provides fewer incentives to take reputational concerns into account, or a reputation of 'being professional' matters more than 'being moral'.

The second variable linked to the characteristics of the policy issue focuses on the impacts the policy (change) has on NGDO funding. Some policies may have direct impacts on the possibilities NGDOs have to access funding in terms of changing the available amount of money donors spend on development aid, or shaping competition for it. Most importantly, donor governments can decide to increase or decrease their spending, which may, depending on the exact forms and aid channels affected, mean more or less funding available for development NGOs. Governments can also alter the rules for other types of NGDO funding (such as tax incentives associated with charitable giving). Eligibility rules for official grant and contract funding also matter hugely for NGDOs: criteria on the nationality of bidding NGDOs, for example, can impact the number of potential groups competing for government funding. As discussed earlier, the funding landscape has indeed become more competitive for NGDOs in most European countries since the 1990s. Government measures which increase competition for official funding can prove to be dilemmas for domestic NGDOs in terms of advocacy. For example, should they support untying aid, and the benefits it brings for developing countries in terms of greater cost effectiveness, or should they oppose it, given how it increases the competition for donor funding by allowing foreign NGDOs to bid as well? If a (proposed) policy measure changes the ability of NGDOs to raise funding, they are likely to engage in more selfish, organisationally driven advocacy, despite reputational concerns. However, it is important to note that not all policy changes have an impact on development NGO funding. Even if they do, their impact can also be indirect or unclear, or they may simply just alter the distribution of resources within the NGDO community. In these cases, development NGOs will have less to lose in terms of funding, and will be more likely to engage in advocacy which does not harm their reputations for being moral actors.

Finally, development NGOs also need to take into consideration how the policy issue in question relates to their moral missions. Simply put, there are significant reputational costs in terms of advocacy and campaigning which does not align with moral missions. NGDOs cannot promote a policy which is squarely against what they say they stand for, and they cannot oppose one which aligns with their moral views. Any such action would have a significantly negative impact on their standing among other NGDOs and also the public, thus harming their ability to collaborate and raise funding. The intrinsic nature of the moral vision of NGDO founders and workers should not be discounted here either: it is possible to argue that there will be organisational and personal resistance to advocacy which is visibly against the humanitarian principles which the NGDO believes in. In itself, a policy area's alignment with moral vision can lead to both morally and organisationally-driven advocacy: for example, in the latter case, if a policy change is positive for NGDO financial interests and aligns with moral vision, it will be difficult to tell which is the driving force. Indeed, in such cases NGDOs can 'disguise' organisationally driven advocacy as being moral. What matters is how moral vision interacts with the other variables related to the issue, and it can provide certain 'red lines' for NGDOs: reputational concerns may mean that morally-driven advocacy is the only option in some cases, such as when an issue is highly politicised.

Figure 2.1. sums up the theoretical model. For any given policy issue relating to development aid, NGDOs will face a choice between advocacy based on moral vision and advocacy based on organisational interests. Given the complexity of these policy issues and the ability of NGDOs to engage in strategically framing them, the choice is not binary, but rather a continuum, and best thought of in terms of determining the appropriate mix of moral and organisational advocacy. The need to ensure their reputation as moral actors will provide an extrinsic incentive for NGDOs to engage in advocacy

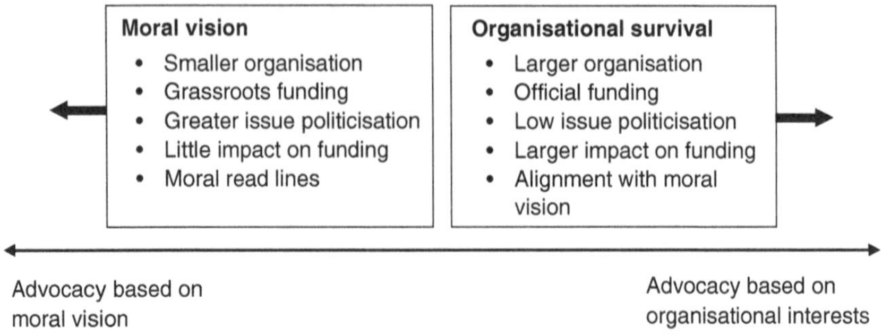

Figure 2.1 Determinants of development NGO advocacy
Source: author.

along their moral vision, which is made more likely in case of smaller, grassroots-funded organisations campaigning on highly politicised issues which have little impact on their funding. Incentives related to organisational survival on the other hand will push towards a greater emphasis on organisationally-driven advocacy, and are likely to be stronger in case of larger organisations with a high degree of funding from official donors. Issues which feature a low degree of politicisation and have direct impacts on NGDO funding will also push groups towards more organisationally-driven advocacy.

This framework allows explanation of advocacy positions both for the entire European NGDO community (using only the variables linked to the policy issue), and can also explain differences between individual organisations if all five variables are used. The book will predominantly do the former, i.e. look at the entire sector's position, but will also examine specific NGDO cases. However, before examining NGDO advocacy, the following chapter provides some descriptive details about the European NGDO sector's history, population ecology and main characteristics.

Notes

1 A shorter and less elaborated version of the theoretical framework presented in this chapter has been published in Szent-Iványi (2021).

2 Although there are perceptions which argue that some NGOs are created outright as profit seeking outfits, with the goal of attracting grant funding from donors.

References

Amagoh, F. (2015). Improving the Credibility and Effectiveness of Non-governmental Organizations. *Progress in Development Studies* 15 (3): 221–239. https://doi.org/10.1177/1464993415578979.

Banks, N., Hulme, D., & Edwards, M. (2015). NGOs, States, and Donors Revisited: Still too Close for Comfort? *World Development* 66: 707–718. https://doi.org/10.1016/j.worlddev.2014.09.028.

BBC (2019). *Oxfam Criticised over Haiti Sex Claims*. BBC. https://www.bbc.co.uk/news/uk-48593401, accessed 08/10/2021.

Bloodgood, E. (2011). The Interest Group Analogy: International Non-governmental Advocacy Organisations in International Politics. *Review of International Studies* 37 (1): 93–120. https://doi.org/10.1017/S0260210510001051.

Bloodgood, E. & Tremblay-Boire, J. (2017). Does Government Funding Depoliticize Non-governmental Organizations? Examining Evidence from Europe. *European Political Science Review* 9 (3): 401–424. https://doi.org/10.1017/S1755773915000430.

Brass, J. N. (2012). Why Do NGOs Go Where They Go? Evidence from Kenya. *World Development* 40 (2): 387–401. https://doi.org/10.1016/j.worlddev.2011.07.017.

Brass, J. N., Longhofer, W., Robinson R. S. & Schnable, A. (2018). NGOs and International Development: A Review of Thirty-five Years of Scholarship. *World Development* 112: 136–149. https://doi.org/10.1016/j.worlddev.2018.07.016.

Carbone, M. (2006). European NGOs in EU Development Policy: Between Frustration and Resistance. In: Lister, M. & Carbone, M. (eds) *New Pathways in International Development. Gender and Civil Society in EU Policy*. Aldershot: Ashgate, pp. 197–210.

Carbone, M. (2014). Much Ado About Nothing? The European Union and the Global Politics of Untying Aid. *Contemporary Politics* 20 (1): 103–117. https://doi:10.1080/13569775.2014.882572.

Care International (2020). Our Aims. https://www.careinternational.org.uk/who-we-are/our-aims.

Cooley, A. & Ron, J. (2002). The NGO Scramble: Organizational Insecurity and the Political Economy of Transnational Action. *International Security* 27 (1): 5–39.

Davis, J-M. (2019). Real "Non-Governmental" Aid and Poverty: Comparing Privately and Publicly Financed NGOs in Canada. *Canadian Journal of Development Studies* 40 (3): 369–386. https://doi.org/10.1080/02255189.2019.1556623.

De Jong, S. (2011). False Binaries: Altruism and Selfishness in NGO Work. In: Fechter, A. M. and Hindmann, H. (eds) *Inside the Everyday Lives of Development Workers: The Challenges and Futures of Aidland*. Lynne Rienner Publishers, pp. 21–40.

DeMeritt, J. H. R. (2012). International Organizations and Government Killing: Does Naming and Shaming Save Lives? *International Interactions* 38 (5): 597–621. https://doi.org/10.1080/03050629.2012.726180.

Edwards, M. & D. Hulme, eds (1995). *Beyond the Magic Bullet: NGO Performance and Accountability in the Post Cold-War World*. London: Earthscan.

Edwards, M. & Hulme, D. (1996). Too Close for Comfort? The Impact of Official Aid on Nongovernmental Organizations. *World Development* 6: 961–973. https://doi.org/10.1016/0305-750X(96)00019-8.

Fechter, A. M. (2014). 'Living Well' While 'Doing Good'? (Missing) Debates on Altruism and Professionalism in Aid Work. In Fechter, A.M. (ed) *The Personal and the Professional in Aid Work*. London: Routledge.

Fruttero, A. & Gauri, V. (2005). The Strategic Choices of NGOs: Location Decisions in Rural Bangladesh. *The Journal of Development Studies* 41 (5): 759–787. https://doi.org/10.1080/00220380500145289.

Gandy, O. H. (1982). *Beyond Agenda Setting: Information Subsidies and Public Policy*. Norwood, NJ: Ablex.

Gibelman, M. & Gelman, S. R. (2004). A Loss of Credibility: Patterns of Wrongdoing among Nongovernmental Organizations. *Voluntas* 15 (4): 355–381. https://doi.org/10.1007/s11266-004-1237-7.

Gourevitch, P. A. & Lake, D. A. (2012). Beyond Virtue: Evaluating and Enhancing the Credibility of Non-Governmental Organizations. In: Gourevitch, P. A., Lake, D. A. & Gross Stein, J. (eds) *The Credibility of Transnational NGOs: When Virtue is Not Enough*. Cambridge: Cambridge University Press, pp 3–34.

Hackenesch, C., Bergmann, J., & Orbie, J. (2021). Development Policy under Fire? The Politicization of European External Relations. *JCMS: Journal of Common Market Studies*, 59: 3–19. https://doi.org/10.1111/jcms.13145.

Hafner-Burton, E. (2008). Sticks and Stones: Naming and Shaming the Human Rights Enforcement Problem. *International Organization* 62 (4): 689–716. https://doi.org/10.1017/S0020818308080247.

Hendrix, C. & Wong, W. (2013). When is the Pen Truly Mighty? Regime Type and the Efficacy of Naming and Shaming in Curbing Human Rights Abuses. *British Journal of Political Science* 43 (3): 651–672. https://doi.org/10.1017/S0007123412000488.

Hill, D. W., Moore, W. H. & Mukherjee, B. (2013). Information Politics Versus Organizational Incentives: When are Amnesty International's "Naming and Shaming" Reports Biased? *International Studies Quarterly* 57 (2): 219–232. https://doi.org/10.1111/isqu.12022.

Hindman, H. & Fechter, A. M. (2011). Introduction. In Hindman, H. & Fechter, A. M. (eds) *Inside the Everyday Lives of Development Workers: The Challenges and Futures of Aidland*. Boulder: Lynne Rienner Publishers, pp. 1–19.

Jones, B. (2017). Looking Good: Mediatisation and International NGOs. *European Journal of Development Research* 29: 176–191. https://doi.org/10.1057/ejdr.2015.87.

Keating, V. C. & Thrandardottir E. (2017). NGOs, Trust, and the Accountability Agenda. *The British Journal of Politics and International Relations* 19 (1):134–151. https://doi.org/10.1177/1369148116682655.

Keck, M. E. (1998). Transnational Advocacy Networks in International Politics: Introduction. In: Keck, M. E. & Sikkink, K. (eds) *Activists Beyond Borders: Advocacy Networks in International Politics*. Ithaca, NY: Cornell University Press, pp. 1–38.

Keck, M. E. & Sikkink, K. (1998). *Activists beyond Borders: Advocacy Networks in International Politics*. Ithaca: Cornell University Press.

Keck, M. (2015). Comparing the Determinants of US-funded NGO Aid Versus US Official Development Aid. *Voluntas* 26 (4): 1314–1336. https://doi.org/10.1007/s11266-014-9464-z.

Korten, D. C. (1990). *Getting to the 21st Century. Voluntary Action and the Global Agenda*. West Hartford: Kumarian Press.

Lasker, J. N. (2016). Global Health Volunteering. Understanding Organizational Goals. *Voluntas* 27 (2): 574–594. https://doi.org/10.1007/s11266-015-9661-4.

Mahoney, C. & Beckstrand, M. J. (2011). Following the Money: European Union Funding of Civil Society Organizations. *JCMS: Journal of Common Market Studies* 49 (6): 1339–1361. https://doi.org/10.1111/j.1468-5965.2011.02197.x.

McGann, J. & Johnstone, M. (2006). The Power Shift and the NGO Credibility Crisis. *International Journal of Not-for-Profit Law* 8 (2): 65–77.

McGillivray, M., Feeny, S., Hermes, N. & R. Lensink (2006). Controversies over the Impact of Development Aid: It Works; it Doesn't; it Can, but that Depends. *Journal of International Development* 18 (7): 1031–1050. https://doi.org/10.1002/jid.1335.

McPherson, E. (2016). Source Credibility as "Information Subsidy": Strategies for Successful NGO Journalism at Mexican Human Rights NGOs. *Journal of Human Rights* 15 (3): 330–346. https://doi:10.1080/14754835.2016.1176522.

Mitchell, G. E. & Stroup, S. S. (2017). The Reputations of NGOs: Peer Evaluations of Effectiveness. *Review of International Organizations* 12: 397–419. https://doi.org/10.1007/s11558-016-9259-7.

Molenaers, N., Jacobs, B. & Dellepiane, S. (2014). NGOs and Aid Fragmentation: The Belgian Case. *Voluntas* 25 (2): 378–404. https://doi.org/10.1007/s11266-012-9342-5.

Mosley, J. E. (2012): Keeping the Lights On: How Government Funding Concerns Drive the Advocacy Agendas of Nonprofit Homeless Service Providers. *Journal of Public Administration Research and Theory* 22 (4): 841–866. https://doi.org/10.1093/jopart/mus003.

Murdie, A. M. & Davis, D. R. (2012). Shaming and Blaming. Using Events Data to Assess the Impact of Human Rights INGOs. *International Studies Quarterly* 56 (1): 1–16. https://doi.org/10.1111/j.1468-2478.2011.00694.x.

Murdie, A. & Urpelainen, J. (2015). Why Pick On Us? Environmental INGOs and State Shaming as a Strategic Substitute. *Political Studies* 63 (2): 353–372. https://doi.org/10.1111/1467-9248.12101.

Okabe, Y., Shiratori, S. & Suda, K. (2019). What Motivates Japan's International Volunteers? Categorizing Japan Overseas Cooperation Volunteers (JOCVs)? *Voluntas* 30 (5): 1069–1089. https://doi.org/10.1007/s11266-019-00110-x.

Oxfam (2021a). History of Oxfam. https://www.oxfam.org.uk/about-us/history-oxfam/.

Oxfam (2021b). How Oxfam is Changing. https://www.oxfam.org.uk/about-us/how-oxfam-changing/.

Paragi, B. (2021). The Price of Getting Donor Money. In: Kalfelis, M. C. & Knodel, K. (eds) *NGOs and Lifeworlds in Africa: Transdisciplinary Perspectives*. New York: Berghahn Books, pp. 172–202.

Pratt, B., Adams, J. & Warren, H. (2006). Official Agency Funding of NGOs in Seven Countries: Mechanisms, Trends and Implications. INTRAC Occasional Paper Series 46.

Rozbicka, P. and Szent-Iványi, B. (2020). European Development NGOs and the Diversion of Aid: Contestation, Fence-sitting, or Adaptation? *Development Policy Review* 38 (2): 161–179. https://doi.org/10.1111/dpr.12417.

Sakue-Collins, Y. (2021). (Un)doing Development: A Postcolonial Enquiry of the Agenda and Agency of NGOs in Africa. *Third World Quarterly* 42 (5): 976–995. https://doi.org/10.1080/01436597.2020.1791698.

Sanchez Salgado, R. (2010). NGO Structural Adaptation to Funding Requirements and Prospects for Democracy: The Case of the European Union. *Global Society* 24 (4): 507–527. https://doi.org/10.1080/13600826.2010.508986.

Sanchez Salgado, R. (2014). Rebalancing EU Interest Representation? Associative Democracy and EU Funding of Civil Society Organizations. *JCMS Journal of Common Market Studies* 52 (2): 337–353. https://doi.org/10.1111/jcms.12092.

Scurlock, R., Dolsak, N. & Prakash, A. (2020). Recovering from Scandals: Twitter Coverage of Oxfam and Save the Children Scandals. *Voluntas* 31 (1): 94–110. https://doi.org/10.1007/s11266-019-00148-x.

Serneels, P., Montalvo, J. G., Pettersson, G., Lievens, T., Butera, J. D. & Kidanu, A. (2010). Who Wants to Work in a Rural Health Post? The Role of Intrinsic Motivation, Rural Background and Faith-based Institutions in Ethiopia and Rwanda. *Bulletin of the World Health Organisation* 88: 342–334. https://doi.org/10.2471/BLT.09.072728.

Serra, D., Serneels, P., & Barr, A. (2011). Intrinsic Motivations and the Non-profit Health Sector: Evidence from Ethiopia. *Personality and Individual Differences* 51 (3): 309–314. https://doi.org/10.1016/j.paid.2010.04.018.

Save the Children (2019). What We Believe, What We'll Do. Save the Children UK's 2019–2021 strategy. https://www.savethechildren.org.uk/content/dam/gb/reports/stgy18-strategy-2019-2021-web.pdf.

Szent-Iványi, B. (2021). Practising What They Preach? Development NGOs and the EU's Emergency Trust Fund for Africa. *Third World Quarterly* 42 (11): 2552–2571. doi:10.1080/01436597.2021.1964358.

Szent-Iványi, B. & Timofejevs, P. F. (2021). Selective Norm Promotion in International Development Assistance: The Drivers of Naming and Shaming Advocacy among European Non-governmental Development Organisations. *International Relations* 35 (1):23–46. https://doi.org/10.1177/0047117820954234.

Tiessen, R. (2012). Motivations for Learn/Volunteer Abroad Programs: Research with Canadian Youth. *Journal of Global Citizenship & Equity Education* 2 (1).

Unerman, J. & O'Dwyer, B. (2010). NGO Accountability and Sustainability Issues in the Changing Global Environment. *Public Management Review* 12 (4): 475–486. https://doi.org/10.1080/14719037.2010.496258.

Vaux, T. (2001). *The Selfish Altruist: Relief Work in Famine and War*. London: Routledge.

Werker, E. & Ahmed, F. Z. (2008). What Do Nongovernmental Organizations Do? *Journal of Economic Perspectives* 22 (2): 73–92. https://doi.org/10.1257/jep.22.2.73.

West, K. (2001). *Agents of Altruism: The Expansion of Humanitarian NGOs in Rwanda and Afghanistan*. London: Routledge.

World Vision (2021). Mission and Values. https://www.worldvision.org/about-us/mission-statement#1468276217335-4d5c9ff3-3760.

Yarrow, T. (2008). Life/history: Personal Narratives of Development Amongst NGO Workers and Activists in Ghana. *Africa* 78 (3): 334–358. https://doi.org/10.3366/E0001972008000211.

Zürn, M. (2014). The Politicization of World Politics and its Effects: Eight Propositions. *European Political Science Review* 6 (1): 41–71. https://doi.org/10.1017/S1755773912000276.

3 The European development NGO community

History, actors, and approaches to advocacy

Introduction

This chapter provides a descriptive account of some key issues associated with the European development NGO sector. It begins with a history of the relations between these NGOs and the EU (including its predecessor the European Economic Community, EEC), with a focus on how advocacy structures and funding evolved between the 1970s and late 2010s. The chapter then discusses the types of NGDOs that make up the sector, ranging from small, single-person organisations to highly professionalised multinational networks. This is followed by an overview of NGDO advocacy platforms, associations which support the engagement of the sector with national governments and the EU institutions. Using data on membership in these platforms, and various other sources, the chapter provides estimates of the numbers of NGDOs in Europe. Finally, the chapter examines the advocacy tools and strategies most commonly used by development NGOs.

Relations between European development NGOs and the EU

Relations between the European development NGO sector and the EEC/EU began to emerge in the mid-1970s. As a result of the European project's enlargement in 1973, most importantly admitting the UK as a member, the EEC needed to re-formalise its partnership agreement with developing countries. The first Lomé Convention, creating a partnership with the Africa, the Caribbean, and the Pacific (ACP) countries, mostly former colonies of member states, came into force in 1976. The convention contained many elements which were seen as highly progressive at the time, including a relative lack of conditionality and automatic support for countries experiencing negative commodity price shocks.

It was in this context, also in 1976, that the EEC first established a budget line to support projects by European NGDOs in developing countries. NGDOs could submit their own proposals for co-financing, without any 'geographic or thematic limits' (Carbone 2006: 199), giving them large discretion in planning their initiatives. This funding system fit into the wider vision of the Lomé

DOI: 10.4324/9780367861872-3

Conventions, i.e. providing assistance with few conditions and thus giving a large degree of ownership to aid recipients. According to Carbone (2006: 199), the opening of the NGDO co-financing budget line meant that the European Commission (EC) acknowledged the importance of European civil society 'as an intermediary force between EU institutions and European public opinion'. The creation of this co-financing also underlined the progressive nature of the EEC's development policies: the EEC was one of the earliest donors to intensify relations with development NGOs, which many donors followed in the 1980s. The EEC also emerged as one of the most important funders of development education targeted at European citizens. This proved an especially crucial source of funding for NGDOs, as national governments provided little funding for such initiatives at the time (Randel and German 1999).

Policy dialogue also intensified between the EEC institutions and NGDOs in the 1970s. Development NGOs established the NGO-EU Liaison Committee (CLONG) in 1975, which represented the sector towards the EEC (Keijzer and Bossuyt 2020). An EC discussion document on EC-NGO relations called CLONG a 'representative European structure' with 'well established working groups' (Prodi and Kinnock 1999: 8). CLONG had formal quarterly meetings with the Commission to discuss both policy and procedural issues, and was vital in providing information to NGDOs about policy developments in the EC. By 2001, CLONG claimed to represent more than 900 NGDOs, albeit indirectly, through 15 national development NGO platforms (Kenety 2001). According to Randel and German (1999), a number of other advocacy NGO networks existed alongside CLONG, representing faith-based NGOs (APRODEV and EURO-CIDSE), or other groups and topics (such as WIDE for women's rights groups, EURODAD for debt issues and Solidar for NGOs with links to trade unions and social democratic parties).

Initially, policy dialogue between the European Commission and the development NGO community focused on financial and administrative issues, including relatively technical aspects of the EEC/EU's NGDO co-financing budget lines. Given how EEC/EU funding for NGDOs rapidly increased during the 1980s and 1990s, reaching about 20 per cent of the total amounts of aid disbursed by the Commission by the mid-1990s (see Randel and German 1999), NGDO interest in maintaining their relatively favourable access grew strong. NGDOs were especially critical about the lack of capacities in the Commission in terms of managing funding and working with NGDOs. However, NGDO advocacy on policy issues gradually gained in importance from the mid-1980s, and by the 1990s there were a number of NGDO campaigns relating to EU policies with impacts on developing countries, including beef dumping, fisheries, arms trade, and the Cotonou Agreement (Randel and German 1999).

However, as documented by Carbone (2006), relations between CLONG and the European Commission, which provided the bulk of CLONG's operating budget, gradually worsened around the turn of the Millennium, with the EU accusing CLONG of financial misconduct (European

Commission 2000). The Commission ordered an independent audit of CLONG's finances, which the NGDOs viewed as harassment driven by political interests (Kenety 2001). Although the audit found no evidence of outright fraud, it did uncover some irregularities and the Commission decided to withhold a portion of CLONG funding. This forced CLONG to suspend its activities, and it was dissolved at the end of 2002.

Some perceived the European Commission's debate with CLONG as part of a shift in the EU's approach towards European NGDOs (Carbone 2006), heralding a new era of less tight relations. The rethinking of the EU's development policy after the turn of the Millennium towards a more coherent and strategic framework questioned the viability of 'NGOs doing what they want' with EU funding, and not contributing to EU strategic objectives. In line with this, after 2000, the Commission phased out the co-financing budget line (Keijzer and Bossuyt 2020), and instead began issuing calls for proposals for NGDOs with more specific thematic guidance. It also partially untied its NGDO funding: while originally eligibility was restricted to European NGDOs, in 1988, direct funding for Southern NGOs became possible (Randel and German 1999). The eligibility criteria were later further expanded to other organisations from developing countries eligible for official development assistance (ODA), as well as to those from OECD countries, although only in case of actions in least developed or heavily indebted poor countries (Maxwell 2017). In the early 2000s, the EC also started using a broader language: instead of singling out NGOs as privileged partners, it began using terms like civil society and non-state actors instead, which also included social partners (trade unions and employer organisations) and private businesses. A Commission paper on non-state actors in 2002 envisioned a rather marginal role for European NGDOs, encouraging them to move away from direct project work in developing countries, and focus instead on capacity building for Southern NGOs and development education in Europe (European Commission 2002; Carbone 2006). European NGDOs where highly critical of these developments, and saw it as a threat to their influence and access to funding. Due to the capacity issues, the Commission also developed a preference for large projects, meaning it had to manage fewer projects overall. While this disadvantaged smaller NGDOs, it has also incentivised greater cross-border collaboration among them.

To replace CLONG, the development NGO community formed a new organisation for advocacy towards the EU institutions in 2003, the European Confederation for Cooperation of Relief and Development NGOs (CONCORD). Interestingly, CONCORD's website makes no mention of its predecessor CLONG, and implies that CONCORD is a result of NGOs (spontaneously) deciding to 'join forces, coordinate and divide the labour, and together through a common confederation called CONCORD, [...] try to change the world' (CONCORD 2020). CONCORD differed in its structure from CLONG: while it remained the 'platform of platforms', i.e. national development NGO associations remained the key members, it also welcomed international NGO networks as direct members. This meant that

CONCORD had even stronger claims of being representative of the sector than CLONG did. According to its website, its members included '28 national associations, 25 international networks and 4 associate members that represent more than 2,600 NGOs' in 2019. CONCORD was also slightly less dependent on the EU in terms of its operations, although between 2016 and 2018 around 60 per cent of its budget was still funded by a Commission grant (CONCORD 2020).

The increase in the number of organisations represented by CONCORD, compared to CLONG, was driven both by the increase in the number of NGDOs in general (Werker and Ahmed 2008), but also by the fact that CONCORD's creation more or less coincided with the 'big bang' Eastern enlargement of the EU in 2004. While development NGOs existed in the Eastern member states before their EU accession (see Drążkiewicz-Grodzicka 2013), joining the EU empowered these organisations, and in general led to the strengthening of development NGO sectors in the new member states (Szent-Iványi and Lightfoot 2016).

Keijzer and Bossuyt (2020) document an important trend in the relations between the EU and NGDOs following the creation of CONCORD, namely increasing requirements for NGDOs to act like professional project implementers. NGDOs needed to meet formal registration requirements (such as registering in the Commission's Potential Applicant Data Online Registration, or PADOR, system), which may have posed additional difficulties for smaller or less formal grassroots groups. NGDOs were mainly encouraged to apply for funding as project implementers, and ring-fenced funding for them had been reduced: for example, the EU's Neighbourhood, Development and International Cooperation Instrument (NDICI), its main source for funding development cooperation between 2021 and 2027, includes €1.36 billion earmarked for civil society out of its total budget of €79.5 billion (European Commission 2021). This lack of emphasis on supporting civil society directly is in marked contrast with the language the EU uses on the importance of civil society in development policy. For example, the 2017 European Consensus on Development prominently acknowledged the 'multiple roles that [civil society organisations] play as promoters of democracy and defenders of rights holders and of the rule of law, social justice and human rights' (Keijzer and Bossuyt 2020: 788).

It is difficult to get an overall picture of how much EU funding actually goes to, and through NGDOs in practice. Figure 3.1., based on data from the European Commission (2019a), shows that between 2011 and 2018, disbursements to NGDOs based in donor countries (overwhelmingly, the EU member states), as well as international NGOs amounted to about 1.1–1.2 billion euros annually, and have remained fairly stable since 2011. A different source, focusing on funds committed to NGDOs instead of actual disbursements, mentions 6.6 billion euros for the years between 2014 and 2017 under the 'Global Europe' heading of the EU budget and the European Development Fund (European Court of Auditors 2018: 8), which is more on an annual average as

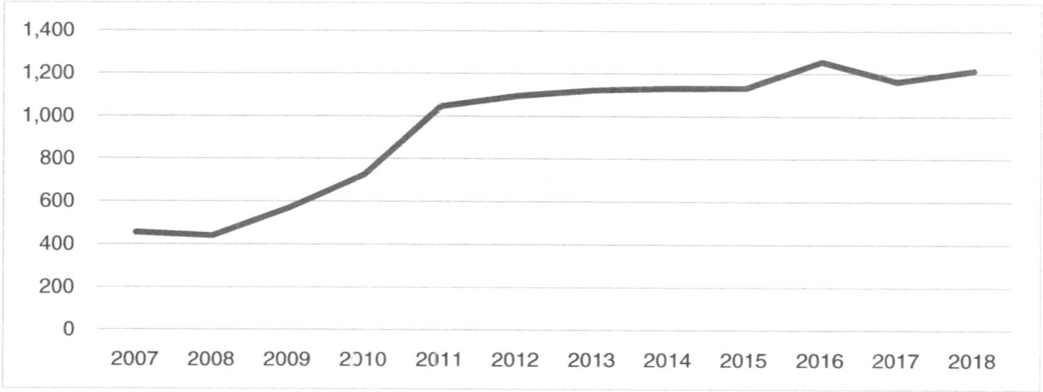

Figure 3.1 Disbursements to donor country based and international NGOs from the EU institutions, 2007–2018, in million euros at current prices

Source: author, based on data from European Commission (2019a).

actual disbursements. However, it is unclear what exactly these data cover, given how NGDOs may receive funds in several forms, including direct contributions, grants and in their role as project implementers (see Chapter 2). Most of the EU funding going to NGOs happens when they act as project implementers on behalf of the EU institutions (European Court of Auditors 2018: 8). The data on disbursements only includes NGDOs if they are the direct beneficiaries of funding, and does not include funds which may end up with NGDO subcontractors. The data on commitments includes funding relating to all forms of EU external actions, and while development assistance makes up the largest share of this, not all expenditures may classify as such. The commitment data most likely also includes funding for partner country NGOs. All this illustrates how difficult it is to get an idea of the exact funding landscape for NGDOs, which Chapter 5 explores in more detail.

There have been a number of policy issues since the creation of CONCORD which development NGOs have been highly vocal on. These include aid volumes, how foreign aid is defined and what counts as aid, aid effectiveness, policy coherence for development, migration, the transparency of development aid, private sector funding, gender, development education, sustainable consumption and production, democratic ownership, and tax justice. Chapter 4 provides a more detailed analysis of these topics, as well as the exact views which NGDOs have promoted in each case.

Types of development NGOs

Treating the European NGDO community as a single entity represented by an organisation like CONCORD of course oversimplifies the diversity of development NGOs. It thus makes sense to explore the structure and hierarchy of the sector in more detail.

Development NGOs come in a wide variety of shapes and sizes. Small groups, which focus on very specific development issues (such as maternal health) and raise resources predominantly in their home country may have little in common with large multinational, multi-issue, professionalised NGDO networks which have larger aid budgets than many official donor agencies. Indeed, the smallest NGDOs, often comprising a single person who raises and channels funds for a single project in their spare time, are often quite detached from the wider aid system and relatively oblivious of its norms and workings, including the policies of official donors (Juffermans 2008; Kinsbergen and Schulpen 2010). Large NGDOs on the other hand work with official donors frequently, receive funding from them, and have a stake in how the norms and rules of the aid system evolve (Werker and Ahmed 2008), giving them strong incentives to attempt to shape these. Given this diversity, it is essential to get a sense of the different types of NGDOs and how they may differ in their work and motivations, especially in terms of advocacy.

It makes sense to distinguish five categories of development NGOs. Of course, all typologies carry some degree of simplification and mask often substantial individual differences within groups. However, a typology of NGDOs is useful as it allows identifying more commonalities within each group than what is possible in the entire population, and so more can be said about each type of organisation's motivations and behaviour. Typologies of NGDOs in the literature have been common. Most famously, David Korten (1990) created an evolutionary typology of four 'generations' of development NGOs, based on the strategies they adopted to promote development (relief, community development, sustainable systems development and people's movements). Vakil (1997) presented an elaborate classification system based on a number of essential and contingent criteria, including orientation (welfare, development, advocacy, networking, or research), level of operation (international, regional, national, or community-based), sectoral focus, and evaluative attributes (funding, accountability, participation, efficiency, etc.). Some classifications emphasise that there are significant differences between advocacy and services provider NGDOs (Yaziji and Doh 2009), while Cousins' (1991) typology focuses on how NGDOs relate to their beneficiaries, and groups them into charitable, service provider, participatory and empowering groups. Further approaches emphasise the differences in the origins of NGDOs, and argue for example that faith-based groups have specific motivations which warrant separate treatment (Dicklitch and Rice 2004).

The typology in this chapter takes a different approach, due to the narrower focus on the advocacy of European development NGOs. The typology is based on two characteristics: the size of the NGDO, and the scope of its activities. Size, measured usually in terms of the NGDO's revenues or expenditures, has been a common approach to distinguishing groups (see Banks and Brockington 2019). However, larger NGDOs are also qualitatively different from smaller ones: they have stronger capacities, more diversified funding streams, and can be active on both the national and the EU level in terms of advocacy. Of course, size is relative: what counts as a large NGDO within a specific member state may be relatively small on the European level. Given the different sizes of member state aid budgets and development sectors, it is difficult to provide uniform definitions of what constitutes mid-size or large NGDOs, at least in terms of budgets or staff numbers – each of these need to be defined within their own national contexts. There is also a matter of perception: some NGDOs may play larger roles in advocacy than what could be expected based on their size, making them more visible. In terms of the scope of an NGDO's activities, these may be restricted to a single issue, but may also span a number of different issues related to development. Some of the largest European NGDO networks have emerged as diverse 'generalist' development NGOs with expertise and interests in a wide range of areas relevant for development, active both as service providers and in advocacy.

As shown in Table 3.1, five types of organisations can be identified based on this typology. The typology does not wish to imply that other characteristics which differentiate NGDOs from each other, as identified in the literature, are not important. Rather, for the purposes of examining the drivers

Table 3.1 Typology of European development NGOs

		Size		
		Very Small	*Small and Medium*	*Large*
Scope of activities	Limited	Citizen's initiatives	Small and medium national NGDOs	EU-wide specialised NGDO networks
	Diverse	-	Large, but predominantly national NGDOs	EU-wide generalist NGDO networks

Source: author.

of advocacy behaviour, the two criteria provide sufficient insights: size is a good proxy for the diversity of a group's funding sources, and the scope of its work gives an idea of the topics it engages in advocacy on.

The first group is composed of the smallest, often single-person NGDOs. While there is significant diversity even within this group, these organisations (if you can call them that) are usually run purely on a voluntary basis, very often by people who are not development professionals. A number of terms have emerged in the literature for these organisations: private initiatives (Kinsbergen and Schulpen 2010), 'citizen's initiatives for global solidarity' (Pollett et al. 2014), micro projects, small charities, or even 'accidental aid agents' (Haaland and Wallevik 2017), 'do-it-yourself (DIY) development' (McLennan 2017), or grassroots international NGOs (Appe and Schnable 2019). Often started by returned expatriates, travellers, volunteers, or diaspora members with first-hand exposure to poverty, these small NGDOs are driven by a genuine desire to help and do good. They usually raise funding within their family, groups of acquaintances and community, and use it to fund small-scale projects (usually in the range of a few ten thousand euros). These include donating second-hand goods, funding the construction of schools or clinics, digging wells, etc. (Kinsbergen and Schulpen 2010: 27; Pollett et al. 2014). The people involved in these small charities develop close links with the communities they support, and travel there frequently. For some, this work becomes a passion and a full-time 'hobby'. Some may formalise their activities through the actual creation of an NGO, but others may do it only on a personal basis. Given the low capacities these small charities have, they are almost always limited in their scope of activities, often to a single project, or a single partner.

People working on these small initiatives are not usually development professionals, and while the longer they do their charitable activities, the more likely they are to be exposed to the workings of the foreign aid system, in general, they have little awareness about the broader implications of their work, or the norms that guide the work of larger donors (Juffermans 2008; Haaland and Wallevik 2017). This has led to a significant amount of criticism towards these small NGDOs: while they are usually highly enthusiastic, their actions involve little strategic analysis. The projects they fund are too small to achieve sustainable and transformative impacts, and local ownership is often questionable (Kinsbergen and Schulpen 2010; Haaland and Wallevik 2017; Kinsbergen et al. 2017), leading some to term them 'amateurish' (Appe and Schnable 2019). These initiatives have also been accused of embodying and perpetuating the white saviour phenomenon (McLennan 2017), i.e. that development and expertise can only from white Westerners 'who know best'.

The second group of NGDOs is comprised of small-to-medium sized organisations which have strong roots in their home countries. In terms of absolute numbers, these groups make up the bulk of European countries' development NGO sectors. For example, based on a detailed mapping for the UK's development NGO sector by Banks and Brockington (2019: 12), around 69 per cent of NGOs can be considered small (with annual expenditures below £500,000), yet they only account for 2.2 per cent of total spending by development NGOs. As opposed to small citizen's initiatives, these organisations may employ professional staff. While they may be engaged in various EU-wide networks and be occasional members of consortia bidding for EU funding, they predominantly raise their funding domestically through individual donations and grants from their national government or other funding bodies. These small to medium sized NGOs often work on single, relatively niche issues, and are only active in a limited number of recipient countries, or even just one. They usually do not have permanent representations in recipient countries, and work with local partners extensively. Many of these smaller groups are also involved in development education and awareness raising projects in their home countries.

The literature generally sees these smaller NGDOs as nimble and flexible, able to adapt quickly to changing needs (Pollett et al. 2014). They are also often seen as innovators, coming up with new approaches to support and empower the poor (Banks and Hulme 2012). Due to their small size and lack of county offices, they have relatively small overheads costs. However, their size also means that they can only carry out smaller scale projects, limiting the impact and transformative effects they can have. Their activities are limited to the community level in most cases, and achieving national, or even regional level change is difficult for these organisations. The advocacy activities of these small to medium sized NGDOs is usually also restricted. While they show a stronger awareness of the policy environment and the workings of the international development system than citizen's initiatives, their capacities to engage in direct advocacy is low. Furthermore, if they do engage in advocacy, it is usually directed to towards their national aid agencies and government. It is highly unlikely that these organisations would engage in direct advocacy with the EU institutions. Even in terms of indirect advocacy nationally, evidence from the UK shows that only a fraction of these small NGDOs see any value in joining national NGDO advocacy platforms, although specialised umbrella organisations for small NGDOs do exist (Banks and Brockington 2019).

Large, but still predominantly national NGDOs make up the third group. These organisations have relatively large professional and permanent staff, including representations in partner countries. Their activities are diverse, and can cover several sectors within the field of development assistance. They are generally active in a larger number of partner countries, and in fact, many may be active domestically as well as social care providers (often with faith-based roots), or may operate charity shops, making them household names within their home countries. This status allows them to draw on volunteers to increase their capacities, as well as raise funds from a number of different domestic sources. Many of them are also active in the humanitarian realm, and have capacities to rapidly react to humanitarian emergencies. While their fundraising includes a mix of grassroots donations, commercial activities, government grants and contracts, as well as grants from the EU and other international organisations, they primarily rely on their home country to raise the bulk of their funding. They have sufficient capacity to lead consortia applying for EU funding, and usually employ professional fundraisers. They are generally highly active in domestic advocacy towards their governments, and may also be active on the EU level, some with small representation offices in Brussels. Given their size and domestic reputation, many of these large NGDOs have direct channels to their national government, and rely on direct advocacy to a significant degree. Finally, they are also the organisations which can initiate and run large national awareness raising and advocacy campaigns. Examples of such organisations include Deutsche Welthungerhilfe (Germany), the Danish Refugee Council (Denmark), People in Need (Czech Republic), or Self Help Africa (Ireland).

The final two groups include NGDOs which are best conceptualised as multinational networks. The main characteristic which differentiates these groups from their more national (or single-nation) counterparts is the fact that they have members or branches in several European countries, which means that both their fundraising and their advocacy is more diverse. Multinational development NGO networks are perhaps the most well-known names in the development sector and beyond: World Vision, CARE, Save the Children, and Oxfam are all widely recognised names in European countries. Depending on the source, the number of such networks active in Europe is usually placed between 25 to 40 (CONCORD 2020; Banks and Brockington 2019). Table 3.2 shows some data for a selection of these networks, including staff numbers and annual revenues. The table reveals that some of these networks are indeed huge, employing tens of thousands of staff and having access to similar numbers of volunteers. Given how these large networks mainly work with local partners in project implementation, they have indirect access to an even larger numbers of development workers. Some of these networks have larger aid budgets than many governmental aid agencies, and thus account for the bulk of development NGO spending.

In-line with the typology in Table 3.1., it is possible to differentiate between specialised NGDO networks and more generalist ones which have

Table 3.2 Selected NGDO networks active in Europe

Name	*Member organisations*	*Activities*	*Staff*	*Volunteers*	*Annual Revenues*
Save the Children	29	Children	25,000	n.d.	2.2 billion USD
World Vision International	90	Children, faith-based	37,000	42,000	2.8 billion USD
Oxfam International	19	Diverse	10,300	50,000	1.05 billion EUR
CARE International	14	Girls and women	n.d.	n.d.	840 million EUR
Plan International	20	Children, especially girls	8,000	n.d.	833 million EUR
Terre des Hommes	10	Children	4,400	6,000	180 million EUR
ActionAid	22	Diverse	4,000 'action aiders'		220 million EUR

Source: collected by the author from NGDO websites and annual reports.

Note: data for staff, volunteers and annual revenues for the 2017/18 financial year. N.d. indicates no data available.

activities in a more diverse set of areas. The former focus their activities on a specific set of issues (such as issues linked to children or women), while others do not make strong limitations on their areas of work. This differentiation makes sense for the purposes of this book, as it has an impact on the nature of advocacy that the groups engage in. Given their size and revenues, many of these multinational NGDO networks are able to engage in development work in several sectors and areas, and have highly diverse activities. Oxfam International, for example, focuses on poverty reduction in its work, and under this heading carries out projects and programmes in the fields of water and sanitation; food, climate and natural resources; conflicts and disasters; reducing extreme inequality; providing essential services; and promoting gender justice and women's rights. A further significant portion of Oxfam's work focuses on responding to emergencies. ActionAid, which aims to work towards 'a world free from poverty and injustice', focuses its activities on four very broad area: women, politics and economics, land and climate, and emergencies, which also make it a generalist, diversified NGDO network.

A stream of criticism questions just how credibly aid agencies (and NGDOs) can really possess expertise in almost all areas related to development, not to mention the fact that the proliferation of generalist organisations is likely to exacerbate duplication and coordination problems which already plague foreign aid (Acharya et al. 2006; Molenaers et al. 2011; Schulpen et al. 2011). Many multinational NGDO networks do aim to specialise their activities by, for example by targeting only specific populations within developing countries, although these may still be perceived as broad. Some groups, including World Vision, Save the Children, or Terre des Hommes focus on the lives, rights, and welfare of children. Plan International and CARE International focus on empowering girls and women. CBM International or Light for the World concentrate their work on disability-inclusive development and supporting people with disabilities.

Given their large size and the potential for influence over policy making this gives them, it makes sense to investigate some general characteristics of multinational development NGO networks in more detail. A more detailed understanding of how these networks are structured can be especially important in terms of understanding their advocacy behaviour, especially since there seems to be variation in this area. Some multinational NGDO networks are relatively centralised: there is a single headquarters which sets strategy and principles for operation, as well as coordinates the network. There is a division of labour between the members, they share financial resources, and all members share the same name and brand. World Vision International, a global faith-based NGDO focusing mainly on child welfare and education, is an example of this structure. Some of the members of its 'partnership', especially the 'support offices' located in developed countries, focus almost exclusively on fundraising, while the 'field offices' in developing countries implement projects. Advocacy towards donors is carried out centrally by the 'Global Centre' located in London, but the support offices also engage in advocacy towards their national governments. However, each national office also has a significant degree of autonomy; many have their own boards and decision making structures, and have a voice in shaping the policies and principles of World Vision as a whole (see World Vision International 2019). A further multinational NGDO networks which can be characterised by a centralised global strategy and a division of labour among members is Plan International, an organisation focused on children, especially girls. Plan International emphasises that its 20 national member organisations are all separate legal entities who are mainly responsible for fundraising, development education, and advocacy towards their national government. Each member takes part in Plan International's highest decision making body. Development work however is carried out by the organisation's over 50 country offices, and the entire network is coordinated by a 'Global Hub' (Plan International 2019).

Some other multinational network NGDOs function with a much less formal structure. Individual members of the network may not only have legal independence, but can have separate brands and identities. The division of labour between members of the network may also be less pronounced, with each member carrying out the full range of development NGO activities, including fundraising, advocacy, and project implementation. The role of the network's centre in these cases mainly relates to coordinating and communicating common standards and principles, usually through a bottom-up process with all members having a voice. The centre may also focus on global advocacy, and promote cooperation and sharing best practices between the members. Actual day-to-day cooperation between the members may be relatively ad hoc in the form of joint grant applications or other various cooperative projects which pool resources. ACT Alliance (formerly APRODEV), a network of more than 150 churches and faith-based development organisations, is an example of such a looser network. All members in the network have different names and identities, and are fully independent. ACT Alliance sets policies and standards towards which members can be held to account, and also operates advocacy offices, such as ACT Alliance EU, which represents the interests of 13 members towards the EU institutions (ACT Alliance 2019). ACT Alliance and other similar loose networks do not produce consolidated annual reports or financial data, unlike more centralised networks, which makes it more difficult to get an overview of the extent of their activities.

The typology above shows that European development NGOs are a highly heterogeneous group, ranging from large, professionalised, multinational networks all the way to single-person NGDOs or citizen's initiatives. The typology presented here does not explicitly cover other, less formal types of civil society advocacy initiatives, such as social movements or transnational advocacy networks (TANs, see e.g. Keck and Sikkink 1998; Della Porta and Diani 2006). While both of these network types are heavily present in development advocacy, they are also conceptually different from NGDOs. Most importantly, while both social movements and TANs are focused on advocacy, they do not engage in actual development work, which means that their incentives for advocacy will differ from those of more formal NGDOs. However, as argued by Keck and Sikkink (1998), TANs usually have NGDOs at their centre, while also include other types of activists, such as less formal groups, researchers and politicians. In this sense, TANs can be conceptualised as one of the vehicles through which NGDOs engage in advocacy, allowing them to present their cause as an issue of broader concern, and distance it from their organisations.

Advocacy platforms

As discussed in the previous section, development NGOs differ in their size and capacities, which has an impact on how they are able to engage in advocacy. To support advocacy, development NGOs in all EU member states have created national advocacy associations, often termed 'platforms'. The main goal of the platforms is to collate and channel the views and interests of the development NGO community towards the national government and the country's aid agency. This allows even the smaller NGDOs to engage in advocacy, albeit indirectly. Many European governments have formally acknowledged the country's national platform as the main voice of the development NGO community, and include it in public consultations on policy. Platforms usually run expert working groups on specific topics, actively involving their members in creating joint positions. Bond, the UK's development NGO platform, for example runs 40 working groups, on topics as diverse as children's rights, sport for development, or ethical approaches to gathering images (Bond 2019).

Beyond channelling development NGO views to the government, platforms also provide various services for their members, including training, support in accessing funding, and providing networking opportunities. Platforms usually fund their activities from membership fees, although some governments regularly provide direct funding to them as well, acknowledging the important role they play in the sector. Platforms may also bid for grant funding themselves. To carry out their activities, platforms usually have a board elected from representatives of the members, as well as secretariat composed of permanent staff.

The national platforms in the EU member states and the UK vary significantly in terms of their membership and capacities, and give a good snapshot of the size and health of the given country's development NGO sector. Table 3.3. lists the platforms of all EU member states and the UK, including details on membership and numbers on the permanent staff they employ. It is clear from the table that some of the platforms are rather large organisations with significant numbers of permanent staff, while others are rather small.

As discussed earlier in this chapter, CONCORD has acted as the EU level 'platform of platforms' for the sector since 2003, serving as the main advocacy body for development NGOs towards the EU. CONCORD monitors, analyses and coordinates NGDO responses to EU development policies, mainly through its structure of working groups centred around four themes: sustainable development, financing for development, civil society space and global citizenship education. The platform provides information to members on EU policy developments and supports the development of their capacities by promoting peer learning. It also provides advocacy resources for members, which they can adapt for their national campaigns. CONCORD itself runs projects and campaigns, and takes part in regular consultations with the EU institutions. CONCORD has a secretariat with permanent staff in Brussels, most of whom work on policy and advocacy.

CONCORD therefore pools the advocacy activity of the development NGO sector towards the EU. This allows it to overcome duplications which might result from individual NGOs engaging in advocacy (Carbone 2006: 203). As mentioned, the major innovation of CONCORD compared to its predecessor CLONG was that it also includes large multinational NGDO networks among its members beyond the national platforms, giving it a stronger and more representative voice. However, almost all multinational NGDO networks (and a number of other NGDOs as well) have advocacy offices in Brussels, and given the resources some of these networks have, it is not surprising that their presence often rivals, or even exceeds CONCORD's in terms of advocacy capacities. The EU's Transparency Register (European Commission 2019b), an online directory of organisations who have been accredited to engage in lobbying and advocacy with the EU institutions, provides information on how many (formal) meetings organisations have

Table 3.3 National development NGO platforms

Country	*Name of development NGO platform*	*Full Members*	*Staff*
Austria	Global Responsibility	35	9
Belgium	Acodev	79	10
Belgium	11.11.11	60	84
Belgium	COPROGRAM	39	8
Belgium	CNCD-11.11.11	90	14
Bulgaria	Bulgarian Platform for International Development	23	n.d.
Croatia	Croatian Platform for International Citizen Solidarity (Crosol)	30	5
Cyprus	CYINDEP: Cyprus NGO Platform 'Development'	25	n.d.
Czechia	Czech Development Cooperation Forum (FORS)	29	5
Denmark	Global Focus (Globalt Fokus)	80	11
Estonia	Estonian Roundtable for Development Cooperation (AKÜ)	33	5
Finland	Suomalaiset kehitysjärjestöt (Fingo)	300	52
France	Coordination Sud	164	16
Germany	Verband Entwicklungspolitik und Humanitare Hilfe (VENRO)	140	n.d.
Greece	Hellenic Platform for Development	6	n.d.
Hungary	Hungarian Association of NGOs for Development and Humanitarian Aid (HAND)	14	4
Ireland	Dóchas, Irish Association of Non-Governmental Development Organisations	42	4
Italy	Concord Italia	51	9
Latvia	Latvian Platform for Development Cooperation (LAPAS)	32	2
Lithuania	National Platform of Non-Governmental Development Cooperation Organisations	20	5
Luxembourg	Le Cercle de Coopération des Organisations Non Gouvernementales de Développement de Luxembourg	87	7
Malta	SKOP	29	n.d.
Netherlands	Partos	102	12
Poland	Grupa Zagranica	53	4
Portugal	Plataforma ONGD	62	n.d.
Romania	FOND	33	5
Slovakia	Platform of Development organisations – Ambrela	19	5
Slovenia	SLOGA	32	5
Spain	Coordinadora de ONG para el Desarrollo	78	10
Sweden	CONCORD Sweden	69	10
UK	Bond	400	40

Source: collected by the author from platform websites. Data for 2019.

with high-ranking European Commission officials. While this is a rather crude indicator of advocacy activity, it shows that CONCORD is more active than most other groups (see section on NGDO approaches to advocacy for more details).

The national platforms rely to differing degrees on CONCORD in their advocacy towards the EU. Some of the larger platforms like Bond or Venro have direct links with the EU institutions (Carbone 2006). CONCORD is therefore clearly not the single voice for the sector which it claims to be, and claims to avoiding duplication should be treated cautiously. However, this set-up also means that if advocacy is coordinated between the organisations, then it can also amplify the voice of the sector. The hierarchy between CONCORD and the national platforms allows smaller NGDOs to have their voices heard on the European level. However, it might also mean that the advocacy pursued by CONCORD represents a lowest common denominator for the sector, which can give an incentive especially for specialist NGDOs to engage in advocacy of their own.

Numbers of development NGOs

Estimating the total number of European NGOs involved in international development is difficult, as there is no single directory which would include all organisations. The diversity of NGDOs outlined above also makes getting a count of each type difficult, especially as the activities of the smaller organisations may be rather sporadic. Furthermore, there are clearly organisations which occasionally engage in activities falling under international development, but it is not their main profile: these may include domestic social care NGOs, environmental NGOs or human rights groups.

The total number of members in the individual national platforms is 2,256 (Table 3.3.). CONCORD (2020) claims that it represents platforms and networks which in turn represent a total of 2,600 NGOs, a slightly higher number, most likely due to the fact that it also includes associate and observer members of the national platforms, which Table 3.3 does not. However, neither of these numbers provides a full picture, for two reasons. First, they obviously do not include the organisations which are not members of national platforms. Not all NGDOs may see value in joining the national platform, especially since membership has costs associated with it. Citizen's initiatives or very small development NGOs, as discussed, may not be aware of the wider sector they work in, and have little knowledge about the national platform or the services it offers. However, there is reason to believe that even some larger NGDOs are left out from platform membership. For example, anecdotal evidence shows that neither of Hungary's two largest development NGOs, Hungarian Interchurch Aid and Hungarian Baptist Aid, are members of the country's platform, HAND (see Szent-Iványi and Lightfoot 2016). The low number of members of the Hellenic Platform for Development also hints at the fact that there may be a substantial group of NGDOs not represented by the platform. Second, even a cursory look at the membership lists of the national platforms reveals that their members often include organisations whose links to development are relatively indirect, or who do not actually engage in development work. These include trade unions, chambers of commerce, or environmental organisations. It would be difficult to conceptualise some of these organisations as development NGOs, although it is understandable that they may see benefits from membership in the national development NGO platform.

A second estimate of NGDO numbers comes from the EU's Transparency Register (European Commission 2019b). Searching this database specifically for NGOs interested in 'International co-operation and development' yields 1,173 organisations. Similar caveats apply however as with the data from the membership of platforms: it only includes organisations with an EU-level interest, most probably leaving out smaller, national groups (which may still be members of their respective national platforms). Furthermore, a careful examination of the list reveals that approximately a fifth of the organisations listed are clearly not development NGOs, but are active primarily in other areas.

Despite these concerns, NGDOs who are members of an advocacy platform, or register themselves with the EU, are relevant because they are the most likely ones to be engaged in advocacy, and thus this population is of key importance for the purposes of this book. However, one must keep in mind that at least in terms of absolute NGDO numbers, they represent only a small share of the European development NGO community. Indeed, very small groups and citizen's initiatives make up most of the sector. Given their high degree of informality, as well as national differences in definitions, it is very difficult to get an idea about the number of these small initiatives in Europe, but as argued by Schulpen and Huyse (2017: 167), the sector is 'no small game'. A mapping exercise, carried out in 2014 in 17 European countries (Pollett et al. 2014) estimated their numbers between 100,000 and 200,000. Even the lower bound implies a significant sector. Given their detachment from the broader international development system, the vast majority of them would not be active in advocacy work. Furthermore, given how their budgets for development work are small, they do not account for a large share of total NGDO spending.

On the other end of the spectrum, there are approximately 25 to 40 large multinational NGDO networks which are highly active in advocacy and as mentioned are significant spenders. This means that there is a high degree of concentration among European development NGOs. This concentration has been increasing in the past decades, and large networks dominate the sector (see also Pratt et al. 2006). The activities of these large networks are the most visible and their advocacy has the highest likelihood of being impactful, thus they will be the main focus of analysis in the following chapters.

Approaches to advocacy

There is a significant literature detailing the strategies, techniques and forms of action which NGOs, interest groups, or social movements use to gain influence in policy making processes (Della Porta and Diani 2006; Beyers and Kerremans 2007; 2012; Tarrow 2011: 99; Dür and Mateo 2016; Rozbicka and Szent-Iványi 2020). This section does not aim to provide a comprehensive overview of these; rather, it briefly presents the strategies, approaches and tools most frequently used by the European development NGO community. What follows is therefore not a thorough, or even fully coherent overview of approaches to advocacy, but rather serves to characterise 'what is typical' in the sector.

The interest group literature divides advocacy strategies into direct (insider) and indirect (outsider) approaches (Dür and Mateo 2016). Direct approaches involve direct contacts between policy makers and interest groups. Interest groups will aim to persuade policy makers through strategic use of information and arguments, usually in relatively closed settings involving direct interaction (such as consultation meetings, submitting written statements, conferences or even less formal settings). Policy makers may see these arrangements as beneficial, since interest groups may be able to provide information which would otherwise not be readily available to them (Keck 1998; Bloodgood 2011; Mosley 2012; Hill et al. 2013). Indirect advocacy relies more on building wider support for a specific policy. Interest groups may offer alternative framings of policy issues and will aim to build support for this through public awareness raising, publications, social media campaigns, building stakeholder coalitions, or engaging in mass mobilisation. Indirect advocacy is always more visible than direct advocacy, and some indirect tactics, such as naming and shaming, or demonstrations and protests can be seen as confrontational by policy makers.

The choice between direct and indirect advocacy will depend on a number of factors related to the policy area and the characteristics of the interest groups (Mosley 2012). Direct advocacy is seen to be more likely in policy areas that are highly technical and not in the forefront of public interest. Professionalised interest groups with significant resources are also more likely to have access to policy makers, allowing direct advocacy. Mosley (2012) argues that direct contacts are also more likely for NGOs which engage in service provision on behalf of government actors. Many groups however may be disadvantaged in terms of direct access due to a lack of resources, reputation, or little capacities to develop relations with the government. These groups will be more likely to engage in indirect techniques.

Based on these arguments, development NGOs are most likely to rely on specific mixtures of direct and indirect advocacy. International development policy represents an area which can be relatively technical, especially in terms of the financial details relating to foreign assistance, or issues surrounding aid effectiveness. As discussed in Chapter 2 and previous sections of this chapter, development NGOs, especially the large ones, are highly professionalised actors in the aid system, and given their roles as project implementers, they have close relations with governments and other funders. On the other hand, simple slogans, like ending poverty, forgiving debts, or saving children have the power to mobilise the public (Busby 2007). Given their grassroots donors and large numbers of volunteers, there is evidence that development NGOs can also mobilise. Furthermore, indirect advocacy around specific topics allows them to raise their profile among potential supporters. These factors mean that NGDOs can, and most likely should, pursue both direct and indirect advocacy.

Looking at the actual advocacy strategies and tools used by development NGOs in their EU level advocacy, there is indeed evidence of both direct and indirect approaches. The fact that CONCORD, most large networks, and even some large national NGDOs have advocacy offices in Brussels shows the value that they place on direct contacts with officials at the EU institutions. A permanent presence in Brussels allows NGDOs to regularly take part in formal meetings with officials, and also network with them at workshops and conferences more informally. The Commission provides ample opportunities for this, for example by organising regular consultations on policy changes which involve inviting written responses, but also specific consultation meetings and other events. As part of a structured dialogue between civil society and the EU institutions, the Policy Forum on Development (PFD) was created in 2018 to provide a regular space for interactions between the Commission and NGDOs through a series of conferences (European Commission 2018).

An example of development NGO direct advocacy relates to the revision of the European Consensus on Development, the EU's main strategic document on development policy, during 2016. The EU launched a public consultation on the revision process between May and August 2016, and received more than 100 written submissions from NGOs, including CONCORD, large networks, and many national platforms. A Commission working document provides further evidence of the scope of direct NGO advocacy in the process (European Commission 2016):

> On 19 October 2016, a high-level consultative discussion with European civil society was organised by the European Commission in Brussels. Around 80 [civil society organisation, CSO] representatives from 63 different networks participated in the event, covering most EU national platforms and encompassing all categories of CSOs, including the private sector, cooperatives and trade unions. The Commission has received and reviewed carefully a range of input papers circulated spontaneously by NGOs and civil society actors and platforms.

As mentioned, the EU's Transparency Register (European Commission 2019b) includes publicly available records of the formal meetings various organisations have with high ranking Commission officials. Based on this, members of

CONCORD's Brussels office have met formally with Commission officials 23 times between February 2015 and September 2019. As further examples, the register records 15 meetings for ACT Alliance, eleven for ActionAid, five for Caritas Europa, 56 for Oxfam EU, 12 for Plan International, and seven for World Vision Brussels during the same period. These numbers clearly show that development NGOs are heavily active in direct advocacy (and the differences between these numbers also implies that some NGDOs are more active in this than others).

European development NGOs also use different indirect advocacy strategies and tools to convince EU (and member state) policy makers to implement reforms. Most importantly, development NGOs engage in different communication and rhetorical strategies, including framing and reframing debates, as well as naming and shaming. Framing refers to selecting 'some aspects of a perceived reality and mak[ing] them more salient in a communicating text, in such a way as to promote a particular problem definition, [...] and/or treatment recommendation' (Entman 1993: 52). Framing allows NGDOs to redefine problems, identify causes, promote their favoured interpretation of these phenomena, pass judgement, apportion blame, and suggest remedies (Kuypers, 2009, 182). NGDOs aim to build support around the frames they promote, with the goal of gradually convincing other actors to act along their preferred frames and interpretations. One way of convincing other actors of the appropriateness of frames is through naming and shaming. This involves identifying actors who do not comply with the frames promoted by NGDOs, or more broadly, with widely accepted norms and behaviour, and publicising their non-compliance. This negative publicity is hoped to create reputational costs for actors, as they would face greater public and peer pressure to reform or otherwise comply with NGDO demands (Hafner-Burton 2008; Hill et al. 2013; Murdie and Urpelainen 2015; Szent-Iványi and Timofejevs 2021).

Framing, naming, and shaming however only work if NGDOs are able to get their messages across to the right audience through specific communication channels. To build external support for their position, or create reputational costs for actors, NGDOs need to ensure that their messages reach not only stakeholders in the sector, but also the wider public. To this end, development NGOs can use a wide variety of tools: online communication, including websites, newsletters and social media, press releases, reports, analyses and research, workshops and other events, as well as more radical tools such as protests and demonstrations. Development NGOs can build networks to ensure a wider reach for their message, and they can also create alliances with NGOs from other sectors whose interests touch on development.

European development NGOs make frequent use of framing, naming, and shaming in their indirect advocacy. Perhaps the most important example, discussed in more detail in Chapter 4, is how development NGOs have attempted to reframe discussions around what counts as foreign aid (specifically, Official Development Assistance). NGDOs have attempted to reframe foreign aid by contrasting what they have termed 'genuine aid', which only includes expenditures which actually reach the recipient country, versus 'inflated aid', which includes a number of items which are actually spent in the donor, such as administrative costs associated with aid, tied aid, costs of hosting developing country students, and debt relief. Led by CONCORD though its annual AidWatch Reports published since 2006 and the campaigns surrounding these, NGDOs have named and shamed EU member states who were the worst 'aid inflators'. These reports have also identified non-compliance by donors in other areas, and have shamed these donors for their behaviour, often with relatively strong language (Szent-Iványi and Timofejevs 2021). These reports are analysed in detail in Chapter 4.

European development NGOs, and especially CONCORD, have a number of other publications, including short notes, 'messages', or longer reports, which serve advocacy purposes, and mostly contain elements of framing, but are perhaps less explicitly aimed at shaming non-performance of the EU or its member states. Many of these focus on establishing and framing the position of the given group, or in case of CONCORD, the common denominator of the development NGO sector on a specific policy issue linked to development. In past decade, these have commonly included topics like sustainable development, the Sustainable Development Goals (CONCORD 2017a; 2019a), private sector funding (CONCORD 2017b), gender (CONCORD 2019b), the EU's migration related funding (CONCORD & CINI 2017), etc. While highlighting shortcomings in the given policy or proposal is usually a part of these publications, they focus on providing recommendations and solutions and include attempts to reframe the issues from an NGDO perspective. These reports are available on CONCORD's website and are also circulated widely among decision makers and aid professionals. Due to their usage of jargon, they are generally written for stakeholders in the sector and not the broader public.

CONCORD has also engaged in campaigns aimed at political leaders and parliamentarians, such as the EU Crystal Ball, in the run up to the May 2019 European Parliamentary elections. This campaign, in the form of an online game, aimed to sensitise decision makers and their advisors to the global impacts their domestic policy choices have (CONCORD 2019c). European development NGOs also engage in indirect advocacy towards the more general public, and promote their framings of development issues through development education and awareness raising (Pratt et al. 2006; De Bruyn 2013; Bourn 2014). Getting 'ordinary' people involved in advocacy has been an often-employed tool among human rights NGOs, for example Amnesty International's letter writing campaigns. Large NGDOs make use of similar techniques as well to engage citizens in their advocacy, although these are clearly less pronounced than advocacy aimed towards policy makers.

NGDOs, and especially large groups and advocacy associations, therefore make use of a wide range of advocacy tools. The actual contents of this advocacy are examined in the following chapter. This looks at CONCORD's advocacy between 2006 and 2018, which, as argued, can be thought of as representing the common denominator of the sector. It also analyses the topics which have featured in Oxfam's advocacy, which is one of the most active transnational groups in terms of its policy work.

References

Acharya, A., Fuzzo de Lima, A. T. & Moore, M. (2006). Proliferation and Fragmentation: Transactions Costs and the Value of Aid. *The Journal of Development Studies* 42 (1): 1–21. https://doi.org/10.1080/00220380500356225.

ACT Alliance (2019). ACT Policies, Standards, Policy Guidance and Strategies. https://actalliance.org/about/standards-and-policies/.

Appe, S. & Schnable, A. (2019). Don't Reinvent the Wheel: Possibilities for and Limits to Building Capacity of Grassroots International NGOs. *Third World Quarterly* 40 (10): 1832–1849. https://doi.org/10.1080/01436597.2019.1636226.

Banks, N. & Hulme, D. (2012). The Role of NGOs and Civil Society in Development and Poverty Reduction. Brooks World Poverty Institute Working Paper 171.

Banks, N. & Brockington, D. (2019). Mapping the UK's Development NGOs: Income, Geography and Contributions to International Development. University of Manchester GDI Working Paper 2019–2035.

Beyers, J. & Kerremans, B. (2007). Critical Resource Dependencies and Europeanization of Domestic Interest Groups. *Journal of European Public Policy* 14: 460–481. https://doi.org/10.1080/13501760701243822.

Beyers, J. & Kerremans, B. (2012). Domestic Embeddedness and the Dynamics of Multilevel Venue Shopping in Four EU Member States. *Governance: An International Journal of Policy, Administration, and Institutions* 25: 263–290. https://doi.org/10.1111/j.1468-0491.2011.01551.x.

Bloodgood, E. (2011). The Interest Group Analogy: International Non-governmental Advocacy Organisations in International Politics. *Review of International Studies* 37 (1): 93–120. doi:10.1017/S0260210510001051.

Bond (2019). Groups. https://www.bond.org.uk/groups.

Bourn, D. (2014). *The Theory and Practice of Development Education. A Pedagogy for Global Social Justice*. London: Routledge.

Busby, J. W. (2007). Bono Made Jesse Helms Cry: Jubilee 2000, Debt Relief, and Moral Action in International Politics. *International Studies Quarterly* 51 (2): 247–275. https://doi.org/10.1111/j.1468-2478.2007.00451.x.

Carbone, M. (2006). European NGOs in EU Development Policy: Between Frustration and Resistance. In: Lister, M. & Carbone, M. (eds) *New Pathways in International Development. Gender and Civil Society in EU Policy*. Aldershot: Ashgate, pp. 197–210.

CONCORD (2017a). The Impact of EU Policies in the World. Seeing the Bigger Picture. Brussels: CONCORD.

CONCORD (2017b). A 10 Point Roadmap for Europe on the Role of the Private Sector in Development. Brussels: CONCORD.

CONCORD (2019a). How Will You Work for Sustainable Development? A Litmus Test for EU Leaders. Brussels: CONCORD. https://library.concordeurope.org/record/2060/files/DEEEP-REPORT-2019-006.pdf.

CONCORD (2019b). Messages on EU Gender Action Plan III. Brussels: CONCORD. https://concordeurope.org/wp-content/uploads/2019/10/CONCORD_Messages_GAP3_Oct2019.pdf.

CONCORD (2019c). EU Crystal Ball. https://concordeurope.org/eucrystalball/.

CONCORD (2020). Who We Are. https://concordeurope.org/who-we-are/.

CONCORD & CINI (2017). Partnership or Conditionality? Monitoring the Migration Compacts and EU Trust Fund for Africa. https://library.concordeurope.org/record/1914/files/DEEEP-REPORT-2018-003.pdf.

Cousins, W (1991). Non-Governmental Initiatives. In: Asian Development Bank (ed) *The Urban Poor and Basic Infrastructure Services in Asia and the Pacific*. Manila: Asian Development Bank.

De Bruyn, T. (2013). Development Education and Awareness-Raising in Belgium: Who Are the Main Actors and Who Are the Target Groups? In: Pollet, I. & Van Ongevalle, J. (eds) *The Drive to Global Citizenship. Motivating People, Mapping Public Support, Measuring Effects of Global Education*. Antwerpen: Garant, pp. 127–140.

Dicklitch, S. & Rice, H. (2004). The Mennonite Central Committee (MCC) and Faith-based NGO Aid to Africa. *Development in Practice* 14 (5): 660–672. https://doi.org/10.1080/0961452042000239805.

Della Porta, D. & Diani, M. (2006). *Social Movements: An Introduction*. Malden, MA: Blackwell.

Drążkiewicz-Grodzicka, E. (2013). From Recipient to Donor: The Case of Polish Development Cooperation. *Human Organization* 72 (1): 65–75. https://doi.org/10.17730/humo.72.1.f115m11742314855.

Dür, A., & Mateo, G. (2016). *Insiders versus Outsiders. Interest Group Politics in Multi-level Europe*. Oxford: Oxford University Press.

Entman, R. (1993). Framing: Towards Clarification of a Fractured Paradigm. *Journal of Communication* 43 (4): 51–58.

European Commission (2000). The European Commission and the Liaison Committee of Development Non-Governmental Organisation to the EU. Press Release, IP/00/1485, Brussels, 18 Decemberhttps://ec.europa.eu/commission/presscorner/detail/en/IP_00_1485.

European Commission (2002). Participation of Non-State Actors in EC Development Policy. COM(2002) 598. Brussels: European Commission.

European Commission (2016). Synopsis Report Summarising the Main Results of the Consultation on the New European Consensus on Development. SWD(2016) 389 final. Brussels: European Commission.

European Commission (2018). The European Policy Forum on Development: Bridging the Global Agenda. https://europa.eu/capacity4dev/articles/european-policy-forum-development-bridging-global-agenda.

European Commission (2019a). EU Aid Explorer. https://euaidexplorer.ec.europa.eu/.

European Commission (2019b). Transparency and the EU. http://ec.europa.eu/transparencyregister/public/homePage.do?redir=false&locale=en.

European Commission (2021). Neighbourhood, Development and International Cooperation Instrument (NDICI) – 'Global Europe' . https://ec.europa.eu/international-partnerships/system/files/factsheet-global-europe-ndici-june-2021_en.pdf.

European Court of Auditors (2018). Transparency of EU Funds Implemented by NGOs: More Effort Needed. Special Report 35. https://www.eca.europa.eu/Lists/ECADocuments/SR18_35/SR_NGO_FUNDING_EN.pdf.

Haaland, H. & Wallevik, H. (2017). Citizens as Actors in the Development Field: The Case of an Accidental Aid-Agent's Activities in Aid-Land. *Forum for Development Studies* 44 (2): 203–222. https://doi.org/10.1080/08039410.2017.1305444.

Hafner-Burton, E. (2008). Sticks and Stones: Naming and Shaming the Human Rights Enforcement Problem. *International Organization* 62 (4): 689–716. https://doi.org/10.1017/S0020818308080247.

Hill, D. W., Moore, W. H. & Mukherjee, B. (2013). Information Politics Versus Organizational Incentives: When are Amnesty International's "Naming and Shaming" Reports Biased? *International Studies Quarterly* 57 (2): 219–232. https://doi.org/10.1111/isqu.12022.

Juffermans, K. (2008). *Tourism, poverty and aid: representations of the Third World Other in Small-scale Development Project Websites*. Tilburg: Tilburg University.

Keck, M. E. (1998). Transnational Advocacy Networks in International Politics: Introduction. In: Keck, M. E. & Sikkink, K. (eds) *Activists Beyond Borders: Advocacy Networks in International Politics*. Ithaca, NY: Cornell University Press, pp. 1–38.

Keck, M. E. & Sikkink, K. (1998). *Activists beyond Borders: Advocacy Networks in International Politics*. Ithaca: Cornell University Press.

Keijzer, N. & Bossuyt, F. (2020). Partnership on Paper, Pragmatism on the Ground: The European Union's Engagement with Civil Society Organisations. *Development in Practice* 30 (6): 784–794. https://doi.org/10.1080/09614524.2020.1801589.

Kenety, D. (2001). NGO Liaison Committee Forced to Disband. www.globalpolicy.org/component/content/article/177/31556.html.

Kinsbergen, S. & Schulpen, L. (2010). *The Anatomy of the Private Initiative. The Results of Five Years of Research into Private Initiatives in the Field of Development Cooperation*. Nijmegen: Radboud University Nijmegen, Centre for International Development Issues Nijmegen.

Kinsbergen, S., Schulpen, L. & Ruben, R. (2017). Understanding the Sustainability of Private Development Initiatives: What Kind of Difference Do They Make? *Forum for Development Studies* 44 (2): 223–248. https://doi.org/10.1080/08039410.2017.1307270.

Korten, D. C. (1990): *Getting to the 21st Century. Voluntary Action and the Global Agenda*. West Hartford: Kumarian Press.

Kuypers, J. (2009). Framing Analysis. In: Kuypers, J. (ed.) *Rhetorical Criticism. Perspectives in Action*. Lanham: Lexington Books, pp. 181–203.

Maxwell, S. (2017). Time to End the Tying of EU ODA?http://www.simonmaxwell.eu/blog/time-to-end-the-tying-of-eu-oda.html.

McLennan, S. J. (2017). Passion, Paternalism, and Politics: DIY Development and Independent Volunteers in Honduras. *Development in Practice* 27 (6): 880–891. https://doi.org/10.1080/09614524.2017.1339780.

Molenaers, N., Nijs, L. & Huyse, H. (2011). The Belgian NGO Landscape and the Challenges of the New Aid approach: Dealing with Fragmentation and Emerging Complexities. Institute of Development Policy and Management Discussion Paper 2011.02.

Mosley, J. E. (2012): Keeping the Lights On: How Government Funding Concerns Drive the Advocacy Agendas of Nonprofit Homeless Service Providers. *Journal of Public Administration Research and Theory* 22 (4): 841–866. https://doi.org/10.1093/jopart/mus003.

Murdie, A. & Urpelainen, J. (2015). Why Pick On Us? Environmental INGOs and State Shaming as a Strategic Substitute. *Political Studies* 63 (2): 353–372. https://doi.org/10.1111/1467-9248.12101.

Plan International (2019). Our Structure. https://plan-international.org/organisation/structure.

Pollet, I., Habraken, R., Schulpen, L. & Huyse, H. (2014). *The Accidental Aid Worker: A Mapping of Citizen Initiatives for Global Solidarity in Europe*. Leuven: KU Leuven HIVA.

Pratt, B., Adams, J. & Warren, H. (2006). Official Agency Funding of NGOs in Seven Countries: Mechanisms, Trends and Implications. INTRAC Occasional Paper Series 46.

Prodi, R. and Kinnock, N. (1999). The Commission and Non-governmental Organisations: Building a Stronger Partnership. *European Commission Discussion Paper*. https://ec.europa.eu/europeaid/sites/devco/files/working-paper-commission-ngo-partnership-com200011-20000118_en.pdf.

Randel, J. & German, T. (1999). European Union. In: Smillie, I. & Helmich, H. (eds) *Stakeholders. Government-NGO Partnerships for International Development*. London: Earthscan Publications and OECD, pp. 263–277.

Rozbicka, P. and Szent-Iványi, B. (2020). European Development NGOs and the Diversion of Aid: Contestation, Fence-sitting, or Adaptation? *Development Policy Review* 38 (2): 161–179. https://doi.org/10.1111/dpr.12417.

Schulpen, L., Loman, B. & Kinsbergen, S. (2011). Worse Than Expected? A Comparative Analysis of Donor proliferation and Aid Fragmentation. *Public Administration and Development* 31: 321–339. https://doi.org/10.1002/pad.619.

Schulpen, L. & Huyse, H. (2017). Editorial: Citizen Initiatives for Global Solidarity. The New Face of European Solidarity. *Forum for Development Studies* 44 (2): 163–169. https://doi.org/10.1080/08039410.2017.1306956.

Szent-Iványi, B. & Lightfoot, S. (2016). Determinants of Civil Society Influence: The Case of International Development and Humanitarian NGOs in the Czech Republic and Hungary. *Comparative European Politics* 14: 761–780. https://doi.org/10.1057/cep.2014.50.

Szent-Iványi, B. & Timofejevs, P. F. (2021). Selective Norm Promotion in International Development Assistance: The Drivers of Naming and Shaming Advocacy among European Non-governmental Development Organisations. *International Relations* 35 (1):23–46. https://doi.org/10.1177/0047117820954234.

Tarrow, S. (2011). *Power in Movement. Social Movements and Contentious Politics* (Third Edition). Cambridge: Cambridge University Pres.

Vakil, A. C. (1997). Confronting the Classification Problem: Toward a Taxonomy of NGOs. *World Development* 25 (12): 2057–2070. https://doi.org/10.1016/S0305-750X(97)00098-3.

Werker, E. & Ahmed, F. Z. (2008). What Do Nongovernmental Organizations Do? *Journal of Economic Perspectives* 22 (2): 73–92. https://doi.org/10.1257/jep.22.2.73.

World Vision International (2019). Our Structure. https://www.wvi.org/about-us/our-structure.

Yaziji, M. & Doh, J. (2009). *NGOs and Corporations: Conflict and Collaboration*. Cambridge: Cambridge University Press.

4 The contents of development NGO advocacy

Introduction

What are the topics NGDOs lobby for? This is the main question which this chapter aims to answer, by mapping the contents of various NGDO advocacy publications. The goal is to identify the main demands and recommendations the European NGDO sector has formulated between 2006 and 2018, especially towards the European Union. The chapter focuses on two organisations: CONCORD, which, as discussed in the previous chapter, is the main advocacy body of the sector towards the EU, and thus its publications can be seen to represent a common denominator; and Oxfam, one of the largest European multinational NGDO networks. The chapter begins with a focus on CONCORD's AidWatch Reports, and first presents the data and methods used to map the advocacy priorities in these publications. This is followed by the analysis of these priorities and how they evolved between 2006 and 2018. The second section presents a similar analysis of CONCORD's other aid-related publications. The third part of the chapter focuses on Oxfam, and similarly, after presenting data and methods, it analyses the shifts in advocacy priorities, although through a shorter time period, encompassing 2008 to 2018.

CONCORD's AidWatch: A common denominator?

Data and methods

Attempting to map the foreign aid related advocacy of the entire NGDO sector towards the EU over a 12-year period is a huge endeavour, given the size of the sector. Even if the number of NGDOs examined are reduced to those which have the strongest presence in Brussels, it would still mean analysing thousands of reports, policy briefs and other publications. Due to the nature of this data, where text and context matter, quantitative analysis would not lead to meaningful results. Therefore, a smaller sample of advocacy publications is required, which can be argued to be representative of the entire sector's views. A good starting point for this are CONCORD's publications, given how CONCORD, as the pan-European 'platform of platform' claims to represent the entire

DOI: 10.4324/9780367861872-4

sector. As discussed in Chapter 3, CONCORD's members include national NGDO advocacy associations from each member state, as well as 25 of the largest pan-European NGDO networks, representing a total of 2,600 organisations across Europe. CONCORD, given that it is a full-time advocacy organisation, publishes a relatively large number of advocacy publications each year related to foreign aid, and more broadly to a wide range of issues linked to development, aimed directly at the EU institutions. The most important aid-related publication of CONCORD are the annual AidWatch Reports, published since 2006. These have emerged as the organisation's flagship publication, and have become an important reference point for the entire NGDO sector (Szent-Iványi and Timofejevs 2021).

The AidWatch Reports follow a similar structure: part one is a narrative section which discusses the main advocacy demands of CONCORD, usually through a critical analysis of European practice, while part two includes individual country pages with demands towards EU member state governments, as well as page for the European Commission. Szent-Iványi and Timofejevs (2021) described the process through which these reports were drafted, based on interviews with CONCORD and other NGDO staff members, as a bottom-up process involving all CONCORD's members, who drafted their individual country pages. The first, critical analysis section, was generally written by members of CONCORD's secretariat, but individual members could also provide inputs, and it also needed to align with any overarching theme emerging from the individual country pages.

Using the AidWatch Reports as a source of data carries a number of advantages. First, they matter. As discussed in Chapter 3, CONCORD is the EU's official partner on development advocacy, and its reports carry weight. Second, they channel the views of a significant part of the NGDO sector, including almost all the major actors, towards the EU institutions and member states governments. CONCORD, as well as the national platforms, organise launch events across the EU for the reports to ensure that policy makers notice the main messages. Third, the AidWatch Reports are published regularly, and thus allow for comparison over time in terms of how the relative emphases on the various themes have shifted. However, there may be reasons to believe that CONCORD's advocacy represents the lowest common denominator among NGDOs, given how it attempts to consolidate the views of a highly diverse sector into a relatively short set of messages (Szent-Iványi and Timofejevs 2021; see also Chapter 3). Therefore, to complement the AidWatch Reports, further, less 'inclusive' publications from CONCORD are also analysed in the next section, while the following section looks at the advocacy of Oxfam, one of CONCORD's network members.

The 12 AidWatch Reports were downloaded from CONCORD's website, and all of them were read in detail twice, focusing on the first, critical analysis sections. Qualitative text analysis was used to identify the main themes in reports. While reading each report, the advocacy-related demands of CONCORD were coded into specific themes. The coding began with a very broad and generic coding scheme, which included four themes: aid quantity, aid allocation, aid effectiveness and the purpose of aid, which can conceivably cover the most important NGDO demands. These themes were refined during coding and a number of further themes emerged. Most of these fit under the original four as sub-themes, while a few did not. The initial reading therefore provided a rich coding scheme, which is shown in Table 4.1. The reports were then read for a second time, and recoded with this more detailed scheme. The aim was to code the entire text of each report, as that would allow identifying which themes were given more space, and thus greater relative emphasis in a specific report. This can be useful in determining shifts in CONCORD's advocacy over the years.

The elements of the coding scheme presented in Table 4.1. proved clear and mutually exclusive in most cases, although there were some minor overlaps: for example, calls to increase aid to reach a specific Millennium Development Goal (MDG) or Sustainable Development Goal (SDG) would fit both under the *Aid quantity* code, but also under the *MDG/SDGs* one. These overlapping discussions were given both codes, but there were not many instances of these in the data.

Table 4.1 The coding scheme for the AidWatch Reports

Aid quantity	*Aid allocation*	*Aid effectiveness*	*Purpose of aid*	*Other*
Increasing levels of aid and meeting aid targets	Aid to Sub-Saharan Africa	Conditionality	Climate change mitigation/ adaptation	EU development policy
Inflated vs genuine aid	Aid to least developed countries	Coordination and joint programming	Funding the private sector	Financial crisis
ODA review process	Human rights and rights-based approach	Country systems	Poverty reduction	MDGs/ SDGs
	Gender	Evaluation	Managing migration	New aid modalities
	Role of civil society	Ownership/ democratic ownership	Security and aid securitisation	Policy coherence for development
		Predictability of aid flows		Public support for aid
		Transparency		Taxation and resource mobilisation
		Untying aid		

Source: author.

Some of the codes in Table 4.1. may require further explanation on exactly what they entail. The *Aid quantity* codes refer to NGDO demands for more aid, or for changing the definition of aid to include only 'genuine' expenditures (see below for more details), or to calls linked to the OECD Development Assistance Committee's (DAC) review process of what counts as official development assistance (ODA), a definition of aid for statistical purposes. The *Aid allocation* codes refer to CONCORD's demands on how the EU should allocate its aid, and what geographic or thematic areas it should focus on, such as allocating more aid to Sub-Saharan Africa, or on gender-related interventions, or on supporting civil society, etc. The *Aid effectiveness* codes are fairly self-explanatory, and include the calls from CONCORD demanding effectiveness enhancing reforms. The sub-codes focus on these specific reforms, such as calls to reduce conditionality linked to aid, increase the use of country systems, reduce tying aid to exports or increase predictability or transparency. The *Purpose of aid* codes focus on what goals donors use aid for, such as poverty reduction or managing migration, and CONCORD views and demands linked to these. Finally, the codes under the *Other* heading include many different topics, such as demands linked closely to specific EU development policy issues, policy coherence for development, or taxation and resource mobilisation.

Results

An overview of the main themes in the AidWatch Reports published between 2006 and 2018 is provided in Figure 4.1. The figure plots the evolution of the relative importance of the codes, based on the share of the report's text devoted to the code. To ensure the figure remains easy to interpret, only the most frequent codes are shown, while the remaining ones are collapsed together into their main code headings. More specifically, all sub-codes of *Aid quantity* are shown on the figure, while *Aid allocation* and *Aid effectiveness* are only shown on the main heading level. For Purposes of aid, some sub-codes appear directly on the figure, while the rest are collapsed into an *Other purposes of aid* heading. Finally, from the *Other* category, only EU development policy appears separately.

Many interesting conclusions are apparent from Figure 4.1 in terms of the themes which CONCORD has chosen to emphasise in its advocacy, and how these shifted during the period. Calling on European donors to increase the quantity of the aid they provide, and closely linked to this, calls for ending aid inflation, have perhaps been the most prominent topics covered in the AidWatch Reports. These themes have regularly taken up around a third of each report, and even more in the early ones. Member state donors have been regularly shamed by CONCORD for not meeting the aid spending pledge of 0.7 per cent of gross national income they had agreed to in the EU in 2005 (Council of the EU 2005), or making sufficient progress towards this. However, CONCORD even claimed that the aid figures published by

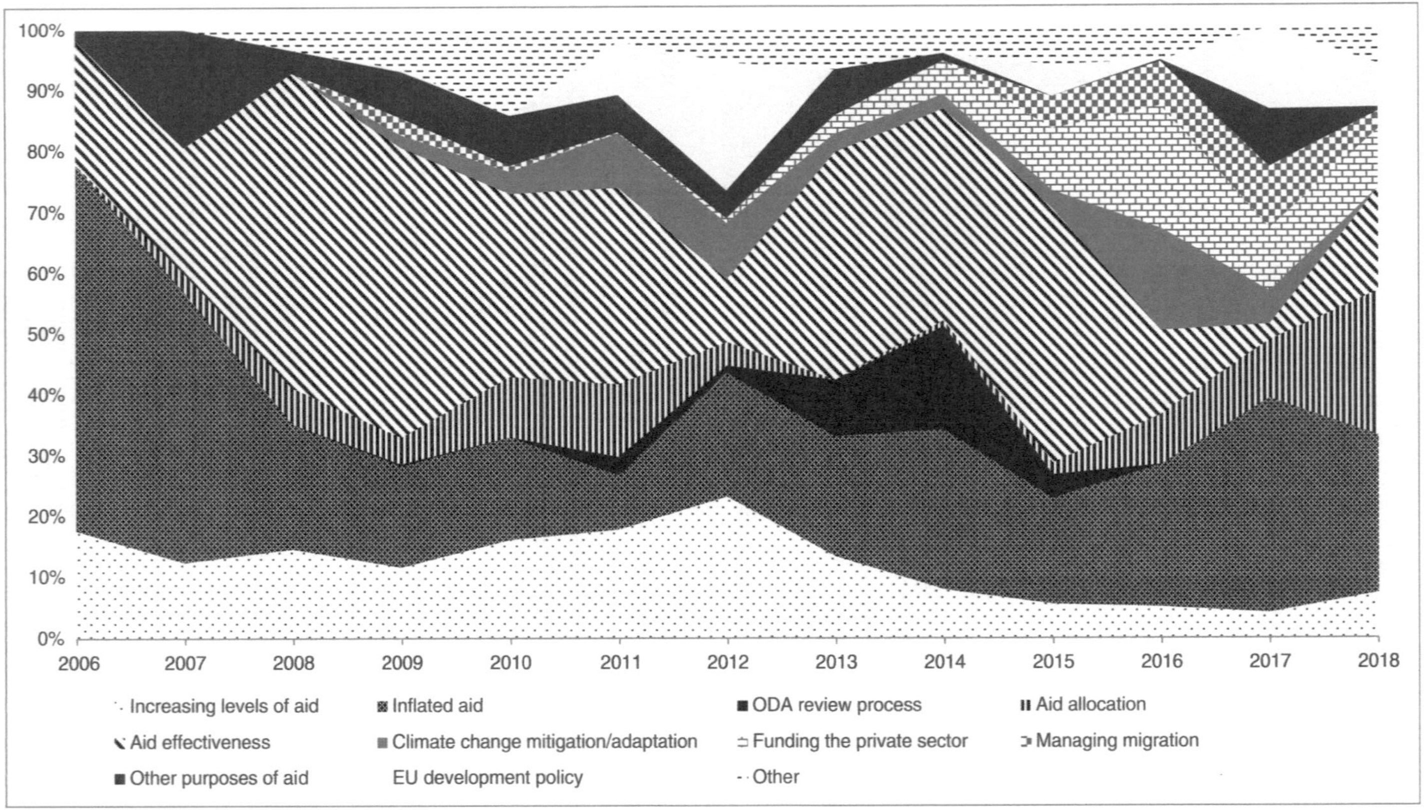

Figure 4.1 Shifts in the themes discussed in the AidWatch Reports, 2006 to 2018

Source: compiled by the author, based on CONCORD (2006; 2007; 2008; 2009; 2010; 2011; 2012; 2013; 2014; 2015a; 2016; 2017c; 2018).

the donors are not true reflections of their efforts to support developing countries. CONCORD argued that many donors artificially inflated their aid figures with expenditures which actually did not even leave the donor country, such as scholarships to developing country students, costs of hosting refugees, debt relief, or tied aid. While these expenses were officially accepted as ODA under the OECD DAC's rules, CONCORD's position was that donors should only count 'genuine' resource transfers as aid. Calling for more aid and contesting aid inflation has been a perennial part of each AidWatch Report, and has made up the bulk of the early ones. The topic has remained an influential part of each report during the period, closely linked to discussions about increasing aid levels in general. CONCORD therefore not only called on donors to increase their aid to meet the collective EU target of 0.7 per cent, but to meet this target using only genuine aid.

Contesting aid inflation is a clear example of pro-active advocacy on CONCORD's part: removing the items which CONCORD sees as non-genuine aid from the OECD DAC's ODA guidelines has never seriously been on the agenda of the DAC, and indeed if anything, most donors have pushed to expand the kinds of expenditures they can include in their foreign aid statistics, such as military and peace-keeping expenses (CONCORD 2009: 2). Indeed, discussions around reviewing the definition of ODA, to make the category even more comprehensive, were ongoing in the OECD DAC and the EU institutions after 2010. CONCORD engaged in reactive advocacy on this in the AidWatch Reports, arguing that the 'current definition of ODA [should be] retained' (CONCORD 2012: 6), and that countries should not meet their aid targets by further inflating their aid statistics with items which do not serve poverty reduction purposes, such as loans or foreign direct investment. As shown in Figure 4.1, CONCORD's advocacy to not dilute the ODA definition with the inclusion of other types of resource flows between developed and developing countries stopped after 2015, when the OECD DAC decided to create a new statistical category, Total Official Support for Sustainable Development (TOSSD), rather than change the accounting of ODA (Fritz and Raza 2017).

Interestingly, aid allocation has received rather little attention in the AidWatch Reports. Most reports included calls on the EU and its member states to increase aid to least developed countries (LDCs), but these calls were hardly ever discussed in depth, or supported with detailed analyses of where donors spend their aid if not in LDCs, which LDCs should be targeted, or how. Most importantly, CONCORD has almost never called on donors to cut aid to certain countries, while clearly, if aid's effectiveness in terms of reducing poverty is to be maximised, it should be concentrated in countries where poverty is high (cf. Collier and Dollar 2002). The 2015 AidWatch Report (CONCORD 2015a) did include a detailed analysis of EU aid to Africa, mainly focused on its effectiveness, however, this was not repeated in other reports, where African countries were in most cases only mentioned to illustrate specific aspects of poverty. In terms of sectoral allocation, CONCORD has mostly called for more and better aid to combat gender inequality and empower women and girls, and also for more aid allocated to civil society organisations. Gender was featured especially prominently in the 2011 AidWatch Report (CONCORD 2011), but received rather detailed treatment in a number of others as well, and has generally been the most frequent sub-theme under the *Aid allocation* heading. Calls for including civil society more strongly in policy level consultations, as well as in implementation, have also been a constant feature of the reports, especially after 2010. The 2011 AidWatch Report for example called on the EU to increase meaningful 'consultations and engagement with [civil society organisations]' and to develop an overarching vision on their role in development (CONCORD 2011: 20).

Figure 4.1 implies that aid effectiveness was as a major element of the CONCORD AidWatch Reports, at times even surpassing the discussions on aid quantity in length. However, the emphasis put on aid effectiveness has varied considerably between reports, and was a less consistent feature than discussions on quantity. Also, while discussions on aid quantity have had a rather specific focus in terms of meeting aid target pledges and what was counted as ODA, the contents of the discussions around aid effectiveness were much more varied, and showed considerable change over time. Figure 4.2 shows a breakdown of the sub-themes within the *Aid effectiveness* heading to illustrate this.

As shown in Figure 4.2, most of the discussions on aid effectiveness in the AidWatch Reports have been on a rather general level, calling on donors to increase the effectiveness of their resources and mentioning broad principles, without going into specific details of what reforms they should prioritise or how these should be implemented. However, CONCORD did go into more details on three topics among the aid effectiveness sub-themes: transparency, untying aid, and (democratic) ownership.

Transparency is actually only partially related to aid effectiveness, even though CONCORD's reports addressed it under the aid effectiveness discussions. The AidWatch Reports called on donors to increase the transparency of their international development policies, mainly in terms of how they reported the details of their aid spending. Greater transparency allows better scrutiny of donor practices by civil society and the media, and while this increased scrutiny can push donors to enhance effectiveness, the link is indirect. Many AidWatch Reports have included detailed comparisons of how transparent donors were, with the less transparent ones regularly highlighted as bad performers. CONCORD called on donors to join the International Aid Transparency Initiative (IATI) and implement its recommendations in their reporting.

Tied aid has been highlighted in the reports as an element of inflated aid, but has also been discussed separately as a practice which undermines aid effectiveness. Donors have committed themselves on several occasions to eliminate the tying of aid to exports (Hall 2011; Fritz and Raza 2017), yet CONCORD highlighted that tied aid remained remarkably resilient. The

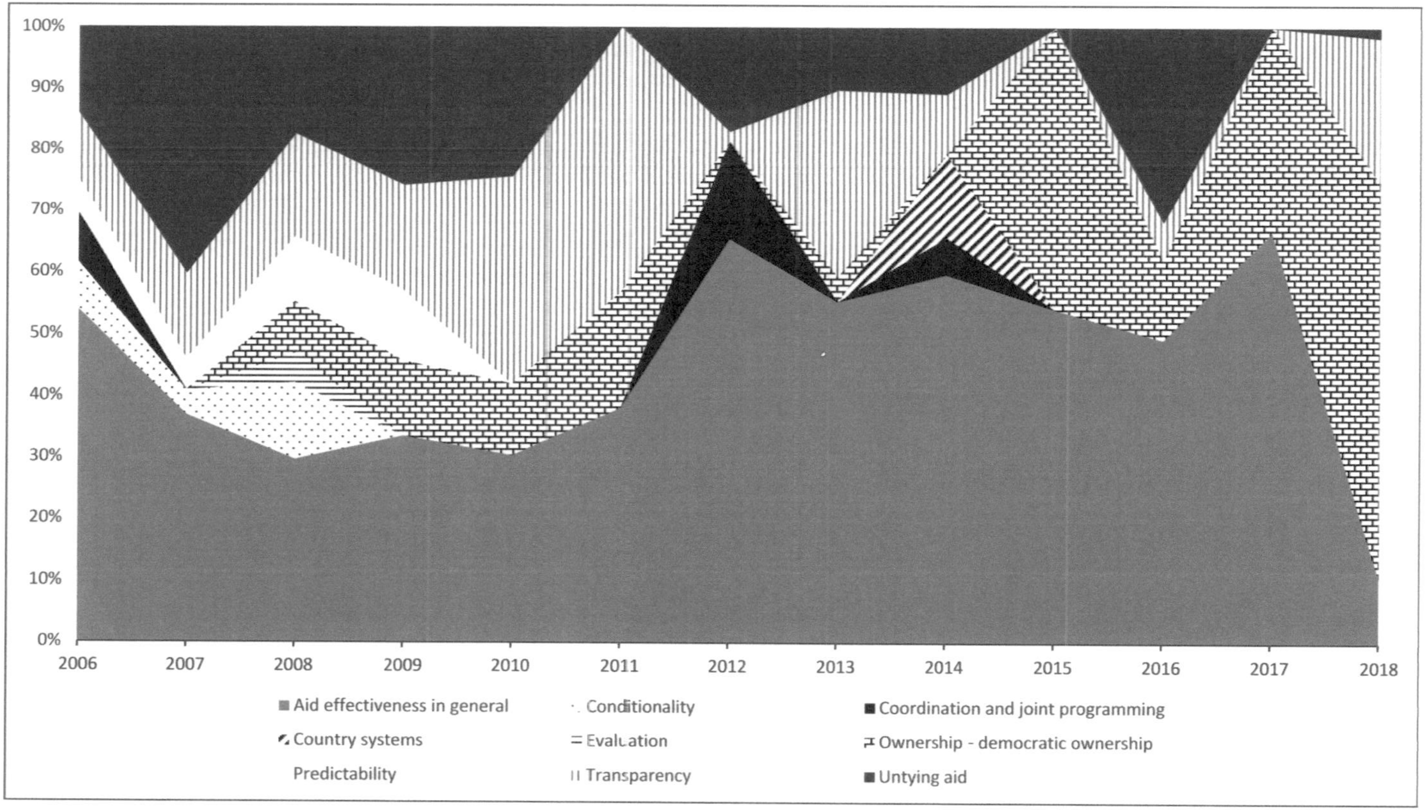

Figure 4.2 Shifts in aid effectiveness sub-themes discussed in the AidWatch Reports, 2006 to 2018
Source: compiled by the author, based on CONCORD (2006; 2007; 2008; 2009; 2010; 2011; 2012; 2013; 2014; 2015a; 2016; 2017c; 2018).

AidWatch Reports showed the loss in the value of aid that developing countries experienced due to tying (see e.g. CONCORD 2007: 15), and also argued that donors informally still continued to tie their aid, despite formal untying (CONCORD 2009). The reports provide many specific examples, emphasising the harm this caused in terms of increasing costs for developing countries.

The final aid effectiveness topic which received more detailed attention was ownership, which CONCORD interpreted in a slightly different way than the more mainstream, official aid effectiveness narratives did, and termed it 'democratic' ownership. Ownership, in the mainstream sense, refers to developing countries making the decisions on their own development priorities, and official donors have generally interpreted this as aligning their activities with local development plans, usually created by national governments. This assumes that developing country governments and elites are actually developmentally minded (Booth 2012). Democratic ownership, in CONCORD's interpretation however recognises the shortcomings of the mainstream view, especially regarding its assumptions about elites, and refers to aid planning processes where the 'voices and concerns of citizens and parliaments are central to national development plans' (CONCORD 2009: 13). In this sense, democratic ownership implies a broad, participatory and consultative process, as opposed to governing elites formulating development plans. CONCORD called on donors to support these processes, and not undermine them by attaching economic and policy conditionalities to their aid, a recent example of which have been the EU's migration compacts under the New Partnership Framework (CONCORD 2018: 22).

Discussions on aid effectiveness in the AidWatch Reports have been much more reactive than those on aid quantity (and especially aid inflation). For example, they were especially prevalent around the various High Level Forums on Aid Effectiveness (Accra in 2008 and Busan in 2011), when CONCORD called on the EU to take a leading role. They also urged EU member states to actually implement the commitments they had agreed to in these High Level Forums and also in the EU, or, in case of untying aid, the OECD DAC. Advocacy related to democratic ownership was however clearly more proactive: similarly to inflated aid, NGDOs have put forward a new concept, which was much broader, inclusive and more demanding than the traditional understanding of ownership used by official donors.

It is also interesting that the AidWatch Reports have been rather silent on many of the specific tools and practices which donors have at their disposal to increase aid effectiveness. Using country systems, greater donor coordination (including working together in joint programming), and budget support have received very few mentions in the reports. It seems that CONCORD was content with calling for adherence to broad principles, but when it came to defining the details, or how implementing these principles should look like in practice, they had relatively little to say.

The fourth main theme in the AidWatch Reports relates to the purposes of aid, or in other words, what donor goals and motivations should foreign aid serve. As shown in Figure 4.1, this topic has gained relative importance in the reports as the years passed. CONCORD took an unequivocal position that the purpose of aid should be poverty reduction, and donors should not use aid resources to promote more 'selfish' goals. While foreign aid, since its inception, had been used to further the strategic interests of donors in terms of improving security, building alliances, or increasing trade flows (see e.g. Alesina and Dollar 2000; Younas 2008; Hoeffler and Outram 2011; Szent-Iványi 2012), the narrative that has been projected by the global development community, especially since the acceptance of the MDGs at the turn of the Millennium, was that aid should serve poverty reduction (Fukuda-Parr and Hulme 2011), and in fact it has a unique role to play in these processes. This gave NGDOs a strong point of reference to call for poverty focused aid, and argue that aid's mission should primarily be the alleviation of human suffering. The AidWatch Reports provided many examples of what poverty-focused aid looks like in practice in terms of its sectoral and country allocation, and often singled out donors which performed weakly in this field. CONCORD often warned the EU that using aid to reduce poverty was a principle to which it had committed itself in its founding treaties, most recently the Lisbon Treaty. For example, the 2011 AidWatch Report (CONCORD 2011: 10), argued that

> The EU must resist the urge to link their aid more formally to their foreign policy and security agendas, since this undermines the poverty-focus of aid and is contrary to Lisbon Treaty obligations. Development aid must be allocated to where it is needed and can help people lift out of poverty. Allocations and policies must not be driven by regional and global security concerns.

As the paragraph above implies, European donors have made increasingly visible attempts to divert aid away from the poverty reduction goal they had committed themselves to, towards other purposes, especially security-related actions, but also combatting climate change, funding the private sector, and reducing/managing migration (Furness and Gänzle 2016; Rozbicka and Szent-Iványi 2020). While discussions around the purposes of aid have been present since the earliest AidWatch Reports, they have become increasingly vocal over the years regarding how aid's main, or indeed sole purpose should be poverty reduction, and how donors should not divert aid towards selfish goals (security or migration); do so only under very strict rules (funding the private sector); or ensure that the resources they use are actually additional to existing, poverty-focused aid spending (climate change).

The securitisation of aid, which includes using ODA to support donor security interests, but also classifying military expenses as ODA and attempts to loosen the definition of ODA to allow for such classification, received significant attention in the earlier reports, especially in 2009

(CONCORD 2009: 17) and 2011 (CONCORD 2011). With the establishment of the EU's External Action Service (EEAS) in 2010, CONCORD feared that foreign policy interests would gain stronger influence over aid spending, leading to an instrumentalisation of aid for foreign and security policy purposes (CONCORD 2011: 6). The 2017 report argued that EU security concerns are clearly undermining the integration's development agenda (CONCORD 2017: 18).

The attempts of the EU and member states to divert aid from poverty reduction intensified, and also diversified from security to other areas in the 2010s, and CONCORD engaged in reactive advocacy in response to all these attempts. The issue of aid for climate change mitigation and adaptation became increasingly prominent after 2009, when the (legally non-binding) political accord coming out of the Copenhagen Climate Conference committed developed countries to raise 'new and additional' resources to help developing countries mitigate the effects of, and adapt to climate change (Copenhagen Accord 2009: 3). CONCORD's advocacy focused on how these resources should indeed be additional, and not a diversion of existing ODA spending, or a simple rebranding of existing ODA as climate spending. Nor should climate funding be counted as ODA, and inflate progress towards the 0.7 per cent goal (CONCORD 2010: 13). The advocacy in the AidWatch Reports concentrated on the fact that there were no unambiguous standards for identifying what climate aid was, and many donors had no policy for defining what 'new and additional' meant (CONCORD 2011: 17). Much of CONCORD's advocacy on climate aid in the later AidWatch Reports concentrated on identifying donor practices in terms of double counting and rebranding existing ODA as climate finance, and calling for the development of clear guidelines and greater transparency on what exactly counted as climate finance.

Funding the private sector emerged as a goal of the EU with the 2011 policy paper *Agenda for Change* (European Commission 2011), and the EU increasingly saw blended financing and using aid to leverage private investments as a way to raise further resources for promoting development in partner countries. The EU External Investment Plan, launched in 2017, provided a formal mechanism for putting these into practice. The AidWatch Reports voiced strong scepticism about the actual development impacts of these arrangements, arguing that there was no guarantee that aid could actually leverage investments which otherwise would not have happened. Furthermore, CONCORD argued that there were no explicit development targets in these private sector arrangements, investments were rarely targeted at the poorest, there was little transparency, and the resources often went to companies from developed countries (CONCORD 2013: 11–12). While in the earlier reports CONCORD strongly contested using aid to fund the private sector, the 2016 AidWatch Report marked a turning point, with CONCORD putting forward a set of recommendations on *how* the EU should fund it. Most importantly, the report argued that when aid was used to support private sector investments, these investments should follow the standard aid effectiveness criteria which aid projects normally should adhere to, including transparency, ensuring country ownership, monitoring and evaluation, and safeguards to minimise social and environmental risks (CONCORD 2016: 19–23; see also Rozbicka and Szent-Iványi 2020).

Finally, migration emerged as a topic after the 2015 European refugee crisis, and the EU's attempts, following the Valletta summit later that year to use aid to manage migration and reduce migratory pressures. These included a 6 billion Euro deal with Turkey, the creation of the EU-Africa Emergency Trust Fund to address the root causes of migration, as well as an emerging practice of tying EU aid to migration related conditionality, including requiring partner countries to sign return and readmission agreements with the EU under the New Partnership Framework launched in 2017 (Castillejo 2016; Szent-Iványi 2021). While CONCORD recognised the 'urgent need to deal with the migratory pressures' (CONCORD 2016: 15), they argued that aid's purpose was reducing poverty. ODA figures should not be inflated with expenses aimed at managing migration, such as funding provided to partner countries to strengthen their border controls, or the expenses of running migrant detention centres. The 2017 and 2018 AidWatch Reports were much more critical of EU and member state practices, and how they portrayed migration as a solely negative phenomenon which needed to be contained (CONCORD 2018: 25). Instead, CONCORD argued for developing pathways for safe and orderly migration, and also creating a more positive narrative of migration.

Finally, the AidWatch Reports have addressed a number of other topics as well, not belonging to either of the four main themes. Most of these made sporadic, and usually short appearances in the reports, such as promoting international financial taxation, policy coherence for (sustainable) development, or the MDGs/SDGs. CONCORD has also used the AidWatch Reports to react and make its position clear on various EU initiatives and processes, most commonly related to negotiations on the EU's Multiannual Financial Frameworks (MFFs). This explains the high emphasis on EU development policy in the 2012 and 2013 Reports (the negotiations of the 2014–2020 MFF), or in 2017 and 2018 (the 2020–2027 MFF). The latter period was also linked to the revision of the EU's main development policy strategy, the European Consensus on Development, where CONCORD was especially vocal on ensuring that poverty reduction remained the primary goal of EU aid.

Summing up the main findings on CONCORD's advocacy in the AidWatch Reports between 2006 and 2018, the topics covered span an extensive range of issues linked to development assistance. A number of conclusions emerge. First, aid quantity, and calling on donors to increase their 'genuine' spending was the single most important topic for CONCORD, although the issue did decline in terms of the relative emphasis the reports placed on it over the years. Second, this decline in relative emphasis was due to how the number of topics covered by the reports expanded over time, making them more complex. Third, aid effectiveness, while important, has mostly been discussed on a general level, and while CONCORD continuously called on EU donors to increase the effectiveness of their ODA, it provided little detail on how exactly this should be done, with few exceptions. Fourth, calling on donors to use aid to reduce poverty and not divert it for other purposes has also been a strong and consistent theme, especially since the early 2010s. Fifth, the AidWatch Reports included a mix of proactive and reactive advocacy. CONCORD has enriched the debate on foreign aid by putting forward concepts like genuine/inflated aid, and also democratic ownership. On the other hand, much of the advocacy in the reports reacted to events and the agendas of the EU or other donors, and so the reports served as a platform for CONCORD to communicate the NGDO position on these.

CONCORD's thematic publications

Data and methods

Beyond the AidWatch Reports, CONCORD also publishes a wide number of other advocacy-related papers and policy briefs which have relevance for debates on foreign aid. Some are detailed reports devoted to a specific topic, while others are short policy briefs, which can be fairly specific in some cases, such as articulating CONCORD's views and demands on a specific EU initiative or legislation. Since these reports and policy briefs are generally devoted to a single topic, there is not much sense in analysing them in the same depth and detail as with the AidWatch Reports above. Furthermore, given how CONCORD makes it positions known on basically all issues linked to aid in the AidWatch Reports, analysing the exact policy changes which CONCORD advocates for its other, stand-alone publications, would be repetitive. However, looking at the topics to which CONCORD decides to devote a separate report to can nonetheless be instructive, as it gives insight into which topics CONCORD may prioritise and place even more emphasis on.

To get of a sense of this, all reports and policy briefs between 2006 and 2018, covering the same period as the analysis of the AidWatch Reports, were downloaded from the publication archive on CONCORD's website (CONCORD 2020). All publications were downloaded from this archive for which CONCORD was the author (with the exception of the AidWatch Reports and the annual reports on CONCORD's activities). Each publication was once read to code its main topics, using the coding scheme in Table 4.1. One difficulty however quickly emerged: CONCORD's website mainly seemed to contain more recent thematic reports, and older ones were more sporadic. It is unclear whether CONCORD started publishing more thematic reports and briefs after 2015, or whether the relative paucity of pre-2015 material is due to a website change and the publication archive not being fully updated. The latter seems more likely. Furthermore, the oldest thematic report was from

2009. It is also unclear whether reports dealing with certain topics are more likely to be missing than others, thus introducing bias into the data. There is not much that can be done with this relative lack of earlier publications, other than keeping it in mind when interpreting the results.

Results

The results of this second coding exercise are presented in Table 4.2, which presents how many thematic CONCORD reports or policy briefs addressed a specific topic in each year between 2009 and 2018. As mentioned, CONCORD's thematic reports generally focused on a single topic, however they may still fit under more than one code under the coding scheme. For example, a policy brief calling on the European Commission to increase its funding for climate change can fit under three codes: increasing levels of aid and meeting aid targets, combating climate change, and EU development policy. To deal with this, a specific publication may be included more than once for a specific year in Table 4.2, and thus the total number of publications row usually includes a lower number than when the topics addressed are added up. Counting such publications more than once also makes sense as these papers are not equal: some policy briefs are only a couple of pages long, while the more substantial reports can run up to 35–40 pages or more. These longer reports are more likely to be coded under more than one topic, giving them more weight in the table.

Looking at Table 4.2, perhaps the most striking finding is that a significant portion of CONCORD's reports and policy briefs were directed specifically towards the EU, whereas the AidWatch Reports had a much broader audience, including member state governments, other actors in the European aid industry, and to a degree, the general public. Most of the reports covered in Table 4.2 focused on CONCORD's position and recommendations on a specific policy, which the EU at the time was discussing. Among the more recent reports, these included the 2021–2027 Multiannual Financial Framework and the new Neighbourhood, Development and International Cooperation Instrument (NDICI) which it introduced, the EU's Emergency Trust Fund for Africa, the post-Cotonou Agreement with the African, Caribbean, and Pacific (ACP) countries, the European Consensus on Development, the EU's financial regulations on how funding is spent, which actors are eligible to apply and how, or how the EU engages with the private sector or civil society. In all of these cases, CONCORD's recommendations and advocacy demands were familiar: more resources for development, an emphasis on partnership and partner country interests as opposed to those of the EU, and calling for a greater role for civil society in development cooperation in general, as well as for greater consultation with it in development of any new EU rules and practices.

Table 4.2 Topics addressed in CONCORD's thematic reports and policy briefs

	2009	*2010*	*2011*	*2012*	*2013*	*2014*	*2015*	*2016*	*2017*	*2018*
Aid quantity										
Increasing levels of aid and meeting aid targets	1	1					2			1
Inflated vs genuine aid							1			
ODA review process										
Aid allocation										
Aid to Sub-Saharan Africa							1	2		4
Aid to least developed countries										1
Human rights and rights-based approach										
Gender		1						1		5
Role of civil society						1	3	2	1	7
Aid effectiveness										
Conditionality										
Coordination and joint programming										
Country systems							1			
Evaluation										
Ownership/democratic ownership										
Predictability of aid flows										
Transparency										
Untying aid							1			

	2009	2010	2011	2012	2013	2014	2015	2016	2017	2018
Aid quantity										
Purpose of aid										
Climate change mitigation/adaptation						1		1		
Funding the private sector							1	1	1	
Poverty reduction		1								
Reducing migration							2	1		4
Security and aid securitisation										
Other										
EU development policy	1	1	1		1	2	5	5	4	15
Financial crisis										
MDGs/SDGs	1			1				3		
New aid modalities										
Policy coherence for development	1		1		2	1	5	2	1	2
Public support for aid										
Taxation and resource mobilisation							3			1
TOTAL number of publications	**2**	**1**	**1**	**1**	**3**	**3**	**14**	**7**	**5**	**21**

Source: author, based on reports and policy briefs collected from CONCORD's website.

A number of further findings also emerge. The themes which were prominent in the AidWatch Reports, especially increasing aid and the issue of genuine/inflated aid, while present in the thematic reports and policy briefs as well, were by no means as visible. Few of these reports dealt explicitly with increasing aid as an end in itself (as the AidWatch Reports sometimes seemed to imply), and where this theme did feature, it was more argued to be a means to achieve development goals such as the MDGs or SDGs. Aid effectiveness was even more conspicuously absent from these reports and policy briefs than it was from the AidWatch Reports. It only featured as the topic of a single publication from the period (CONCORD 2015b), and while there were references to aid effectiveness in some of the others, these remained vague and general.

The thematic reports however also covered a number of topics in much greater depth than the AidWatch Reports did. These were, most importantly, around policy coherence for (sustainable) development (PC(S)D), gender, and the role of civil society. PC(S)D has been a constant fixture among these publications, with at least one report or policy brief dealing with it each year. These have been rather proactive: compared to CONCORD's EU development policy related advocacy publications, these did not react to ongoing policy discussions, but rather focused on specific recommendations on how EU policies could be made more coherent with the goal of (sustainable) development, and thus not undermine the impact of aid. While PC(S)D appeared in some AidWatch Reports (especially CONCORD 2008), these separate reports were much more ambitious in their analysis and the recommendations they provided. Publications on civil society were similarly proactive, and were focused not only on the EU's approach to working with civil society organisations, but also provided guidance for these organisations, both Northern and Southern, on how to engage with EU delegations. These went well beyond the relatively generic calls in the AidWatch Reports for donors to work more with civil society. Finally, publications on gender were more reactive and focused on ongoing EU policy debates, although they perhaps had a stronger evaluative approach, such as a report evaluating the EU's Gender Action Plan (GAP) II (Allwood 2018).

Based on this brief analysis, CONCORD's thematic reports and policy briefs seem to complement and add to the AidWatch Reports, but are also more targeted in their audience. This latter observation is also reinforced by the fact that while the AidWatch Reports are professionally produced with high quality graphics and layout, many of the policy briefs are fairly rudimentary, focusing on the message and not the packaging.

Do individual NGDOs do advocacy differently? The case of Oxfam

CONCORD claims that its advocacy is representative of the entire sector's interests, which implies that the in-depth analysis of their publications in the previous two sections should give us a comprehensive picture of what the

European NGDO sector stands for. However, there are reasons to think that this may not necessarily be the case. Most importantly, given its broad direct and indirect membership, CONCORD's positions may actually reflect the lowest common denominator in the sector, the topics that 28 (pre-Brexit) national NGDO platforms and 25 large networks could agree on. While NGDOs across Europe are tied together by a shared moral vision of supporting the poor in the Global South, the national platforms differ widely in their capacities, and many of the transnational networks are specialised on certain topics (see Chapter 3), which will have an impact on their advocacy preferences.

Whether CONCORD's views are representative or not of the sector is difficult to cross-check, as it would require analysing the advocacy of at least its 25 large network members. Given how the national platforms all have separate country pages in the AidWatch Reports, their views enter more directly and can thus be assumed to be represented by CONCORD. However, their country pages mainly include advocacy demands towards their national governments, and less so towards the EU. CONCORD, with its relatively limited staff numbers, is not a prolific publisher. The large network member NGDOs on the other hand have much larger capacities for research and producing advocacy related material, and some of them publish several dozens of outputs each year. The sheer number of these documents make qualitative analysis impossible, and quantitative methods, such as comparing the frequencies of certain keywords in publications by different organisations can easily be misleading, as context matters significantly in these cases.

The remainder of this chapter cross-checks CONCORD's advocacy by analysing the advocacy publications of one of its member networks, Oxfam. While looking at just one member does not give a full picture of the diversity of the European NGDO scene's advocacy, it can serve to illustrate how individual organisational advocacy can differ from advocacy on the collective level. The reason for selecting Oxfam is that it is a generalist organisation active in a wide range of areas linked to development and foreign aid, as opposed to most CONCORD networks members which are specialised, such as on women or children. This means that Oxfam is likely to have a similarly broad-based advocacy as CONCORD, covering a number of topics linked to foreign aid.

Data and methods

Oxfam's advocacy-linked publications are included in its research/policy paper archive on its website (Oxfam 2021). The papers go back to 2008, and coverage seems full, which is a much better situation than with CONCORD's archive, although still not ideal, given how the analysis of the AidWatch Reports started from 2006. Nonetheless, a search in Oxfam's archive between 2008 and 2018 returns 577 papers, which is an order of a magnitude larger than CONCORD's (online accessible) output over the same period. Most of these papers were published solely by Oxfam, some were collaborative advocacy endeavours with other like-minded NGDOs, and a limited few were published by other organisations to which Oxfam is indirectly linked to (an AidWatch Report from CONCORD for example was also uploaded in one year). A striking feature is how robust these papers often are even from an academic perspective, underpinned by methodologically grounded empirical research and data. Many of Oxfam's papers are country-level case studies. All of this is evidence of the significant capacities Oxfam has built in research, including gathering data on the ground, and channelling the findings into advocacy.

The first step in analysing this huge dataset was to sort out the papers that were actually relevant, i.e. the ones which focused on development aid. This was not necessarily clear-cut, as the boundaries between aid and other topics linked to development in the Global South is blurry. For example, as briefly mentioned, the AidWatch Reports deal with issues around taxation and domestic resource mobilisation in developing countries, which is linked to aid because aid and taxes have often been viewed as substitutes (Clist 2016), and both serve as resources for funding development. However, taxation is also a distinctly different topic from aid, and while donors may have a role in supporting domestic resource mobilisation in developing countries, it is distinctly the partner country's responsibility. The guiding principle therefore to decide what was relevant from Oxfam's papers was to ensure comparability with CONCORD's advocacy. Specifically, the following steps were made:

1 The paper was deemed relevant if it could be coded using the scheme in Table 4.1.
2 If it did not fit into the scheme, but had a strong link to development aid, it was also deemed relevant.
3 Papers where the link to aid was more tenuous have been classed as irrelevant and excluded from the analysis.
4 Papers in which the advocacy was not directed towards a European actor were also classed as irrelevant for the analysis

There were four main topics which accounted for the bulk of irrelevant papers: humanitarian aid/disaster relief, conflict resolution, the arms trade, and advocacy directed towards businesses. Oxfam is a significant humanitarian actor besides its development work, which means that much of its advocacy was focused around humanitarian assistance, disaster relief, conflict management and resolutions, etc. While humanitarian aid has strong links to development aid, it is also conceptually different from it, and outside the scope of this book. The global regulation of the arms trade is a relatively distant topic from development aid, and so is Oxfam's advocacy towards businesses and multinational companies, which focuses mostly on their environmental impacts and working conditions in their supply chains.

Once the irrelevant papers were sorted out, 394 publications remained. To analyse these, a similar approach was followed as with the standalone

CONCORD papers and policy briefs, i.e. each was coded according to the main themes it addressed. The overwhelming majority of Oxfam papers focused very tightly on a specific topic, but as with coding the CONCORD papers, each paper could nonetheless receive multiple codes. The coding scheme in Table 4.1 was used, but additional codes not included in the table also emerged (see below).

Results

The analysis reveals that Oxfam's advocacy was much broader than that of CONCORD, and it covered many topics which were not really present in the AidWatch Reports. The most important of these 'new' themes included various sectoral aspects of development cooperation, such as agricultural aid and food security, health aid, education aid, or support for water and sanitation. Such sectoral level discussions were very rare in the AidWatch Reports, which was understandable given their summative nature. Going into sectoral analysis of aid seems much more feasible with standalone policy and research papers. Oxfam has also placed significant attention on inequalities, and instead of using aid to reduce poverty per se, the emphasis has often been on reducing inequalities. This goes beyond calls for supporting the poor, to include greater demands around the redistribution of income through taxation of those well-off.

The large number of publications and topics each year means that it is possible to track the evolution of relative emphasis put on each topic over the years, similarly to CONCORD's AidWatch. Figure 4.3 shows the evolution of the 12 most frequent themes in Oxfam's 394 policy/research papers with links to foreign aid, between 2008 and 2018. The figure is especially instructive when compared with Figure 4.1, and it illustrates how an individual NGDO can have different advocacy priorities than the entire NGDO community as represented through CONCORD. Oxfam placed a much lower relative emphasis on increasing aid volumes than CONCORD did (Chapter 6 looks at potential reasons for this in more detail), and the debate around inflated/genuine aid hardly entered its policy papers. Aid effectiveness, while making sporadic appearances and even having some dedicated papers (see e.g. Oxfam 2010), was not a strong theme either. Finally, while Oxfam often called on donors to provide aid to a specific country in need, its publications hardly featured any overall discussions of aid allocation.

What does appear strongly and very consistently with Oxfam is climate change adaptation and mitigation, often in conjunction with other topics, such as food security and inequality/poverty. The discussions on climate change are less about the technical aspects around accounting climate finance as in the case of CONCORD's AidWatch Reports (although these feature as well, see e.g. Oxfam 2015), but more around the impact climate change is having on livelihoods in developing countries, and how donors and other stakeholders should react to this. Oxfam's advocacy on climate change was

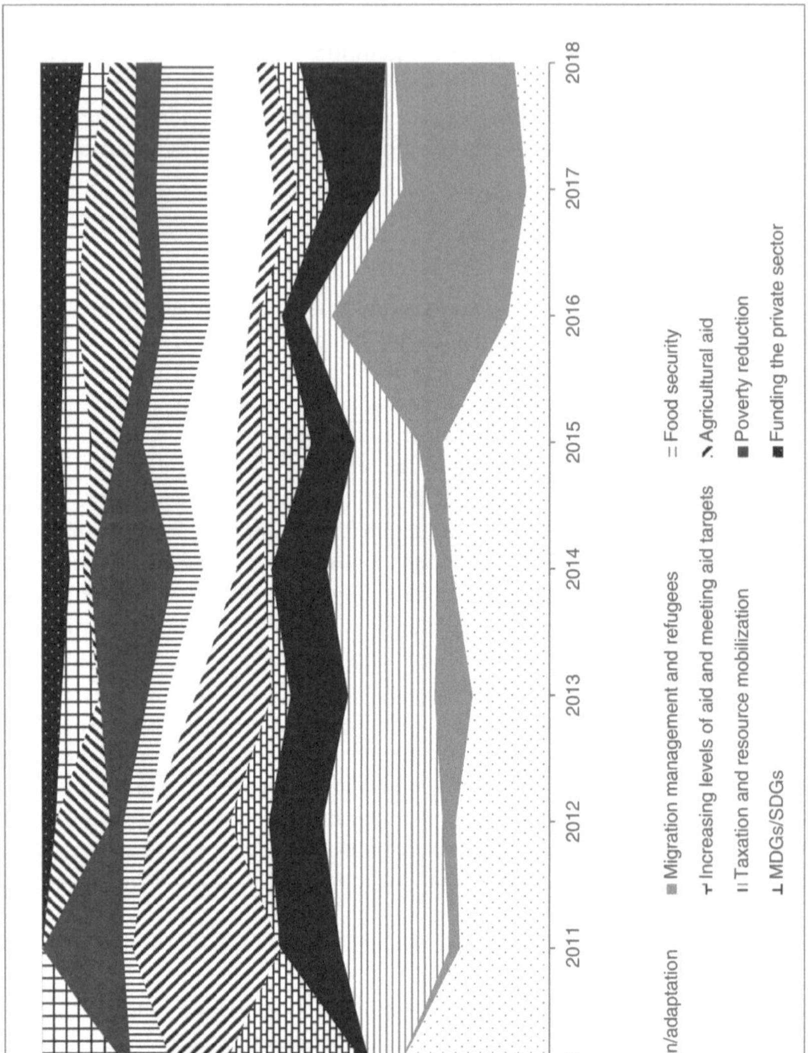

Figure 4.3 Evolution of the twelve most frequent themes in Oxfam's publications between 2008 and 2018
Source: compiled by the author, based on publications from Oxfam (2021c).

also much more constant and not only linked to various high-profile events. Linked to climate change, Oxfam has also put significant emphasis on supporting agriculture in developing countries and ensuring food security and rural livelihoods. Much of the advocacy in this area focused especially on small scale farmers in the Global South, as Oxfam saw their livelihoods most threatened by climate change, and aimed to proactively draw attention to the situation of these often neglected people.

Taxation and domestic resource mobilisation, often linked to advocacy on the tax behaviour of multinational corporations and the need for global taxation and tax justice, were also strong themes in Oxfam's advocacy, present throughout the period, and much more visibly so than in the case of AidWatch. Strengthening governance using donor funding and dialogue with partner countries, although not on the list of the most relevant themes and thus not included in Figure 4.3, also featured more heavily in Oxfam's papers than it did with CONCORD. Oxfam adopted the concept of democratic governance promoted by CONCORD (see e.g. Oxfam 2013), but also used governance in the more mainstream understanding.

Oxfam's advocacy does not differ much from CONCORD's on a number of other topics however. It is similarly reactive on EU development policy issues, and on the MDGs and SDGs. Advocacy on EU issues included the EU's linking of aid and migration (Oxfam 2016c), the implementation of the SDGs (Oxfam 2016a), or the European Consensus on Development (Oxfam 2016b). EU-related advocacy was also often done together with other like-minded organisations through open letters and joint statements (see e.g. Joint NGO statement 2016), especially regarding migration and refugees. Furthermore, some of Oxfam's EU-related advocacy went beyond EU development policy, and criticised the EU in areas like its energy policy and biofuel mandate, which it saw as promoting global food price increases (Oxfam 2012; 2014). As further evidence of being reactive, Oxfam only started putting more emphasis on issues like using aid to fund the private sector or managing migration through aid after these increasingly became practices in the EU following 2011 and 2015 respectively. Managing migration through aid, and also the whole issue of increasing arrivals of refugees and migrants to Europe, especially from the Middle East, emerged as possibly the most important topic in Oxfam's advocacy post-2015.

The dynamic topic map of Oxfam's advocacy between 2008 and 2018 has therefore revealed both similarities with CONCORD's work, but also some differences in emphasis, most notably lower attention to aid volumes and aid effectiveness, and more to issues like climate change, food security and the livelihoods of the poor. Both cases support the idea that NGDO advocacy follows the topics which are on the European Commission's agenda, and is thus reactive: for example, in both cases, we see the appearance of advocacy linked to private sector funding after the publication of the EU's Agenda for Change in 2011. However, Oxfam is also proactive on certain issues, although not fully the same ones as CONCORD emphasises.

The comparison of two topic maps shows how there are differences in advocacy within the European NGDO sector. These are not differences in the policies that NGDOs promote, rather differences in emphasis placed of different themes. Further comparisons with other groups would be instructive, but are beyond the scope of this text. Nonetheless, a number of interesting puzzles emerge. Why does collective NGDO advocacy through CONCORD focus so much on aid volumes? Why is aid effectiveness relatively neglected in both cases? Chapter 6 aims to explain these differences using insights from the book's theoretical framework. First however, Chapter 5 analyses the main characteristics of how the European NGDO sector is funded.

References

Alesina, A. & Dollar, D. (2000). Who Gives Foreign Aid to Whom and Why? *Journal of Economic Growth*, 5 (1): 33–63. https://doi.org/10.1023/A:1009874203400.

Allwood, G. (2018). *Transforming Lives? EU Gender Action Plan II, From Implementation to Impact*. Brussels: CONCORD.

Booth, D. (2012). Aid Effectiveness: Bringing Country Ownership (and Politics) Back in. *Conflict, Security & Development* 12 (5): 537–558. https://doi.org/10.1080/14678802.2012.744184.

Castillejo, C. (2016). The European Union Trust Fund for Africa: A Glimpse of the Future for EU Development Cooperation. DIE Discussion Paper 22/2016.

Clist, P. (2016). Foreign Aid and Domestic Taxation: Multiple Sources, One Conclusion. *Development Policy Review* 34: 365–383. https://doi.org/10.1111/dpr.12154.

Collier, P. & Dollar, D. (2002). Aid Allocation and Poverty Reduction. *European Economic Review* 46 (8): 1475–1500. https://doi.org/10.1016/S0014-2921(01)00187-8.

CONCORD (2006). AidWatch Report 2006. EU Aid: Genuine Leadership or Misleading Figures?Brussels: CONCORD.

CONCORD (2007). AidWatch Report 2007. Hold the Applause! EU Governments Risk Breaking Aid Promises. Brussels: CONCORD.

CONCORD (2008). AidWatch Report 2008. No Time to Waste: European Governments behind Schedule on Aid Quantity and Quality. Brussels: CONCORD.

CONCORD (2009). AidWatch Report 2009. Lighten the Load: In a Time of Crisis, European Aid Has Never Been More Important. Brussels: CONCORD.

CONCORD (2010). AidWatch Report 2010. Penalty Against Poverty: More and Better EU Aid Can Score Millennium Development Goals. Brussels: CONCORD.

CONCORD (2011). AidWatch Report 2011. Challenging Self-Interest. Getting EU aid it for the fight against poverty. Brussels: CONCORD.

CONCORD (2012). AidWatch Report 2012. Aid We Can: Invest More in Global Development. Brussels: CONCORD.

CONCORD (2013). AidWatch Report 2013. The Unique Role of European Aid – The Fight Against Global Poverty. Brussels: CONCORD.

CONCORD (2014). AidWatch Report 2014. Europe's Role in Financing and Implementing Sustainable Development Goals Post-2015. Brussels: CONCORD.

CONCORD (2015a). AidWatch Report 2015. Looking to the Future, Don't Forget the Past. Aid Beyond 2015. Brussels: CONCORD.

CONCORD (2015b). What's in the Commitment? Unlocking 0.7%. Policy Paper, May. https://library.concordeurope.org/record/1720/files/DEEEP-PAPER-2016-056.pdf.
CONCORD (2016). AidWatch Report 2016. This is Not Enough! Brussels: CONCORD.
CONCORD (2017). AidWatch Report 2017. EU Aid Uncovered. How to Reach the Target on Time. Brussels: CONCORD.
CONCORD (2018). AidWatch Report 2018. EU Aid: A Broken Ladder? Brussels: CONCORD.
CONCORD (2020). Resources/Our Publications. https://concordeurope.org/resources/our-publications/.
Copenhagen Accord (2009). Copenhagen Accord. UN Framework Convention on Climate Change, Conference of the Parties, 15th Session, Copenhagen, 7–18 December 2009. http://unfccc.int/resource/docs/2009/cop15/eng/l07.pdf.
Council of the EU (2005). Presidency Conclusions of the Brussels European Council (16 and 17 June 2005). Doc. 10255/1/05.
European Commission (2011). Increasing the Impact of EU Development Policy: An Agenda for Change. COM(2011) 637 final. Brussels: European Commission.
Fritz, L. & Raza, W. (2017). Living up to Policy Coherence for Development? The OECD's Disciplines on Tied Aid Financing. *Development Policy Review* 35: 759–778. https://doi.org/10.1111/dpr.12264.
Fukuda-Parr S. & Hulme, D. (2011). International Norm Dynamics and the End of Poverty: Understanding the Millennium Development Goals. *Global Governance* 17 (1): 17–36.
Furness, M., & Gänzle, S. (2016). The European Union's Development Policy: A Balancing Act Between 'a More Comprehensive Approach' and Creeping Securitization. In: Brown, S. & Grävingholt, J. (eds) *The Securitization of Foreign Aid*. Basingstoke: Palgrave Macmillan, pp. 138–162.
Hall, S. (2011). Managing Tied Aid Competition: Domestic Politics, Credible Threats, and the Helsinki Disciplines. *Review of International Political Economy* 18 (5): 646–672. https://doi.org/10.1080/09692290.2011.599522.
Hoeffler, A. & Outram, V. (2011). Need, Merit, or Self-interest? What Determines the Allocation of Aid? *Review of Development Economics* 15 (2): 237–250. https://doi.org/10.1111/j.1467-9361.2011.00605.x.
Joint NGO Statement (2016). EU Leaders Can Save Lives this Winter if They Change Migration Policies. Joint NGO Statement ahead of the European Council of 15 December 2016. https://www.oxfam.org/en/research/eu-leaders-can-save-lives-winter-if-they-change-migration-policies.
Oxfam (2010). 21st Century Aid. Recognizing Success and Tackling Failure. https://www.oxfam.org/en/research/21st-century-aid.
Oxfam (2012). The Hunger Grains. The Fight is on. Time to Scrap EU Biofuels Mandates. https://www.oxfam.org/en/research/hunger-grains.
Oxfam (2013). Held to Account. Putting Democratic Governance at the Heart of Development Finance. https://www.oxfam.org/en/research/held-account.
Oxfam (2014). The EU's 2030 Energy and Climate Change Package. Fit for a Food and Energy-secure World?https://www.oxfam.org/en/research/eus-2030-energy-and-climate-change-package.
Oxfam (2015). The Roadmap to $100bn Per Year by 2020: A Foundation for Success in Paris. https://www.oxfam.org/en/research/roadmap-100bn-year-2020-foundation-success-paris.

Oxfam (2016a). From Agenda 2030 to Post-Paris Climate Action: Six Areas in Which the Dutch Presidency Can Drive EU Implementation of Global Deals. https://www.oxfam.org/en/research/agenda-2030-post-paris-climate-action-six-areas-which-dutch-presidency-can-drive-eu.

Oxfam (2016b). Red Lines for the EU's New Development Framework. Position Paper on the Review of the European Consensus of Development. https://www.oxfam.org/en/research/red-lines-eus-new-development-framework.

Oxfam (2016c). Causing Suffering and Problems. Europe's Approach to Migration. https://www.oxfam.org/en/research/causing-suffering-and-problems.

Oxfam (2021). Policy Papers. https://www.oxfam.org/en/research.

Rozbicka, P. and Szent-Iványi, B. (2020). European Development NGOs and the Diversion of Aid: Contestation, Fence-sitting, or Adaptation? *Development Policy Review* 38 (2): 161–179. https://doi.org/10.1111/dpr.12417.

Szent-Iványi, B. (2012). Aid Allocation of the Emerging Central and Eastern European Donors. *Journal of International Relations and Development* 15: 65–89. https://doi.org/10.1057/jird.2011.19.

Szent-Iványi, B. (2021). Practising What They Preach? Development NGOs and the EU's Emergency Trust Fund for Africa. *Third World Quarterly* 42 (11): 2552–2571. https://doi.org/10.1080/01436597.2021.1964358.

Szent-Iványi, B. & Timofejevs, P. F. (2021). Selective Norm Promotion in International Development Assistance: The Drivers of Naming and Shaming Advocacy among European Non-governmental Development Organisations. *International Relations* 35 (1):23–46. https://doi.org/10.1177/0047117820954234.

Younas, J. (2008). Motivation for Bilateral Aid Allocation: Altruism or Trade Benefits. *European Journal of Political Economy* 24 (3): 661–674. https://doi.org/10.1016/j.ejpoleco.2008.05.003.

5 Patterns of European NGDO funding

Introduction

Chapter 5 addresses the third objective of the book by analysing the funding of European development NGOs. It focuses mainly on examining the role of the EU in funding the sector, and provides macro-level data on the EU NGDO funding patterns. The chapter then proceeds to analyse the funding structures of the NGDOs which have been the most successful in winning EU funding. The findings of the chapter reinforce some well-established facts in the literature. For example, Western NGDOs are far more successful in winning funding from the EU than those from the Eastern or Southern member states. The findings also add new insights to the study of these groups: the largest NGDOs are highly adapt at mixing different funding streams and are not reliant on any single one, while smaller NGDOs, often thought to be closer to and more in touch with their grassroots, are actually often highly dependent on official funding.

EU funding: Macro-level patterns

Chapter 2 provided a theoretical overview about the different funding sources NGDOs may have access to, including official grants and implementing contracts from member state governments, the European Commission, or other multilateral funders; grassroots donations; grants from private philanthropic foundations (although these are less common in Europe than they are in the United States); and income from their own commercial activities, such as through charity stores selling second-hand donated items.

The EU provides a multilevel funding environment for development NGOs, and they can engage in 'venue-shopping' to ensure an optimal funding mix (Sanchez Salgado 2017). There are significant variations between how member states fund their NGDO communities, leading to different funding mixes (Pratt et al. 2006). France, for example, has a relatively weak national NGDO funding system, which forces NGDOs to seek funding on the EU level and from grassroots donations (Cumming 2008). In federal countries like Belgium, the regional level can also provide significant funding for

DOI: 10.4324/9780367861872-5

development NGOs (Molenaers et al. 2014). Countries like the Netherlands have traditionally been highly active in funding NGDOs, although such funding was cut in the mid-2010s, and also redirected from larger NGDOs to smaller ones (Schulpen 2016). National funding systems continuously change, including the amounts governments devote to funding NGDOs, the types of mechanisms they use, eligibility and reporting criteria, etc., which forces NGDOs to adapt (Pratt et al. 2006).

These differences in official funding systems have an impact on the size, strength, and composition of national NGDO sectors across Europe. However, NGDOs also face different conditions in access to funding due to broader historical legacies, including a history of colonialism or the generosity of the welfare state, rules on charitable giving, and how ingrained charitable giving is in various societies (Pennerstorfer and Neumayr 2017). In countries with strong traditions of charitable giving, NGDOs will find it easier to raise grassroots donations than in countries with weaker ones. These differences, coupled with the heterogeneity in size and organisational types discussed in Chapter 3 make it difficult to establish clear sector-wide patterns in funding for the whole of the European NGDO sector. Instead, they emphasise the need to investigate these patterns and country-level differences further.

The EU's data on the funding it provides for NGDOs is a good starting point for this, but it is also one of convenience, given that there are no member state level, comparable datasets. While some member states are more transparent than others in terms of how much funding they provide to non-state actors, others are not, making it difficult to create an EU-wide picture. Data on grassroots donations raised by NGDOs, aggregated on the national level, are even more difficult to obtain. This means that any assessment of the differences in NGDO funding between member states needs to start from the EU level. The EU publishes an online searchable database, the Financial Transparency System (FTS), which provides information on all contracts and grants concluded by the EU institutions, including the purpose of the funding (or title of the project), date of the award, the names and home countries of the direct beneficiaries, and the total amount of funding. It can be filtered based on type of receiving/beneficiary organisation (including NGOs), and also based on EU service or Commission Directorate General responsible for the funding, allowing the identification of international development-related funding. Previous research on NGOs has made use of this and other similar EU transparency databases (see e.g. Nancy and Yontcheva 2006; Mahoney and Beckstrand 2011; Sanchez Salgado 2014; Szent-Iványi 2014).

However, there are some limitations with the data in the FTS, which make it slightly less ideal. In the overwhelming majority of cases, it only includes total funding amounts for contracts and grants, and these are not broken down for individual beneficiaries. Many development projects are implemented by consortia involving several partners, and so it is not possible to attribute the exact shares of the funding received by each partner. This can be especially problematic in cases where NGOs/NGDOs receive only minor shares of the funding in large projects. This means that the information can only tell us the total value of projects NGDOs are involved in, but not the amount of funding they actually receive from these. While this is far from ideal, the value of projects NGDOs are involved in is not a bad proxy for EU funding. It is reasonable to expect that lead partners in consortia account for the largest share of the funding, and so looking at data with NGDOs as lead partners can provide a reasonably accurate picture, (even if the lead partner is not indicated in all cases, and seems to be missing for most funding awarded in 2017). The FTS also seems to lack project level details, such as short descriptions or details on implementation such as project start and completion dates. These limitations significantly reduce the possibilities for more sophisticated quantitative analysis of the data, but even by providing lists of NGDOs involved in EU funding, the FTS can help in gauging the presence and visibility specific NGDOs have towards the EU. A final issue with the FTS is that searching specifically for projects which involve NGDOs is only possible for the years between 2016 and 2019, which makes longer time series comparisons difficult.

The first dataset downloaded from the FTS includes all funding for NGOs/NGDOs located in EU member states managed by the Directorate-General for International Cooperation and Development between 2016 and 2019. This includes funding for grants and implementation contracts, both from the EU's budget (mainly, but not exclusively from the Development Cooperation Instrument, DCI) and the European Development Fund (EDF). Table 5.1 presents some descriptive details about the data. Between 2016 and 2019, about a fourth of the development actions funded by the EU included at least one NGDO. Approximately two thirds of these actions with an NGDO included a group from an EU member state, while the remainder either included only NGDOs from Southern partner countries, or from other developed countries (most notably Norway, Switzerland, and the United States). This shows that Northern NGDOs dominated the EU's development funding (at least when it came to direct funding relations between the Commission and various beneficiaries; Southern NGOs may have been indirect or final beneficiaries in many cases, but there was no information on this in the dataset). There was no clear trend in the data on

Table 5.1 NGDO participation in actions managed by the Commission's Directorate-General for International Cooperation and Development, 2016–2019

	2016	*2017*	*2018*	*2019*
Total number of actions	2,819	2,557	2,185	2,326
Actions including at least one NGDO	623	705	478	574
Actions with EU NGDO participation	408	468	307	408

Source: calculations of the author, based on EU FTS (2021).

the evolution of the share of NGDOs in these projects, although the four year period is too short to draw any conclusions on this.

To get a sense of the differences between member states, Table 5.2 shows a breakdown of the actions which include at least one EU NGDO, based on the NGDO's home country. Given the caveat mentioned above with the data, it is impossible to break funding amounts down to individual partners in each project. Therefore, each NGDO is attributed the full value of the project. This is of course problematic, as it can lead to significant instances of double counting in case of actions including more than one NGDO, as all of them will be attributed the full value of the project. Therefore, the amounts in each of the cells in Table 5.2 do not actually represent incomes to a given member state's NGDOs, but rather the total value of projects they are involved in. Despite this problem, the data is still useful for cross-country comparisons, and reveals a number of interesting findings.

The data in Table 5.2 reveals large differences in the success of NGDOs from different member states in terms of their participation in EU-funded development actions, with organisations from some countries being more successful than others. In absolute terms, it is no surprise that the largest member states do the best in terms of involvement, simply due to their larger number of NGDOs. However, even among them, countries which have strong traditions of voluntary action, such as the UK, stand out. It is therefore more instructive to look at the data in relative terms, on a per capita basis. The final column in Table 5.2 includes total values of actions which NGDOs from each country have participated in between 2016 and 2019, divided by the country's population for 2019. According to this metric, Irish and Belgian NGDOs have been the most successful ones over this period, followed by organisations from Denmark, the Netherlands, and (surprisingly) Slovenia. The average across the EU is 9.9 euros per person, and almost all of the countries below this average are Eastern and Southern member states (but interestingly also Germany and Sweden), with Poland being the country which's NGDOs participated in the fewest international development actions during the period.

A similar different picture emerges if, using a different approach, we attribute the entire project values to the lead organisation only, and other members of beneficiary consortia are simply left out. This means a slightly reduced dataset, as data on lead organisations, as mentioned, are not available for 2017. Table 5.3 presents a simplified view of this, with only total per capita amounts for 2016, 2018, and 2019. Due to the omission of 2017, the results are not fully comparable with those in Table 5.2. Nonetheless, Irish NGDOs are still the most successful, followed by the Dutch, Luxembourgish, Belgian and Danish ones. At the other end of the spectrum, there are very few instances of NGDOs from the Eastern member states, or indeed Southern ones such as Portugal or Greece, leading projects. This points to important capacity issues in these countries, and a lack of large NGDOs which are able to successfully organise and lead consortia in EU funding

Table 5.2 Total value of EU funded international development actions including an NGDO from each member state (and the UK), 2016–2019

	Total value of actions with an NGDO from the MS					*Population (2019)*	*Total 2016–2019 value per capita*
	2016	*2017*	*2018*	*2019*	*Total*		
Austria	10.30	49.59	24.41	28.76	113.06	8.86	12.8
Belgium	45.05	118.14	92.32	209.33	464.85	11.46	40.6
Bulgaria	2.25	37.64	5.31	14.04	59.24	7.00	8.5
Croatia	–	13.48	1.79	–	15.27	4.08	3.7
Cyprus	–	11.58	–	9.23	20.80	0.88	23.8
Czech Republic	8.85	45.60	6.86	21.97	83.28	10.65	7.8
Denmark	41.80	92.98	32.66	31.16	198.59	5.81	34.2
Estonia	7.17	9.89	–	10.72	27.77	1.32	21.0
Finland	9.30	22.71	17.62	9.69	59.32	5.52	10.8
France	133.24	192.63	143.09	208.72	677.68	67.18	10.1
Germany	109.82	159.37	119.89	138.91	527.99	83.02	6.4
Greece	–	19.54	3.96	18.43	41.93	10.72	3.9
Hungary	4.00	29.00	0.79	18.85	52.65	9.77	5.4
Ireland	10.53	73.48	73.63	64.17	221.80	4.90	45.2
Italy	81.62	173.02	89.62	178.92	523.17	59.82	8.7
Latvia	4.00	9.25	–	12.46	25.70	1.92	13.4
Lithuania	0.56	11.50	0.75	4.81	17.62	2.79	6.3
Luxembourg	1.20	4.19	2.23	1.00	8.63	0.61	14.1
Malta	4.60	6.21	–	0.30	11.11	0.49	22.5
Netherlands	88.58	171.68	96.97	145.58	502.81	17.28	29.1
Poland	0.40	40.32	0.94	19.95	61.62	37.97	1.6
Portugal	8.48	47.12	11.01	50.08	116.70	10.28	11.4
Romania	4.00	42.51	1.79	11.81	60.11	19.41	3.1
Slovakia	–	36.69	3.21	16.28	56.19	5.45	10.3
Slovenia	4.00	37.40	5.31	16.22	62.94	2.08	30.2
Spain	44.35	101.61	43.70	76.86	266.52	46.94	5.7
Sweden	21.83	26.22	16.65	15.02	79.72	10.23	7.8
United Kingdom	179.33	274.35	149.03	113.55	716.26	66.65	10.7
EU average							9.9

Source: calculations of the author, based on EU FTS (2021) and Eurostat (2021).

Note: project values in million euros. Population in million persons. Values per capita in euros.

bids. In the three years examined, there were no lead organisations from Croatia, Cyprus, Poland, Romania, or Slovenia. There was only one organisation from Bulgaria, Latvia, and Lithuania each, and two from Greece, Hungary and Slovakia each. The Czech Republic and Estonia are exceptions, however. In the former case, we see three organisations, and one of them, People in Need (Člověk v tísni), has led eight actions in these three years, including multi-million-euro ones. Looking at Estonia, we see a single NGDO, Mondo MTÜ, leading a very large action. In comparison, for example, there are nine Irish, five Austrian and eleven Swedish NGDOs as organisations leading EU-funded actions, underlining the significant differences in NGDO capacities between East and West.

Irish NGDOs seem to be most successful in winning EU funding. Ireland has channelled a significant part of its aid budget through development NGOs, and has seen them as a 'unique resource' that needs to be utilised fully in the delivery of Irish bilateral aid (O'Neill 2005: 314). Between 2006 and 2019, Ireland consistently channelled between 20 per cent and 26 per cent of its bilateral ODA as core contributions to NGDOs, compared to the OECD DAC average of around 3.5 per cent during the same period (OECD 2019). This strategic support to NGDOs has strengthened them and seems to have crowded-in EU funding as well. A DAC peer review already in 1999 highlighted how adept Irish NGDOs are at raising money not only from the state, but also the EU and the public (O'Neill 2005: 315).

None of the other well-performing countries is a surprise, as they all have strong bilateral development policies and vibrant domestic NGDO sectors. The success of Belgian NGDOs is fairly self-explanatory, given how many large networks have headquarters or representative offices in Brussels to ensure proximity to the EU institutions. Despite many positive changes since their accession to the EU, the development NGOs from the Eastern member states are still, on average, smaller, fewer in numbers, and financially weaker than their Western counterparts. Although membership in CONCORD and exposure to the EU level has had significant learning and socialisation effects on these Eastern NGDOs (Szent-Iványi and Lightfoot 2016), they have found it difficult to compete with Western ones for international, including EU funding (Szent-Iványi 2014), a finding from the previous literature which Tables 5.2 and 5.3 clearly support. There is also evidence that there are differences in the discourses and interests between Eastern and Western development NGOs (Profant 2019). The Slovenian NGDO sector has generally been seen as stronger than most in the Central and Eastern European region (Bučar 2012), explaining their relatively successful participation in projects, even though no NGDO from Slovenia has led projects between 2016 and 2019. The Czech NGDO community is also seen to stand out, mostly due to People in Need emerging as a major European NGDO (Szent-Iványi and Lightfoot 2016).

Table 5.3 Breakdown of per capita EU funding to NDGOs in EU member states (and the UK), with full action values attributed to lead organisations, total for 2016, 2018, and 2019

Country	*€/capita*	*Country*	*€/capita*	*Country*	*€/capita*
Austria	2.9	Germany	2.0	Poland	0.0
Belgium	6.7	Greece	0.4	Portugal	1.6
Bulgaria	0.1	Hungary	0.1	Romania	0.0
Croatia	0.0	Ireland	17.3	Slovakia	0.3
Cyprus	0.0	Italy	2.6	Slovenia	0.0
Czech Republic	1.3	Latvia	0.5	Spain	1.1
Denmark	6.3	Lithuania	0.1	Sweden	2.8
Estonia	2.8	Luxembourg	7.2	United Kingdom	3.3
Finland	3.1	Malta	1.2	**EU average**	**2.5**
France	3.2	Netherlands	7.9		

Source: calculations of the author, based on EU FTS (2021) and Eurostat (2021).

Note: per capita values in euros.

The micro level: Individual NGDOs

The data in the FTS allows going beyond the macro level and analysing the individual NGDOs which receive EU funding. It especially makes sense to look at the largest organisations in more detail. Table 5.4 lists the largest NGDOs in terms of the total value of EU development actions they participated in, also between 2016 and 2019. For the purposes of this analysis,

Table 5.4 The largest organisations in terms of involvement in EU-funded international development actions

Organisation	*Total value*	*Organisation*	*Total value*
Oxfam	227.4	Danish Refugee Council	66.1
CARE	187.0	Plan International	66.1
Save the Children	134.3	Action Aid	61.3
World Vision	94.1	WWF	58.0
Action Contre La Faim	90.7	Gorta/Self Help Africa	53.0
Deutsche Welthungerhilfe	82.2	Mercy Corps	47.9
Caritas	74.1	Handicap International	47.7
ADRA	73.5	Aga Khan Foundation	44.7
Concern Worldwide	73.4	GRET	40.8
ACTED	69.0	People in Need	39.4

Source: calculations of the author, based on EU FTS (2021) and Eurostat (2021).

Note: values represent the total value of actions the NGDO participated in between 2016 and 2019, in million euros. Transnational NGDOs consolidated into one organisation.

NGDOs with branches or network partners in more than one EU member state have been consolidated into a single actor. This makes sense, given how the book's interest in the advocacy these organisations carry out, which, especially towards the EU, is generally unified for the entire group or network.

Most of the NGDOs listed in Table 5.4 are not surprising: they are the ones with vast networks both globally and within Europe, and as discussed in Chapter 3, their European network members are mainly engaged in fundraising. Thus, Oxfam for example actually represents seven organisations across Europe (in Denmark, France, Germany, Italy, the Netherlands, Spain, and the UK). Similarly, in Save the Children's network, members from Germany, Italy, the Netherlands, Spain, Sweden, and the UK have been active in bidding for EU funding. On the other hand, some NGDOs are active in only one member state, such as Deutsche Welthungerhilfe, the Danish Refugee Council, Gorta or GRET, although these single-country organisations are a minority among the larger ones.

While these organisations have been the most successful in bidding for EU funding, in most cases acting as lead partners in consortia, the funding amounts in the EU FTS do not allow us to gauge just how important source the EU is in their funding mix. As mentioned, there is no single comparable EU-wide database where information on NGDO total incomes and their sources would be available, so it is very difficult to establish any sector-wide patterns. Data on funding mixes needs to be collected individually from NGDOs. Most of the larger groups and networks aim to be transparent and provide breakdowns of their funding sources, however, the collection of these is a highly labour-intensive process, as data need to be individually transferred from annual financial reports on NGDO websites. To smooth out annual fluctuations, several years need to be covered for all organisations. This makes the creation of a comprehensive dataset prohibitive, and only a sample of organisations is possible.

Therefore, to examine the significance of EU funding for NGDOs further, a sample of 14 organisations was selected. These 14 organisations were selected from the list in Table 5.4 of the largest EU funding recipients. The sample is mainly one of convenience: the original aim was to examine the financial accounts of all 20 NGDOs in Table 5.4, but not all of these organisations publish consolidated data for the entire group. Caritas and ADRA, for example, are highly decentralised organisations, and no network level financial data are available for either. CARE, World Vision, and Plan International, while more centralised than the loose networks of Caritas and ADRA, do not publish consolidated data, or if they do either, like Plan International, it does not provide details on funding sources. All five of these organisations have large global networks, making it extremely difficult to patch together network level data from the financial reports of their individual members. Finally, WWF was excluded, as it is not primarily a development NGO. The resulting 14 groups represent a mix of large EU-wide networks (such as Oxfam or Save the Children), as well as nationally significant organisations like Deutsche Welthungerhilfe or People in Need. While this approach clearly does not allow generalisation for the entire European development NGO community, it does allow the analysis of the balance between various forms of official funding and private donations for the NGDOs which are most likely to be active in advocacy.

The main international websites of all 14 organisations were searched to locate their annual financial reports. The reports covered the period between 2015 and 2019; it was not feasible to cover earlier years, as many of the groups did not have 2014 or earlier reports on their websites. Most of these financial reports included breakdowns of funding sources along rather similar (although not identical) categories; the data collection focused on five of these: income from (1) bilateral donor governments, (2) the EU, (3) other multilateral funders (especially the UN family), (4) individual donations, and (5) other income. This last category primarily includes trading activities (such as running charity shops), investment income, income from foundations or other NGOs, and corporate donations. While it would have been interesting to break down this category into further details, this was the area where there with the lowest degree of consistency between how NGDO reporting, thus lumping them together was the only way to achieve comparable data. Furthermore, some NGDOs reported corporate donations together with individual donations, which warrants caution, however corporate donations are unlikely to be significant for any of the groups.

The results of this exercise are summarised in Figure 5.1, which breaks down the incomes of the 14 NGDOs between 2015 and 2019 along the five sources of income (the note to the figure mentions some further caveats with the data not covered above).

A striking finding from Figure 5.1 is how little these large NGDOs rely on individual donations/grassroots funding, and, overall, how dependent they are on official donors (governments and multilateral agencies). The share of official funding of course varies between the organisations. Not taking the Danish Refugee Council and the Aga Khan Foundation into account, both of which have deficiencies in the data they publish, making it difficult to identify the volume of official sources (see notes to Figure 5.1), official funding is the lowest for Action Aid (26 per cent) and Oxfam (38 per cent). Both of these are NGDOs which raise the majority of their income in the UK, the country which has perhaps the strongest traditions of charitable giving in Europe. They are followed by another organisation of British origins, Save the Children (59 per cent). The remaining NGDOs receive on average a staggering 74 per cent of their income from official donors. Individual donations represent on average 20 per cent of the incomes of these 14 NGDOs, which underlines arguments on just how detached these organisations have become from their grassroots in Europe.

Despite this overall situation, some of these organisations clearly have healthier funding mixes than others, at least in terms of the diversification of

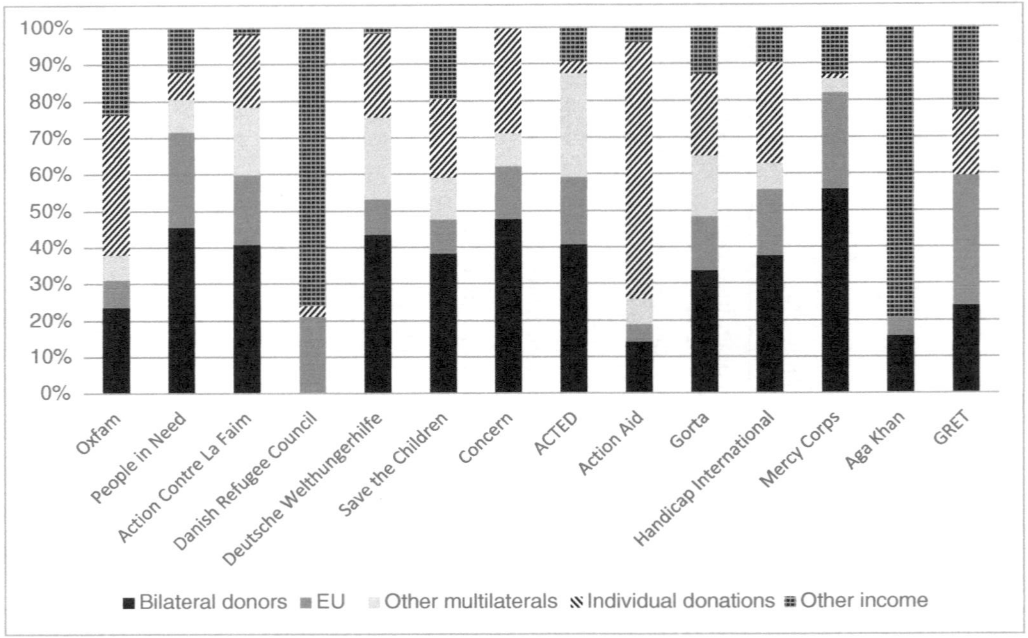

Figure 5.1 Income sources of selected NGDOs, 2015 to 2019

Notes: income shares for ACTED and Handicap International are based on data for 2016 to 2019, Danish Refugee Council and Action Contre La Faim on 2017 to 2019, and Gorta for 2015 to 2018. For the Danish Refugee Council, there is no data on bilateral donors and other multilateral donors, and these are subsumed into the 'Other' category. A similar caveat applies to the Aga Khan Foundation, which does not provide data for other multilateral donors and individual donations.

Source: collected by the author from NGO financial reports.

their income sources. It is not difficult to see how a diverse set of funders leads to greater organisational resilience. Being specialised on a limited number of funders makes the organisation vulnerable to situations where those funders decrease their overall aid levels (as has been the case for many European governments following the global financial crisis of 2008 and the subsequent European debt crisis), or specifically change their approach to funding NGDOs. There are also differences in the types of funding: most importantly, funding from official sources is generally restricted in its usage, i.e. tied to a specific project. While some of these may carry allowances for overhead costs, not all do. In some cases, such as EU grants, NGDOs bidding for funding may need to add their own resources as well to the project. It is therefore important for NGDOs to ensure a variety of different funds, including ones which are not restricted in their usage, as these are what allow them to operate smoothly as an organisation, and also build permanent capacities for fundraising, marketing, and core corporate functions like human resources, IT, and finance. While some governments may provide operating grants to NGDOs, unrestricted funds generally come from grassroots donations and own incomes, such as commercial activities, and so these have a key role to play in ensuring long term organisational viability.

NGDOs operate in a multilevel funding environment (cf. Sanchez Salgado 2017), and need to be adept at shifting between these levels. Increasing funding from another source in case one falls out is of course not straightforward even for organisations with relatively diversified funding mixes. The experience of Save the Children UK is highly instructive here. In 2018, the NGDO made a decision to withdraw from bidding for funding from the UK's Department for International Development (DfID). Members of Save the Children UK's senior management were accused of sexual harassment towards female employees, which the organisation at first tried to cover up. When the allegations where revealed, they led to a statutory inquiry, and the NGDO decided to not bid for UK government funding until it can rebuild public trust in itself (Abrahams 2018). This impacted not only its official funding, but also its public image and thus ability to raise donations, resulting in a fall of income of around £100 million between 2017 and 2018 (a quarter of its total). Save the Children UK stated in its accounts that it 'did not win enough new income to compensate for' the drop in income from DfID (Preston 2019), which shows exactly how difficult it can be for an organisation to substitute sources of funding with others, at least on a relatively short term. Nonetheless, a diversified funding stream gives more opportunities for an NGDO to make up for such lost income, even if this may not happen quickly.

Looking specifically at the role of the EU in funding in the 14 large organisations, there again seem to be significant variation. On average, the EU accounts for around 16 per cent of the income of the NGDOs in Figure 5.1, but the share seems the lowest for UK-based organisations, such as Oxfam, Save the Children, ActionAid, and the Aga Khan Foundation. This may be driven by Brexit, although during the period of analysis, British organisations where still fully eligible to participate in EU development actions. It may also be explained by the higher share of individual donations: funding from the EU is actually quite large for some of these organisations, as shown in Table 5.4, but the diversity of their funding, especially their ability to attract grassroots funding, means the EU is altogether less significant in their overall income.

At the other extreme, there seem to be few commonalities between the organisations which are the most dependent on EU funding. Size may be one explanation however: People in Need, GRET, and Mercy Corps (at least its European operations) are all relatively small in terms of their total incomes (varying between 30 and 100 million euros annually in the period under analysis), especially compared to giants like Oxfam or Save the Children. Figure 5.2 therefore analyses the data further, by comparing organisational size, measured by total incomes between 2017 and 2019, and the share of this income which originates from the EU. While a sample of 14 organisations is rather small for strong conclusions, the figure does imply a correlation between size and dependence on the EU: larger organisations generally derive a lower share of their funding from the EU, and this relationship holds, although in a weaker form, even if the British organisations are removed from the sample. This is not an unexpected finding: participation in a just a few EU projects (which tend to be large) can skew the balance for a small NGDO. However, there are some exceptions even for large NGOs: large French groups, like Action Contre La Faim and Acted derive close to a fifth of their income from the EU, and so does the Danish Refugee Council.

Similar comparative research into EU funding could reveal further details, however, NGDO financial reports are generally not granular enough for this. For example, it would be interesting to see specifically which EU funding instruments these NGDOs get funding from, including a differentiation between humanitarian and development funding, and potentially further breakdowns of the latter (such as, for the 2015–2019 period, between European Development Fund, EU budget, or funding from specific EU trust funds). Many, including Save the Children, GRET, Action Contre La Faim, and Oxfam, simply lump together all EU funding, making any further analysis difficult. Some organisations differentiate between development funding and humanitarian funding from the EU's DG ECHO (such as Concern Worldwide, Welthungerhilfe, the Danish Refugee Council, or Action Aid). The most transparent however are People in Need, which provides breakdowns of EU funding from each DG or service, or if it is a member in a consortium, also names the lead partner; and Handicap International, which provides project-level breakdowns of EU funding. Nonetheless, all this raises questions regarding just how committed NGDOs are to the transparency of their funding sources, especially if they bid for funding from more controversial EU aid instruments, such as the EU Emergency Trust Fund for Africa, which Chapter 7 analyses in more detail.

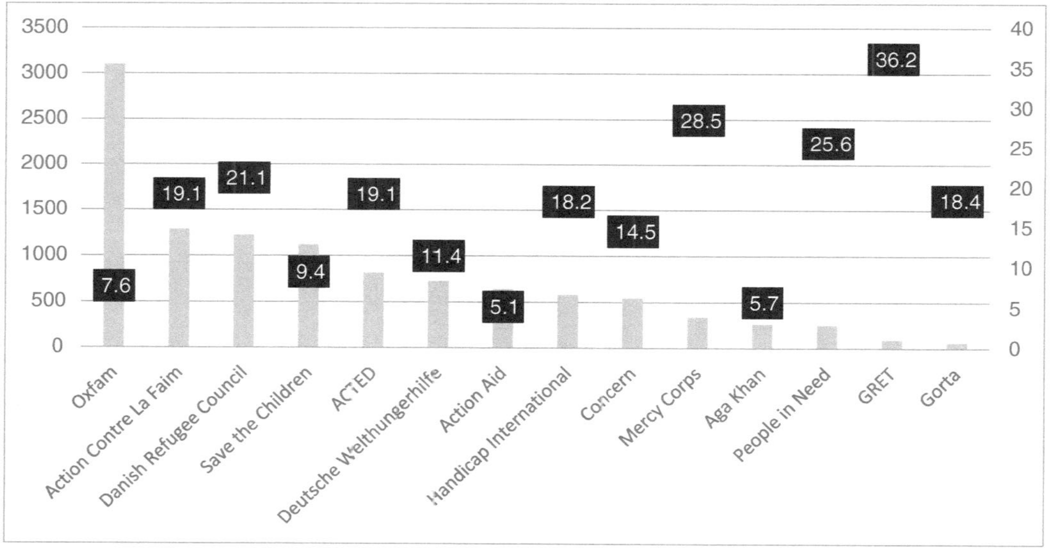

Figure 5.2 Total NGDO incomes and the share of EU funding, 2017–2019
Notes: Total incomes for 2017 to 2019, expect for Gorta which is 2017 to 2018. Incomes are represented by the bars, in million euros (left axis), the share of this coming from the EU is shown in the bubbles in percentage (right axis).
Source: collected by the author from NGO financial reports.

References

Abrahams, J. (2018). Save the Children Suspends DFID Bidding amid Sexual Misconduct Scandal. *Devex*. https://www.devex.com/news/save-the-children-suspends-dfid-bidding-amid-sexual-misconduct-scandal-92634.

Bučar, M. (2012). Involving Civil Society in the International Development Cooperation of 'New' EU Member States: The Case of Slovenia. *Perspectives on European Politics and Society* 13 (1): 83–99. https://doi.org/10.1080/15705854.2011.64917.

Cumming, G.D. (2008). French NGOs in the Global Era: Professionalization 'Without Borders'? *Voluntas* 19: 372–394. https://doi.org/10.1007/s11266-008-9069-5.

EU FTS (2021). Financial Transparency System. https://ec.europa.eu/budget/financial-transparency-system/index.html.

Eurostat (2021). Population on 1 January. https://ec.europa.eu/eurostat/databrowser/view/tps00001/default/table?lang=en.

Mahoney, C. & Beckstrand, M. J. (2011). Following the Money: European Union Funding of Civil Society Organizations. *JCMS: Journal of Common Market Studies* 49 (6): 1339–1361. https://doi.org/10.1111/j.1468-5965.2011.02197.x.

Molenaers, N., Nijs, L. & Huyse, H. (2011). The Belgian NGO Landscape and the Challenges of the New Aid approach: Dealing with Fragmentation and Emerging Complexities. Institute of Development Policy and Management Discussion Paper 2011.02.

Nancy, G. & Yontcheva, B. (2006). Does NGO Aid go to the Poor? Empirical Evidence from Europe. IMF Working Paper WP/06/39.

OECD (2019). Total Flows by Donor (ODA+OOF+Private) [DAC1]. OECD.stat. https://stats.oecd.org/Index.aspx?datasetcode=TABLE1.

O'Neill, H. (2005). The Foreign Aid Policy of Ireland. In Hoebink, P. & Stokke, O. (eds) *Perspective on European Development Cooperation. Policy and Performance of Individual Donor Countries and the EU*. London: Routledge.

Pennerstorfer, A. & Neumayr, M. (2017). Examining the Association of Welfare State Expenditure, Non-profit Regimes and Charitable Giving. *Voluntas* 28: 532–555. https://doi.org/10.1007/s11266-016-9739-7.

Pratt, B., Adams, J. & Warren, H. (2006). Official Agency Funding of NGOs in Seven Countries: Mechanisms, Trends and Implications. INTRAC Occasional Paper Series 46.

Preston, R. (2019). Save the Children UK's income drops by a quarter. Civil Society News. https://www.civilsociety.co.uk/news/save-the-children-s-income-drops-by-a-quarter.html.

Profant, T. (2019). *New Donors on the Postcolonial Crossroads. Eastern Europe and Western Aid*. London: Routledge.

Sanchez Salgado, R. (2014). Rebalancing EU Interest Representation? Associative Democracy and EU Funding of Civil Society Organizations. *JCMS Journal of Common Market Studies* 52 (2): 337–353. https://doi.org/10.1111/jcms.12092.

Sanchez Salgado, R. (2017). Europeanization of Civil Society Organizations in Times of Crisis? Exploring the Evolution Grant-seeking Strategies in the EU Multi-level System. *European Politics and Society* 18 (4): 511–528. https://doi.org/10.1080/23745118.2017.1286283.

Schulpen, L. (2016). *The NGO Funding Game. The case of the Netherlands*. Nijmegen: CIDIN, Radboud University, Nijmegen.

Szent-Iványi, B. (2014). The EU's Support for Democratic Governance in the Eastern Neighbourhood: The Role of New Member State Transition Experience. *Europe-Asia Studies* 66 (7): 1102–1121. https://doi.org/10.1080/09668136.2014.927646.

Szent-Iványi, B. & Lightfoot, S. (2016). Determinants of Civil Society Influence: The Case of International Development and Humanitarian NGOs in the Czech Republic and Hungary. *Comparative European Politics* 14: 761–780. https://doi.org/10.1057/cep.2014.50.

6 How do moral, reputational, and organisational incentives impact advocacy?

Introduction

Building on the previous chapters, Chapter 6 analyses the main themes in European NGDO advocacy. Using the theoretical framework from Chapter 2, it discusses how the themes NGDOs have selected for advocacy and how they deal with them provide evidence of their underlying motivations. Specifically, the chapter deals with six of the most prominent themes from CONCORD's advocacy: increasing levels of 'genuine' aid, aid effectiveness, aid allocation, and three instances of aid diversion: using aid to manage migration, fund climate change adaptation or mitigation and leverage private sector investments. For each of these, the chapter discusses the potential impact the policies advocated for would have on NGDOs' access to funding, how they relate to NGDO moral vision and specifically moral red lines, and what reputational risks or opportunities emerge. This last issue, as discussed in Chapter 2, will mainly be analysed by looking at the degree of the theme's politicisation.

The chapter uses academic and media sources to establish arguments on these three variables for all six of the themes. These sources are complemented by 31 interviews, carried out in several rounds between 2012 and 2017 by the author and various co-authors on past papers (Szent-Iványi and Lightfoot 2016; Rozbicka and Szent-Iványi 2020; Szent-Iványi and Timofejevs 2021). These interviews were with NGDO officials in Brussels (working at CONCORD and other networks, including Save the Children, Oxfam, World Vision, Solidar, etc.) and also in various member state capitals (mainly from national NGDO platforms). Respondents were usually those who worked on advocacy at each organisation, and in some cases the director of the NGDO's Brussels office. A full list of the interviews is available at the end of the chapter, however, interviewees have been anonymised to ensure confidentiality. The interviews focused on a number of topics related to NGDO advocacy, and contain a significant degree of information on the process of how development NGOs decide which topics enter their advocacy. About half of the interviews were carried out in person, and the other half were over the phone or via online video links.

DOI: 10.4324/9780367861872-6

The chapter proceeds along seven subsections, the first six of which address each of the advocacy themes mentioned above, along the theoretical framework's three variables. The final subsection synthesises the results and draws conclusions on the drivers of NGDO advocacy.

Increasing levels of 'genuine' aid

The most consistent element in CONCORD's advocacy has been the calls on donors to increase the amounts of aid they provide, and also to ensure that what they count as aid actually reaches the partner countries, i.e. it is 'genuine'. As discussed in Chapter 4, these calls for increasing aid and ensuring that it is genuine are closely linked, and made up the bulk of CONCORD's early advocacy. They remained an important topic in it ever since, and while potentially less of an important issue in the advocacy of individual groups as shown by the case of Oxfam, there is no evidence of any NGDO arguing against higher aid levels.

Politicisation

Generally, foreign aid has not been a highly politicised topic in most European countries, or at the EU level. The rationale behind this is usually seen in how the amounts European countries spend on aid are small compared to government spending in other areas, and how this spending generally has little visibility to voters. Unlike spending on domestic issues like education, healthcare or transport infrastructure, foreign aid does not impact the daily lives of voters in direct or visible ways. However, if either the amounts spent or foreign aid, or aid's impact on the lives of donor country citizens changes, the level of politicisation around it may change as well. Decisions to increase spending on aid relative to other government expenditures, or conversely, to not cut foreign aid when all other policy areas are experiencing austerity (see the case of the UK in Heppell and Lightfoot 2012), will conceivably increase politicisation. These decisions raise the alternative costs of aid: if more is spent on aid, where is the money taken away from? Foreign aid can also become more politicised when it links to policies which have impacts on the everyday lives of voters, such as immigration and security, thus increasing aid's visibility to the public (Raunio and Wagner 2021). Hackenesch et al. (2021) call this horizontal, or cross-politicisation. The 2015 European refugee crisis has been seen as an event that promoted such cross-politicisation of aid. Kiratli (2021) argues that aid has become more politicised after the 2015 European refugee crisis, and European electorates emerged as more supportive of aid, especially in countries which were experiencing higher inflows of migrants and refugees. This implies that voters may see a role for foreign aid in managing migration. Following the refugee crisis, governments and the EU did exactly that, and diverted significant amounts of aid for migration management purposes (Rozbicka and Szent-Iványi 2020; see also later in this section). Furthermore, Bergman et al. (2021) argue that populist radical right parties in Europe, while generally relatively silent on foreign aid, have also played a role in increasing political discussions on the usage of aid in managing migration.

This observation means that while the politicisation of aid spending may generally be low and it may not feature heavily in political debates, there may be sudden upticks which draw the public's attention to it. It would therefore be reasonable to expect similar periodic increases in NGDO advocacy on aid volumes in times when politicisation is higher. CONCORD's and Oxfam's advocacy however provides only weak support for this. CONCORD was relatively consistent in calling for more (genuine) aid between 2006 and 2018 (Figure 4.1 in Chapter 4), in fact its calls were the most pronounced on these before the austerity brought in by the financial crisis. The picture for Oxfam is slightly different: calling for more aid was actually highly pronounced in the aftermath of the financial crisis, supporting the idea that higher politicisation leads to more advocacy (Figure 4.3)

Impact on funding

The impact of greater official aid levels on development NGOs is reasonably straightforward: more government aid spending is likely to translate into more possibilities for NGDOs to access funding, although much depends on what form the increases take, and what share of the increases governments decide to channel through NGDOs. Governments can increase funding for facilities directly aimed at NGDOs, such as core funding or calls for grant proposals. NGDOs may also benefit if the government increases funding to sectors where NGDOs generally have advantages and are well placed to compete, such as healthcare or education. Counting only genuine aid when measuring progress towards aid targets means that governments have to increase their aid even more. While NGDOs may benefit from some inflated aid items, such as in-donor refugee costs given how some groups are often service providers for refugees or run refugee camps, they do not benefit from other forms of inflated aid, such as debt forgiveness, or hosting students from developing countries. Therefore, increasing genuine can be more beneficial for NGDOs.

Elucidating whether funding concerns actually drive NGDOs is difficult, because given how they portray themselves as morally driven actors, it is not something they would admit to openly. There is one telling bit of evidence however in CONCORD's publications, which are also present, albeit to a lesser degree, in Oxfam's papers: calls for the greater inclusion of NGDOs (both Northern and Southern) in development policy planning and implementation processes. A stronger role in these processes would allow NGDOs to exert influence on the types of projects donors fund, and lobby for interventions in areas where they have advantages. This in turn would potentially lead to more funding. Furthermore, the added value of donors involving NGDOs more is not always spelt out clearly, which raises feelings of these calls being self-serving.

Among the interviewees, some have expressed frustration over the funding landscape, and have argued that governments should increase NGDO funding or reverse cuts (Interview#14; Interview#15; Interview#19; Interview#21). There was however only a single interviewee who openly admitted that demands for more aid are indeed driven by NGDO funding concerns (Interview#21). A more widely shared argument however among the NGDO staff interviewed was that official funding and the size of the country's aid budget is not a chief concern for survival, due to diversified funding streams and an ability to engage in venue shopping (Interview#14; see also Sanchez Salgado 2017). Diversified funding streams, especially for larger NGDOs, therefore mean that they are able to detach their funding concerns from their advocacy priorities. One interviewee even argued that lower government funding should actually be seen in a positive light by NGDOs, as it would provide an incentive for them to engage more with their grassroots (Interview#24).

In all, there is some evidence that NGDO calls for increasing aid volumes are driven by funding concerns, but it is indirect and not particularly strong, and there are also arguments to the contrary.

Moral vision

Increasing aid is in line with NGDO moral visions of supporting the poor, although again the way donors increase their resources matters. Development NGOs will support poverty-focused aid, which has been a strong theme in both CONCORD's and Oxfam's advocacy, and may contest increases from a moral perspective in areas which they see as not supporting poverty reduction (such as increases for funding the private sector, see below). Nonetheless, it is difficult to argue that increasing aid in general would contradict NGDO moral visions, even though some have criticised the commitment to increasing aid as the way to eradicate poverty as being driven by a 'headless heart' (see e.g. Collier 2007). While the intentions of NGDOs may be sincere, there are strong, although debated arguments around how increasing foreign aid can cause more harm than good. These range from the creation of unintended macroeconomic distortions such as the Dutch Disease (Rajan and Subramanian 2011), through negative impacts on institutions and governance (Jones and Tarp 2016) and distorting donor interests (Bearce and Tirone 2010), to creating and maintaining relationships of dependency between donors and recipient communities (Moss et al. 2006). Proposals for 'better' or 'smarter' aid abound in the literature (see e.g. Joseph and Gillies 2008), and some have argued that making aid more effective is a better way to help the poor than increasing aid.

These arguments in the literature about the impacts of aid therefore imply that NGDOs may not be fully driven by moral motivations when calling for more aid, or disregard the debates on the negative impacts of aid for other reasons. These reasons may be linked to their motivations related to aid effectiveness, which is examined next.

Aid effectiveness

Aid effectiveness has figured prominently in CONCORD's advocacy, and has received attention in all AidWatch Reports, as well as other publications. As discussed in Chapter 4 however, most of the discussions have treated the topic on a highly general level. The subthemes within the aid effectiveness topic receiving more detailed treatment were transparency, democratic ownership, and untying aid, while many of the others were neglected. In Oxfam's papers, aid effectiveness was a rather marginal topic.

Politicisation

It is difficult to argue that aid effectiveness is politicised to any significant degree. While occasional media stories of wasteful projects or corruption associated with aid may surface, the topic receives even less public and political attention than aid volumes do. The main likely reason for this is that as opposed to the idea of giving more aid, improving the effectiveness of existing funds is rather abstract and technical. The potential impact of more aid on the lives of the Southern poor, as well and its alternative costs in donor country government budgets, can easily be understood by the public. Generating public understanding is more difficult in case of aid effectiveness, due to the technical nature of many aid effectiveness enhancing reforms. For example, looking at the five main themes of the 2005 Paris Declaration (OECD 2005), ownership, alignment, harmonisation, results-orientation, and mutual accountability, explaining these and the impacts of their implementation on the lives of the poor to the wider public can be challenging. Aid volumes can also be measured much more easily than aid effectiveness, and government spending on aid resonates much more strongly with publics than indicators measuring progress on partner country ownership or harmonisation. Data from the interviews support these ideas. One respondent has argued that the Paris/Accra/Busan aid effectiveness process has become highly technical (Interview#13), and it is difficult to communicate in advocacy. Another interviewee mentioned how discussions on donor coordination 'do not catch the eye of the readers' (Interview#15). Furthermore, readers of advocacy publications are interested in numbers and comparative tables, and it is difficult to quantify progress (or the lack of it) for aid effectiveness (Interview#17).

The lack of a high degree of politicisation means that NGDO advocacy relating to aid effectiveness will either be general and vague, or directed towards aid professionals in governments instead of the wider public. It may therefore be more emphasised in direct/insider advocacy than in advocacy publications. However, evidence has emerged from the interviews which may question this: one interviewee from a Western EU member state stated for example that they do not really engage their governments on aid effectiveness, as it is 'not really a topic in the policy debates' (Interview#19).

A lack of politicisation of aid effectiveness, due at least partly to the topic's technical nature, therefore seems to discourage NGDOs from raising it in their advocacy on a too detailed level.

Impact on funding

The diversity of themes under the broad umbrella of aid effectiveness makes it difficult to draw simple conclusions on what impact implementing these would have on NGDO funding. It makes sense to look at the sub-themes which have received the most emphasis first, transparency, democratic ownership, and untying aid.

Increasing the transparency of donor aid spending is most likely neutral in terms of its impact on NGDO funding, as it would simply require donors to publish more data on how they spend their resources. However, greater transparency would serve NGDO interests, as it would allow them to be more informed in their scrutiny of donor practices. Greater (democratic) ownership most likely also has only indirect impacts on NGDO funding. Increasing ownership by the partner country, i.e. ensuring that decisions relating to aid spending and development planning are made by the partner, can increase the influence of Southern and locally present Northern NGDOs over these processes. This is why CONCORD calls for 'democratic' ownership instead of the 'simple' ownership concept found in the Paris Declaration and other aid effectiveness initiatives. Democratic ownership is a much broader concept, and instead of focusing only on the partner government's role in aid planning, it refers to involving local communities and their organisations in these processes, thus giving NGDOs a role as well.

Untying aid is the area which has the most direct impacts on NGDO funding. Tied aid reduces the competition for aid implementation contracts and grants, putting donor country NGDOs at an advantage, compared, for example to groups from other donors or from the Global South. Northern NGDOs clearly have a financial disincentive to campaign for untying aid, and this has been documented rather explicitly in the literature by some observers (Carbone 2006). The relative prominence of calls to untie aid in CONCORD's advocacy are therefore not consistent with the funding argument, although there may be other factors at play here as well.

First, many donors have significantly reduced the de jure tying status of their aid since the mid-1990s (Clay et al. 2008), and NGDOs have already been adapting to this trend, or at least accepting it as inevitable. However, despite de jure untying, much aid in Europe remained de facto tied, or at least partially tied (Carbone 2014). While this topic has not received significant attention in the literature, there are indications that national

NGDOs still tend to be favoured by their governments in aid implementation procurement, and are more likely to win such contracts than foreign groups are (Meeks 2018). There are several channels through which such favouritism may happen, most importantly the informal ties that exist between policy makers and national NGDOs. These ties may allow more advance notice of new procurement tenders, better information for national NGDOs, or a better understanding of the needs and priorities of policy makers. According to Meeks (2018: 9), in 2016 around 51 per cent of ODA contracts 'were awarded back to firms in the country providing the ODA', even if that ODA was de facto untied. This means that NGDOs may not particularly worry about the impacts untying aid would have on their funding.

Second, the largest NGDOs may actually benefit financially from untying. There are strong parallels between the debates on untying aid and those around free trade. Both reforms create winners and losers. In the case of free trade, the competitive export companies will benefit, as reductions in tariffs abroad will open new markets for them (Baldwin and Robert-Nicoud 2015). Other companies, which focus on the domestic market, will face competition from imports, and while the weaker ones will suffer, the stronger ones will be incentivised to increase innovation and efficiency, thus becoming more competitive in the process. A similar logic applies to NGDOs and untying aid: if other countries untie their aid, large and competitive groups will gain access to new sources of funding, and they will also be well-placed to continue competing for resources from their home governments. Thus, this argument means that there is a group of NGDOs which may actually gain from untying aid, and these are exactly the groups which are also the most vocal in advocacy. Evidence from the interviews shows that competitive Western European NGDOs are indeed not concerned about untying (Interview#14), but this is not the case for Eastern European groups who are less competitive internationally and much more dependent on funding from their governments (Interview#12).

These two arguments around untying aid shows that while initially NGDOs may have been opposed it for financial reasons, they now seem to support it, possibly because it may even improve access to funding for the largest groups.

It also makes sense to have a more detailed look at other aspects of aid effectiveness on which CONCORD and Oxfam's advocacy publications are relatively silent on. Take budget support, for example. This aid modality was highly popular in the early 2000s, and heralded as a way to increase partner country ownership and reward well performing countries by giving funding which they could spend relatively freely, not linked to specific development projects. It was however conspicuously missing from CONCORD's advocacy between 2006 and 2018, never receiving more than sporadic references. Budget support takes partner country ownership a step further, by not only placing responsibility for development planning on the recipient, but also taking financial spending decisions away from the donors. Northern NGDOs have lower levels of access to partner country governments, and processes for lobbying and influence are often less transparent in these settings, putting these groups at a disadvantage in terms of funding.

Moral vision

Clearly, making aid more effective or efficient at reducing poverty aligns with the moral visions of helping the poor put forward by NGDOs. There should also be a moral imperative to use scarce resources as effectively as possible, to reach the greatest number of poor. This requires research and the identification of the types of interventions which work, to continuously amend practice based on these findings.

Therefore, from a moral perspective, it is extremely difficult for NGDOs to argue against increasing aid effectiveness, and given the potential impacts on funding discussed above, they need to ensure that their reputation is not harmed. The nature of their advocacy supports this: NGDOs generally call for increasing aid effectiveness on a general level without going into details, which allows them to show alignment with their moral incentives. However, they are very selective when it comes to the specific sub-themes under this category. Advocacy either seems to focus on aid effectiveness topics which have minimal impact on NGDO funding (such as increasing donor transparency), or may actually benefit the strongest groups (untying aid). They are relatively silent, or aim to modify the framing on issues which may take decision making on aid planning and programming farther away from them, decreasing their influence (ownership, budget support). The fact that aid effectiveness is simply not a politicised topic is also convenient for NGDOs, as it means that there is little external pressure on them to engage in advocacy on it.

Aid allocation

Aid allocation has not been a strongly prominent theme in CONCORD's or Oxfam's advocacy. Calls for shifts in the geographical allocation of aid were present in both cases, demanding that donor countries spend more aid in Sub-Saharan Africa, and/or in least developed countries, but neither was ever really discussed or developed in detail. Calls to change the sectoral allocation of aid, or give more aid for certain themes has been stronger, especially in case of gender: demands on donors to better support the empowerment of women and girls have been a constant fixture in both CONCORD's and Oxfam's advocacy publications.

Politicisation

Aid allocation has a low degree of politicisation, as in general, it shares a similar technical nature as aid effectiveness. However, calls to give more aid to the poorest countries can have public resonance, and so can be politicised. There are some examples of such politicisation between 2006 and 2018, but even these seem rather low intensity and sporadic. Two example are discussed below.

First, on the EU level, there has been a long-standing debate between member states on aiding the Global South versus the Eastern Neighbourhood. In essence, Central and Eastern European member states have been keener on using EU aid to support countries in the EU's Eastern Neighbourhood, (see Szent-Iványi 2014). This is mainly linked to the geopolitical interests of these member states, who would like to see prosperous and stable countries in the former Soviet space. However, most of these Eastern Neighbourhood countries are middle income, and while poverty is an issue, it is not as acute as in countries of the Global South. The Western and Northern member states have aimed to maintain the focus of EU development policy on Africa and other poorer regions of the Global South. How EU resources are allocated between these two broad groups has been a constant source of tensions within the EU since its 'big bang' enlargement in 2004 (Lightfoot and Szent-Iványi 2014: 1265). While these rarely made it into national presses, the politicisation of aid allocation along the foreign policy priorities of member states has clearly been present on the EU level. This divide is reflected in public opinion polls as well. While more than 80% of respondents in countries like Spain, Denmark, Germany or Finland agreed in 2019 that the EU should strengthen its partnership with Africa, the ratio was only 68 per cent in Poland, 65 per cent in Romania, 60 per cent in Slovakia, and 54 per cent in the Czech Republic (European Commission 2019). NGDOs therefore can point to popular support for their positions on the need for more aid to Sub-Saharan Africa, at least in most Western or Northern member states, whereas in the Eastern members such advocacy would not resonate as strongly with popular opinions.

The second example of politicisation happens on the national level in member states, and revolves around questions, often raised by the media, of where the government spends foreign aid. These debates focus on whether a given donor indeed supports 'the partner countries it should be supporting'. There are perceptions that aid should not be given to countries which are highly corrupt, relatively rich (especially the 'booming emerging giants') or hostile to the donor country. Aid to China seems to have especially become politicised in the past two decades, with the media and opposition politicians in several countries questioning why their governments continue to provide aid to the country (see e.g. Express 2021). For example, a politicised debate on China in the UK arose when the government announced cutting foreign aid to a number of countries in 2021, including China. An opposition politician called it 'astounding that the UK still gives any [official development assistance] to China' (*Express* 2021). Another politician argued that '[t]axpayers have every right to pose these questions as to why a penny is being spent there given where China is taking Hong Kong, how it treats Uighurs and its growing authoritarian stance beyond its shores' (Sky News 2021). Similar debates have happened in other countries as well, including Germany (DW.com 2007; The Local Germany 2009), or Sweden (The Local Sweden 2007). However, such debates are usually linked to a specific revelation which sparks media or political attention, and seem to quickly dry up.

The sporadic nature of these debates can provide NGDOs with opportunities to engage and raise their profiles. However, politicisation of the topic remains relatively low even when it does enter the media or the EU level, and this can explain why NGDOs do not give aid allocation a greater weight in their advocacy.

Impact on funding

Given how NGDOs have comparative advantages in some sectors and regions compared to other development actors, shifts in how aid is allocated will have an impact on their ability to raise resources. Simply put, the more donors spend in countries and sectors where NGDOs are competitive, the more funding they may be able to access. It is reasonable to assume that the sectoral allocation of aid matters more than the geographical, given NGDOs are present across the developing world. As discussed in previous chapters, NGDOs generally have expertise in working with local communities to improve social welfare, including areas like healthcare or education. Working with vulnerable groups, such as women and girls, is also an area where NGDOs are generally seen as having an advantage. Indeed, many of the largest development NGOs are specialised on supporting the empowerment of women and girls, or the livelihoods and rights of children; these include Plan International, Save the Children or World Vision. More EU or government aid for these topics increases the overall pot of money these and other groups can bid for, although as discussed earlier, the exact nature of the increase matters. As shown in Chapter 4, calls for greater donor focus on the empowerment of women and girls has indeed been a strong element in NGDO advocacy, and this is consistent with these funding concerns. However, it was not a topic which respondents mentioned in the interviews.

Geographical shifts in EU aid allocation, while overall probably neutral for the NGDO community as a whole, can disproportionately benefit or harm NGDOs in some member states. As discussed above, NGDOs in the Central and Eastern European member states have experience of working in the EU's Eastern Neighbourhood and the Western Balkans, and are thus presumably less interested, from a funding perspective at least, for resources to be shifted to Sub-Saharan Africa or least developed countries, where they have less experience and presence. Large Western NGOs however may have a strong presence in both regions, and so their funding interests would not really play a role. Interviews with NGDO representatives from the Central and Eastern European member states support this: there are strong notions on how they cannot compete with large Western groups on their 'home turf', i.e. Africa (Interview#2, Interview#3). These groups, together with their national governments, have lobbied within the EU to ensure not only that the countries in the Eastern Neighbourhood remain a priority for EU spending, but also that these NGDOs are compensated in some form for their lack of competitiveness, such as through ring-fenced funding for them (Lightfoot and Szent-Iványi 2014).

This 'East versus West' conflict between the national platform members of CONCORD may explain why CONCORD has not been more forceful in calling for a re-allocation of EU aid to least developed countries and Sub-Saharan Africa. CONCORD may have found it easier to not engage in strong advocacy on the topic, rather than attempt to reconcile differing interests among its members.

Moral vision

Development NGOs champion the interests and rights of the poorest and most vulnerable groups, thus calls to increase aid to least developed countries, 33 (out of 46 on the UN's 2020 list) of which are in Sub-Saharan Africa, makes sense from a moral perspective. Although many least developed countries are relatively small, poverty is significantly concentrated in them: despite years of decline, the share of people living below the World Bank's international poverty line of 1.9 dollars per day was 45.6 per cent in 2017 in low-income countries.[1] The share in Sub-Saharan Africa was 41.2 per cent in the same year. Such concentrations of poverty make it easier for donors to have an impact, potentially reaching more people with the same amounts of resources (Collier and Dollar 2000). Similar conclusions can be made for sectoral allocation, especially regarding gender: women and girls are significantly disadvantaged in most developing countries compared to men, and increasing aid to fund programs which target their specific needs and empower them is morally the right thing to do. All this means that from a moral perspective, NGDOs can do little else but to call for a re-allocation of aid towards the poorest and most vulnerable.

Aid allocation therefore seems to be an area where NGDOs face conflicting motivations. While more aid to the poorest countries or most vulnerable groups resonates with their moral incentives, the topic is not highly politicised, and changing the allocation of aid will create winner and losers within the NGDO community from a funding perspective. These can explain why the calls for shifts in aid allocation are not particularly strong in CONCORD's advocacy. The situation is slightly more puzzling in case of Oxfam, which is highly competitive and thus does not need to worry about how shifts in aid allocation would impact its funding, and could instead campaign based on its moral motivations. The low degree of the topic's politicisation however can be a key explanatory factor here as well, as Oxfam may decide to focus its advocacy work on topics which have higher levels of political salience instead.

Migration

The theme of using foreign aid to manage migration has gradually gained prominence in the advocacy of both CONCORD and Oxfam during the 2006–2018 period, and became a key topic following the 2015 European refugee crisis. As discussed in Chapter 4, NGDO advocacy seems to have been reactive, and called out the EU's approach not only regarding its treatment of migrants, but also how it began using aid to create counter-incentives to migration. Given how prominent an issue migration has been for NGDOs, it is dealt with in more detail in Chapter 7 through a case study of how NGDOs have reacted to and engaged with the EU's Emergency Trust Fund for Africa. This section nonetheless provides some more general insights based on the book's analytical framework.

Politicisation

Migration has been a strongly politicised issue in most European countries for decades, and its degree of politicisation has increased significantly further following the 2015 migration crisis. While the general public often has little interest in development aid, leading to relatively low levels of politicisation on issues related to it, this is not the case for migration, which has been a significant concern for many.

According to the Eurobarometer polls, Europeans regularly cited migration as their foremost concern (European Commission 2018a; Desvignes 2019). Although the COVID-19 pandemic has led to a decrease in concerns around migration, it remained among the top issues for European citizens even in 2021 (European Commission 2021a). A number of political parties across the continent, especially on the populist right, but also more established centrist parties, have aimed to mobilise voters, often successfully, by appealing to this concern (Lutz 2019). Issues related to migration figure prominently in the national political discourses in almost all member states. The politicisation of migration has several dimensions, including economic, cultural, and security related (Gattinara and Morales 2017). The dominant narratives on migration are generally negative, and have shifted towards the security dimension, portraying migrants as potential threats not only to jobs and national culture, but more importantly to the safety of citizens. While more positive narratives of migration are also present, focusing on the skills migrants bring and the benefits of cultural diversity, these are clearly on the defensive. The role migration can play in promoting development in the Global South is practically absent from these debates (Lauwers et al. 2021). Furthermore, political discourses on migration often make no distinction between the various reasons that drive people to migrate, and there is thus little differentiation between, for example, people fleeing from conflict and economic migrants. Labels used by politicians and commentators, such as 'illegal migrant' further serve to construct a negative picture of migration (Tétényi et al. 2019).

This high degree of politicisation has spilled over to the area of development aid following 2015, as the EU and member states increasingly began using aid to manage migration flows. The migration/development nexus has therefore also been politicised. One of the 'solutions' politicians routinely mention to reduce migratory pressures to Europe focuses on 'addressing the root causes', or 'preventive development cooperation' (Lauwers et al. 2021), or the 'instrumentalisation of development aid for reducing migration flows' (Bergmann et al. 2021). As shown by Lauwers et al. (2021), even more radical discourses are also present, which call for a complete rethink of how aid is used, redirecting it to fund counter-migration security measures. These arguments resonate with European citizens. According to a Eurobarometer poll, 71 per cent of Europeans think that providing financial assistance to developing countries is an effective way to address irregular migration (European Commission 2019: 36–37).

The high politicisation of using aid to manage migration means that NGDOs have an incentive to engage in advocacy around it, as it helps them raise their profiles. We see clear evidence of this in Chapter 4, and most interviewees agreed that advocacy related to migration, and specifically the use of aid to manage migration, was the most important element of their work between 2016 and 2017 (Interview#22; Interview#23; Interview#25; Interview#29). Advocacy was highly visible, and included joint open letters and statements by the NGDO community (Joint NGO Statement 2016a; 2016b; 2016c; 2016d; 2016e) and viral campaigns (Interview#29), thus going beyond the 'usual' advocacy aimed at policy insiders.

Impact on funding

Migration-related aid can come in many forms, including humanitarian support to people displaced by conflict and living in refugee camps, efforts to create jobs in home communities to decrease incentives for migration (or increase incentives for return), information campaigns to deter potential migrants, legal aid to migrants, and more securitised measures aimed at supporting sending countries in better policing their borders. NGDOs, especially the large global organisations, have significant experience in providing humanitarian services (e.g. medical assistance, sanitation, and education) for displaced people, and in 'protecting vulnerable groups like women and children from exploitation and human trafficking, supporting migrants and refugees with legal assistance, providing shelter and generally improving the conditions under which migrants are housed, or sensitising law enforcement and other government officials on the rights of migrants' (Szent-Iványi 2021). However, they have lower capabilities and expertise in other areas of migration-related aid. Clearly, development NGOs do not work in the fields of border management and law enforcement, and projects in these areas often involve the delivery of surveillance technology, as well as police and military equipment. Other types of migration-related aid, such as those aimed to decrease the incentives to migrate by creating better conditions and increasing resilience in local communities are more grey areas, as these could conceivably involve NGDOs as well. NGDOs have expertise in carrying out such projects, but other types of project-implementing agencies and organisations are also possible competitors here.

Due to this diversity of the types of migration aid, the exact impact on NGDO funding will depend on which forms donors favour. The emergence of more securitised types of aid aimed at supporting law enforcement actions clearly signals a tilt in the past decade, and especially since 2015, towards actions which NGDOs are excluded from. Without increases in the total amount of aid spent, this reduces the overall amounts available for more 'traditional' aid projects, and thus indirectly also the resources which NGDOs can bid for.

The EU's Emergency Trust Fund for Africa (EUTFA), which is discussed in more detail in Chapter 7, is a good example of this kind of aid diversion. Created in 2015 as a response to the European migration crisis, the fund aimed to address the full range of potential migration-related issues, including both more securitised projects, as well as supporting refugees and increasing resilience in home communities. Most of this fund's resources were diverted from the European Development Fund (EDF). While the EDF's resources were used to address a wide range of objectives, not only poverty reduction, the EUTFA's programming led to a much higher share of securitised projects than was generally the case in EU development funding (Szent-Iványi 2021). While the EUTFA did raise some additional contributions from member states, these only made up around 12 per cent of the fund, and thus overall, it represented existing aid being diverted away from poverty reduction into areas where NGDOs had fewer possibilities to compete for funding. This case therefore shows migration-related aid having a negative impact on NGDO access to funding.

There is some evidence that NGDOs were concerned with funding impacts. They argued that migration aid should be additional to aid focused on poverty reduction, and both are needed to reduce the root causes of migration (Interview#23; Interview#31). Despite contesting the shift in aid resources to migration management, NGDOs did not want to miss out from funding, and bid for projects falling under the theme of migration management (such as from the EUTFA), arguing that they aimed to 'change the policy from within' (Interview#25; Interview#29). The discussion in Chapter 7 on the EUTFA nuances these motivations and NGDO strategies further.

Moral vision

NGDOs generally view migration, at least in its organised form, as positive. It allows people in the Global South to escape poverty, find better livelihoods, but also to support the reduction of poverty in their home through remittances, and potentially through eventual return with new skills and capital to invest. In this sense, migration is a catalyst for development and poverty reduction, and NGDOs have argued for either larger levels of (legal) migration, or genuinely solving the root causes of poverty and inequality which incentivise or outright force people to move (CONCORD 2016a: 16). There are however some caveats to this line of reasoning, as NGDOs acknowledge the negative developmental impacts of certain forms of migration, especially brain drain, and so some groups favour temporary schemes which incentivise people to return home. NGDOs are often attacked by opponents of migration, including populist governments, as promoting a 'letting everyone in' approach, which is not the case. NGDOs' moral motivations simply call for increasing regular and orderly migration and treating migrants with the same human dignity all people deserve.

Human dignity is especially important in cases of forced displacement. NGDOs call for a better differentiation of the types of migration, and argue that forced displacement needs to be treated separately. The moral motivations of NGDOs dictate a humanitarian approach in these cases, including compassion, and ensuring that the fundamental rights of those displaced, guaranteed in international law, are protected (Joint NGO Statement 2016d). According to this, refugees need to be treated humanely and provided with decent living standards. Everyone who has a reasonable claim for asylum should be granted asylum, and treated well while awaiting their decision.

These moral motivations were strongly present in NGDO advocacy, and in fact the topic's high degree of politicisation meant that NGDOs would risk their reputation as moral actors if it were not. The lives of the poor were indeed placed at the centre of NGDO advocacy, and the groups emphasised how the EU is looking only at its own selfish interests at the expense of the global poor (CONCORD 2016a: 20; Oxfam 2016). Opposing the diversion of aid to manage migration was clearly presented as a matter of principle for NGDOs

Climate change adaptation and mitigation

Using aid to support climate change adaptation and mitigation was strongly present in Oxfam's advocacy, but only appeared gradually in CONCORD towards the end of the period under investigation. There were also some differences in emphasis between the two: Oxfam's advocacy focused on the impacts climate change would have, and indeed was already having, on the livelihoods of the global poor, while CONCORD, at least in the AidWatch Reports, placed significant emphasis on ensuring the additionally of climate finance, in a relatively technical manner.

Politicisation

There is little doubt that the politicisation of acting against climate change has been increasing since the turn of the Millennium. Discourses on climate change have shifted from it being a technical issue among scientist in the 1990s to a strong general concern; and has gradually gone from being a politically contested issue to a general consensus that action is necessary, with mounting pressure on political decision makers (see Carter 2014; Pepermans and Maeseele 2014). The degree of politicisation of the topic has always been lower in most EU member states than in the USA, where climate change scepticism still continues to be strong and even relatively mainstream. In Europe, the issue has got to a point where the need to act is no longer contested, rather the question of how to act, and how to ensure that these actions do not lead to unfair distributional consequences, have emerged as the key political issues. These are illustrated by the debates around the European Commission's Fit for 55 package, a series of climate legislative proposals with the aim of decreasing greenhouse gas emissions, published in 2021 (see Galgóczi 2021).

Public opinion surveys reflect this evolution. A 2021 Eurobarometer survey revealed that the feeling that climate change is a very serious problem has become more prevalent across the EU since 2015 (European Commission 2021b: 24). Nine out of ten Europeans agreed that greenhouse gas emissions needed to be reduced to the minimum, reflecting a strong consensus around the topic (European Commission 2021b: 90). Furthermore, citizens increasingly expected their national governments, as well as the EU to take action to tackle climate change (European Commission 2021b: 27). There were indications however that citizens would be less willing to bear higher costs in order to ensure transition to a low carbon economy (Carlsson et al. 2021).

Climate change also featured more frequently in EU and member state parliamentary debates (Marcinkiewicz and Tosun 2015), and the EU Parliament has become increasingly active in pushing the climate change agenda (Burns and Carter 2010; Burns 2016). Furthermore, environmental sustainability figures much more strongly in the post-2015 global development framework, the Sustainable Development Goals (SDGs), than it did in its predecessor, the Millennium Development Goals. The SDGs have helped raise the profile of climate change in the development profession, and both the EU and its member states have adapted their development cooperation strategies and legislation to align with the SDGs (De Roeck et al. 2018). Close to 90 per cent of European citizens agreed in 2021 that it was important for the EU to tackle the impacts of climate change specifically in developing countries (European Commission 2021c: 27).

As with migration, a high degree of politicisation allows NGDO to raise their profile if they engage in advocacy around climate change. However, it seems that development NGDOs came rather late to the game: most of them had not worked traditionally on environmental issues or climate change, and an interviewee even argued that they had poor understandings of it (Interview#22). Many NGDOs interviewed had either not worked on climate change at all (Interview#24; Interview#27), or saw it a more marginal part of what they did (Interview#22; Interview#25; Interview#30). A greater NGDO focus on climate change seems to have come with the SDGs. The SDGs have caused a shift in the global development system, and NGDOs needed to adapt to this by incorporating sustainability issues more strongly into their advocacy. NGDOs therefore reacted not to the public or general level of politicisation around climate change, but its increasing politicisation specifically within development politics. This is reinforced by the fact that CONCORD's advocacy on the topic was rather technical, focusing on climate finance and the need to avoid double counting it by separating climate aid and poverty-focused aid (CONCORD 2014; 2016a).

While CONCORD did not engage in more public-facing advocacy on climate change funding, despite the topic's relatively high level of politicisation, the situation is perhaps different for Oxfam. Oxfam, which lists climate change as one of its priority areas of work, has focused less on technical issues related to aid diversion in its advocacy, and has been more concerned with convincing donors to change their approach and take the already visible consequences of climate change more seriously. Oxfam seems to have taken a more holistic approach and has integrated climate change adaptation and mitigation, and poverty focused aid in its advocacy, arguing that the two need to go hand-in-hand (Interview#29). Oxfam did call for more funding for climate change adaptation and mitigation, but rarely portrayed this as competing with poverty-focused aid.

Impact on funding

As with migration-focused aid, the impact climate adaptation and mitigation funding has on NGDO financial positions depends on the exact forms donors favour, whether development NGOs can plausibly bid for such funding, and whether it opens up competition to new actors who were previously not so active in development cooperation. However, the impact is less clear than in the case of migration aid, as there is no clear boundary between development aid and climate aid, and many types of projects may serve both purposes (Stadelmann et al. 2011). A common example relates to installing solar panels in villages, which has strong developmental impacts through providing access to electricity. Furthermore, by decreasing the use of carbon-intensive cooking fuels, it also reduces greenhouse gas emissions. Development NGOs, who have significant experience in poverty reduction projects, can conceivably be involved in actions similar to this, but so can environmental NGOs.

A further question is how donors provide climate aid, especially whether it is additional to existing development resources, or a diversion of these. Practice implies that diversion seems to be the more common case (CONCORD 2010: 13; Interview#31), or due to the difficulties in defining what exactly constitutes climate aid, donors may simply double-count existing resources. This means that not only do development NGOs have to compete with other actors, but the overall pot of money available remains limited as well.

These financial considerations are clearly present in advocacy, as shown by how the additionality of climate funding to existing aid commitments was the key element in CONCORD's advocacy. The interviews revealed that NGDOs clearly saw environmental NGOs as competitors for funding (Interview#24; Interview#26; Interview#30), and there was relatively little cooperation between the two communities. CONCORD, for example, did not engage in any integrated lobbying with the Climate Action Network, the main umbrella group for environmental NGOs (Interview#31).

Moral vision

As discussed, development NGOs have generally focused on poverty reduction and the livelihoods and rights of the poor, with environmental concerns being rather marginal in their activities. However, with the shifts in general understanding of climate change, which have become increasingly reflected in the international development system through the SDGs and the activities of official donors, the approach and understanding of NGDOs has also gradually changed (Interview#28; Interview#30). Climate change impacts the poor most, especially through its effects on agriculture and more frequent extreme weather events. Both of these are more severe in regions with highly concentrated poverty such as the Sahel or the around the Bay of Bengal. Poverty reduction is thus increasingly unimaginable without taking environmental aspects into consideration (Interview#30).

There is evidence that during the period under investigation, NGDOs shifted their normative positions to gradually include the climatic aspects of development and poverty reduction. While climate change was never something at odds with NGDO moral positions or something they contested, it just simply did not figure strongly in their work (Interview#22). The global discourse running up to the SDGs, and eventually their acceptance however 'forced' NGDOs to take climate issues into greater consideration, and to incorporate sustainability more strongly into their normative positions. NGDOs needed to acknowledge that poverty reduction cannot happen without it being environmentally sustainable. They also needed to accept that climate change will continue to throw up new challenges which hit the global poor disproportionately. This modified normative position has become visible in NGDO publications (e.g. CONCORD 2016b; 2016c). Therefore, climate change is an example of how NGDO normative positions can evolve, based on how general understandings of development change.

Funding the private sector

The final theme examined in this chapter is how NGDOs have reacted to the increasing role of the private sector in development cooperation, given how the EU and other donors have increasingly been using development aid to support or at least incentivise private sector investments. As discussed in

Chapter 4, NGDOs have continuously contested this shift, following its first appearance in EU policy documents in the early 2010s, arguing that it was 'not good value for money' in terms of reducing poverty.

Politicisation

Using official developmental resources to leverage private sector investments seems to be a relatively technical topic, and its politicisation more akin to that of aid effectiveness and less similar to other instances of aid diversion. While the topic has been discussed extensively within the aid profession (see e.g. CONCORD 2017), it is difficult to argue that it is politicised to any significant degree. The issue hardly appears in the press beyond specialist websites. There has been some level of politicisation within the EU: the European Parliament (EP) adopted a resolution on the private sector and development in 2016, which was broadly supportive of the practice, although it called on the Commission to implement a number of improvements. The resolution was accepted however with relatively little plenary debate, and with the support of all mainstream EP parties (European Parliament 2016). Parliamentary debates on the topic in the member states have been close to non-existent.

The Eurobarometer surveys have asked respondents twice about their views on how important the role of private companies is in the sustainable development of developing countries, in 2018 and 2019 (European Commission 2018b; 2019). According to these, 75 to 80 per cent of respondents across the EU have judged the private sector's role to be very important or fairly important. This implies, that in public opinion at least, the topic is relatively uncontroversial, and has strong support. Indeed, then Commissioner for International Cooperation and Development, Neven Mimica argued that '[t]his shows that our proposal to deepen our economic relationship with Africa by focussing on private investment is on the right track with citizens' (European Interest 2018). It must be noted however that the question asked in the two surveys was rather superficial, and did not break down what exactly is meant under the private sector in detail. This is a recurring criticism from NGDOs: the EU's discourse on the topic regularly conflates a diverse set of private sector actors, including European multinational companies and micro enterprises in Africa into a single category (Brachet 2017). Furthermore, people have not specifically been asked about using foreign aid to support the investments of various private sector actors, nor are they informed about the opportunity costs of this.

The low level of politicisation around the EU's private sector development funding agenda clearly does not explain NGDO engagement around it, which has been rather substantial. It does however provide some explanation on the nature of this advocacy: low levels of politicisation should imply that advocacy will be more focused towards policy makers and not the broader public, and will also be more technical. NGDOs did not engage in any similar large-scale campaigns or joint lobbying as in the case of managing migration. Interviews confirm that the topic has been important for NGDOs, and also how advocacy on it was less public facing (Interview#24).

Impact on funding

The increasing role given to private sector actors in EU and also member state development policies means the appearance of new actors with whom NGDOs have to compete for funding. This competition is not direct, as the EU and donor states would in most cases have separate financial instruments and institutions to work with these two sets of actors: private sector funding mainly happens through development finance institutions (DFIs), such as the European Investment Bank, or in the case of member states, Germany's KfW group or France's Proparco. However, funding DFIs and setting up any new private sector funding instruments with them may come at the expense of the funds for the instruments dedicated to NGDOs. As opposed to aid diverted to managing migration or supporting climate change adaptation and mitigation, where NGDOs may find possibilities to bid for funding from the resources diverted, there is no similar 'grey' area here: NGDOs are generally not eligible for DFI funding.

As early as 2003, some of the resources of the EDF were placed under the supervision of the European Investment Bank, 'to support private sector development in [African, Caribbean and Pacific] states' (Van Waeyenberge 2015: 18). In 2016, the European Commission announced the European External Investment Plan, which aimed to support private sector investments in Africa and the EU Neighbourhood. The European Fund for Sustainable Development (EFSD) was created to support implementation of the plan, worth 5.1 billion euros (European Commission n.d.). The EFSD has two facilities to support investments: a guarantee facility, which aims to reduce risks for private sector investments, and a blending facility, which provides grants to co-finance projects. The European Parliament's 2016 resolution on the private sector and development also pressed for a stronger role for the European Investment Bank in EU development policy (European Parliament 2016).

At the same time, member state governments have been putting larger emphasis on increasing the role of their DFIs as well (Van Waeyenberge 2015; Mah 2018; Kenny 2019). All of these changes were happening when there were no significant increases in European aid levels: the aid budgets of many member countries stagnated between 2006 and 2014, or only grew very slowly, implying a clear redistribution of resources from existing aid modalities towards ones aimed at funding private sector investments (Van Waeyenberge 2015: 25). NGDOs would therefore have reasons to feel their access to funding was under threat, or that it brought an 'unhealthy competition for EU funding' (Interview#23). According to CONCORD, EU private sector funding suffered from a 'total lack of transparency, accountability and regulatory framework' (CONCORD 2016a: 3), which put NGDOs at an unfair disadvantage, as they have to abide by strict aid effectiveness criteria. An interviewee also argued that private companies do not care about, or understand poverty, whereas NGDOs do, and are therefore much better at reducing it (Interview#13).

Moral vision

Whether using aid to fund the private sector is at odds with the moral vision of development NGOs depends on what impacts it has on the poor, and how efficiently it uses aid resources. The vast literature on the impacts of foreign direct investments (FDIs) on poverty has highly ambiguous results. At the one end of the spectrum, FDI creates jobs, which are usually better paid than what domestically owned companies offer, with better working conditions. Foreign investors can support the development of infrastructure, are more likely to observe regulations (including paying taxes), and can bring new technology to the country. Others however argue that foreign investments often harm communities and the host country as a whole, through the expropriation of land, driving local companies out of business, the large tax breaks they often receive, pollution, and governments turning a blind eye to sweat shop conditions in supply chains. There is a wide range of anecdotal evidence of cases where FDI has led to positive, and equally to negative outcomes for the local poor. The literature agrees that the actual effects are highly context specific, and making any ex-ante generalisations difficult (see Cohen 2007 or Magombeyi and Odhiambo 2017 for general overviews of the literature).

NGDOs, while generally acknowledging the role of the private sector in development, especially the role that local small enterprises play, tend to view large private companies and FDI highly suspiciously. Indeed, Oxfam's advocacy placed significant focus on the need to support small scale businesses, especially in rural areas. The suspicion towards large companies may come from several factors. Cases of abuse by foreign investors are often highly publicised, leading to skewed perceptions. Furthermore, many people working in NGDOs have strongly left-wing, even anti-capitalist views, and may thus be prejudiced against large companies. Indeed, an interviewee argued that some in CONCORD have been especially dogmatic and against all private sector involvement in development as a matter of principle (Interview#28). NGDOs argued that the motivations of foreign investors centred solely around profits, and they cared little about poverty reduction. This means that any development-related objectives in private sector aid projects may be treated as secondary by companies, with little efforts to meet them (Interview#24; Interview#28). Furthermore, interviewees voiced concerns on how private sector projects suffered from a lack of accountability and transparency, further undermining potential development gains. Funding for the private sector was therefore not seen as an effective way of reducing poverty (CONCORD 2016a: 3; 2016b: 40).

However, there are some indications that, from a normative perspective at least, NGDOs could accept private sector aid if it is 'done right'. CONCORD published a '10 Point Roadmap' on how the EU should fund the private sector (CONCORD 2017), which included principles like giving poverty reduction a central role in these projects, implementing safeguards to ensure there are no human rights abuses, increasing transparency and carrying out independent impact evaluations. If private sector aid adheres to these principles, it may be reconcilable with NGDO normative vision.

The patterns of motivations behind development NGO advocacy

The drivers of NGDO advocacy are complex, and they have different interplays with each other in case of the six themes. Table 6.1 summarises the analysis in the previous sections, and includes the main findings for each driver/theme combination.

The analysis shows that NGDO motivations need to be looked at in the policy context, and they need to be considered jointly, as they will have different interplays in each context. The different motivations lead to different types and forms of advocacy as well.

Politicisation clearly matters, and generally, as expected, greater politicisation leads to more morally driven advocacy. Diverting aid to manage migration is clearly an example of this, where NGDOs publicly took a strong moral position after 2015, even though this position was not generally shared by the public. While funding issues may have also mattered, these were not visible at all, and indeed some NGDOs ended up benefitting from the changes they campaigned against (such as through the EUTFA). At the other end of the spectrum, we see issues such as aid effectiveness and aid allocation, where politicisation is minimal, and this deters NGDOs from strong advocacy. Advocacy on these topics is made even more difficult by a lack of common interest among the NGDO community, as making aid more effective or changing its allocation creates winners and losers from a funding perspective. Using aid to fund climate change adaptation and mitigation is an interesting area in between: while the topic's politicisation would have predicted more visible advocacy, its ambiguous and shifting relationship with NGDO moral vision made this more difficult.

Politicisation also helps in explaining patterns over time: migration and climate change both became increasingly important topics in NGDO advocacy as their politicisation increased. Furthermore, politicisation clearly limits NGDOs' ability to campaign along lines which would focus entirely on ensuring their funding. Funding concerns can never become too dominant or visible, as NGDOs need to uphold their reputation as morally driven actors, and a topic's high degree of politicisation means that their actions would be more visible. There are also moral red lines that they cannot cross.

Table 6.1 Summary of analysis of the main themes in NGO advocacy

	Politicisation	*Impact on funding*	*Moral vision*
Increasing (genuine) aid	Low, but shifts over time. These shifts have little impact on advocacy however.	Potentially strong impact, but limited direct evidence that funding concerns are a driver.	Strongly consistent, but negative effects of 'too much' aid are disregarded.
Aid effectiveness	Very low, and there is evidence that this deters advocacy on the topic.	Winners and losers. This explains selective advocacy: the NGDOs which do campaign on the issue are the ones which would benefit.	Strongly consistent, NGDOs cannot speak out against aid effectiveness reforms.
Aid allocation	Very low, only some sporadic instances. This explains the low degree of advocacy.	Winners and losers; Western NGDOs vs Eastern ones.	More aid for Africa/LDCs or marginalised groups is strongly consistent.
Migration	High politicisation, which leads to very visible, public-facing advocacy.	Potentially strong due to aid diversion, but little evidence that it actually drives advocacy. Many NGDOs ended up benefitting from migration aid though.	Using aid to reduce migration is difficult to reconcile with normative positions.
Climate change	Medium to high: gradually increasing during the period and shifting from contestation to consensus	Potentially strong due to aid diversion. Concerns around funding clearly present.	Reconcilable with normative positions, which changed during the period. Climate aid diversion not as problematic as in case of migration.
Private sector funding	Low, advocacy is mostly technical and focused towards policy makers.	Potentially strong due to aid diversion, and no grey areas as in case of migration and climate change. Funding concerns strong around 'level playing field'.	Suspicion towards private companies and criticism on aid effectiveness grounds.

Source: compiled by the author.

Calling for more NGDO participation, more aid, less aid diversion, etc., are all consistent with funding motivations. But in most cases, it is difficult to actually tell just how important funding concerns are: much of the advocacy by NGDOs is highly coherent not only with their funding concerns, but also their moral motivations. Increasing levels of aid benefit NGDOs financially, and for the most part, global poverty reduction as well. The analysis in this chapter has been able to separate these motivations, and even though it is difficult to gain direct evidence (such as from interviews) about the importance of funding concerns, there are telling signs in many cases which add up. These include calls for greater NGDO participation and consultation, more aid to sectors and themes where NGDOs have advantages, neglecting aid effectiveness, and opposition to changes which would increase competition for aid funding.

The case of climate aid is further interesting because it may be construed as an instance when NGDOs shifted their moral vision to increase their own compatibility with the international development system's shifting norms towards sustainable development, and thus enhance their ability to obtain funding. It is unclear however whether these shifts were indeed made with funding concerns in mind, or more driven by changing understandings of how to support the global poor.

The main implication of these findings is that NGDO motivations cannot be simplified to a single factor, especially funding-related concerns. While funding concerns are undoubtedly present, it would be a strong exaggeration to say that this is the only, or even the most important driver of NGDO advocacy. Motivations need to be examined in their complexity, taking into account the specific policy context, and how one set of motivations may dampen or amplify the effects of another.

Note

1 The World Bank does not use the UN classification of least developed countries. Its low-income country group is slightly more restrictive in its membership (only 29 countries in 2021), but all of these are also LDCs (see World Bank 2021).

References

Baldwin, R. & Robert-Nicoud, F. (2015). A Simple Model of the Juggernaut Effect of Trade Liberalisation. *International Economics* 143: 70–79. https://doi.org/10.1016/j.inteco.2015.04.008.

Bearce, D. H. & Tirone, D. C. (2010). Foreign Aid Effectiveness and the Strategic Goals of Donor Governments. *The Journal of Politics* 72 (3): 837–851. https://doi.org/10.1017/S0022381610000204.

Bergmann, J., Hackenesch, C., & Stockemer, D. (2021). Populist Radical Right Parties in Europe: What Impact Do they Have on Development Policy? *JCMS: Journal of Common Market Studies* 59: 37–52. https://doi.org/10.1111/jcms.13143.

Brachet, I. (2017). Private Sector and Development: The EU is Not Doing Enough! EurActiv. https://www.euractiv.com/section/development-policy/opinion/private-sector-and-development-the-eu-is-not-doing-enough/.

Burns, C. & Carter, N. (2010). The European Parliament and Climate Change: From Symbolism to Heroism and Back Again. In: Wurzel, R. & Connelly, J. (eds) *The*

European Union as a Leader in International Climate Change Politics. London: Routledge.

Burns, C. (2016). The European Parliament and Climate Change: A Constrained Leader? In: Wurzel, R., Connelly, J. & Liefferink, D. (eds) *The European Union in International Climate Change Politics. Still Taking a Lead?* London: Routledge.

Carbone, M. (2006). European NGOs in EU Development Policy: Between Frustration and Resistance. In: Lister, M. & Carbone, M. (eds) *New Pathways in International Development. Gender and Civil Society in EU Policy*. Aldershot: Ashgate, pp. 197–210.

Carbone, M. (2014). Much Ado About Nothing? The European Union and the Global Politics of Untying Aid. *Contemporary Politics* 20 (1): 103–117. https://doi:10.1080/13569775.2014.882572.

Carlsson, F., Kataria, M., Krupnick, A., Lampi, E., Löfgren, Å., Qin, P., Sterner, T., & Yang, X. (2021). The Climate Decade: Changing Attitudes on Three Continents. Resources for the Future Working Paper 21–02.

Carter, N. (2014). The Politics of Climate Change in the UK. *WIREs Climate Change* 5: 423–433. https://doi.org/10.1002/wcc.274.

Clay, E. J., Geddes, M., Natali, L. & te Velde, D. W. (2008). The Developmental Effectiveness of Untied Aid: Evaluation of the Implementation of the Paris Declaration and of the 2001 DAC Recommendation on Untying ODA to the LDCs. https://www.oecd.org/dac/evaluation/dcdndep/41537529.pdf.

Cohen, S. D. (2007). *Multinational Corporations and Foreign Direct Investment. Avoiding Simplicity, Embracing Complexity*. Oxford: Oxford University Press.

Collier, P. (2007). *The Bottom Billion*. Oxford: Oxford University Press.

Collier, P. & Dollar, D. (2000). Aid Allocation and Poverty Reduction. *European Economic Review* 46 (8): 1475–1500. https://doi.org/10.1016/S0014-2921(01)00187-8.

CONCORD (2010). AidWatch Report 2010. Penalty Against Poverty: More and Better EU Aid Can Score Millennium Development Goals. Brussels: CONCORD.

CONCORD (2014). AidWatch Report 2014. Europe's Role in Financing and Implementing Sustainable Development Goals Post-2015. Brussels: CONCORD.

CONCORD (2016a). AidWatch Report 2016. This is Not Enough!Brussels: CONCORD.

CONCORD (2016b). Transforming EU Development Policy: Concord Calls for a Long-Term Vision for Sustainable Development. www.globaleverantwortung.at/download/?xml:id=1631.

CONCORD (2016c). Sustainable Development. The Stakes Could Not Be Higher. Brussels: CONCORD.

CONCORD (2017). A 10 Point Roadmap for Europe on the Role of the Private Sector in Development. Brussels: CONCORD.

De Roeck, F., Orbie, J., Delputte, S. (2018). Mainstreaming Climate Change Adaptation into the European Union's Development Assistance. *Environmental Science & Policy* 81: 36–45. https://doi.org/10.1016/j.envsci.2017.12.005.

Desvignes, B. (2019). Eurobarometer: What challenges for Europe? *The New Federalist*. https://www.thenewfederalist.eu/eurobarometer-what-challenges-for-europe?lang=fr.

DW.com (2007). German Development Minister Defends Aid to China. *Deutsche Welle*. https://www.dw.com/en/german-development-minister-defends-aid-to-china/a-3018362.

European Commission (2018a). Standard Eurobarometer 89. Public Opinion in the European Union. Spring 2018. Brussels: European Commission.

European Commission (2018b). Special Eurobarometer 476. EU Citizens and Development Cooperation. Brussels: European Commission.

European Commission (2019). Special Eurobarometer 494. EU Citizens and Development Cooperation. Brussels: European Commission.

European Commission (2021a). Standard Eurobarometer 94. Public Opinion in the European Union. Winter 2021. Brussels: European Commission.

European Commission (2021b). Special Eurobarometer 513. Climate Change. Brussels: European Union.

European Commission (2021c). Special Eurobarometer 512. EU Citizens and Development Cooperation. Brussels: European Commission.

European Commission (n.d.). The EU External Investment Plan. A Quick Overview. https://ec.europa.eu/eu-external-investment-plan/sites/default/files/documents/eip_factsheet_web-en.pdf.

European Interest (2018). EU Citizens Back Private Sector Development Cooperation. *European Interest*. https://www.europeaninterest.eu/article/eu-citizens-back-private-sector-development-cooperation/.

European Parliament (2016). European Parliament Resolution of 14 April 2016 on the Private Sector and Development. 2014/2205(INI). https://www.europarl.europa.eu/doceo/document/TA-8-2016-0137_EN.html.

Express (2021). Foreign Aid: Why Does the UK Give Aid to China? *Express*. https://www.express.co.uk/news/world/1426455/foreign-aid-why-does-the-uk-give-aid-to-china-evg.

Galgóczi, B. (2021). Is Europe Socially Fit for the 'Fit for 55' Package?https://socialeurope.eu/is-europe-socially-fit-for-the-fit-for-55-package.

Gattinara, P. C. & Morales, L. (2017). The Politicization and Securitization of Migration in Western Europe: Public Opinion, Political Parties and the Immigration Issue. In: Bourbeau, P. (ed.) *Handbook on Migration and Security*. Cheltenham: Edward Elgar, pp. 273–295.

Hackenesch, C., Bergmann, J., & Orbie, J. (2021). Development Policy under Fire? The Politicization of European External Relations. *JCMS: Journal of Common Market Studies*, 59: 3–19. https://doi.org/10.1111/jcms.13145.

Heppell, T. & Lightfoot, S. (2012). 'We Will Not Balance the Books on the Backs of the Poorest People in the World': Understanding Conservative Party Strategy on International Aid. *The Political Quarterly* 83: 130–138. https://doi.org/10.1111/j.1467-923X.2012.02279.x.

Joint NGO Statement (2016a). EU Leaders Can Save Lives this Winter if They Change Migration Policies. Joint NGO Statement ahead of the European Council of 15 December 2016. https://www.oxfam.org/en/research/eu-leaders-can-save-lives-winter-if-they-change-migration-policies.

Joint NGO Statement (2016b). Open letter: Development Aid Must Not Aim at Stopping Migration. Joint NGO Statement ahead of the October European Council. https://www.oxfam.org/en/research/open-letter-development-aid-must-not-aim-stopping-migration.

Joint NGO Statement (2016c). The European Parliament Must Immediately Address the Joint Way Forward Agreement between the EU and Afghanistan. https://www.oxfam.org/en/research/ngos-call-scrutiny-over-eu-afghanistan-agreement.

Joint NGO Statement (2016d). Stop Discriminatory and Dangerous Border Closures. Joint Statement by 26 Organisations Working with People on the Move https://www.oxfam.org/en/research/stop-discriminatory-and-dangerous-border-closures.

Joint NGO Statement (2016e). Don't Use Migrants as Bargaining Chip! Open Letter to European Leaders on Refugee and Migration Crisis Signed by 20 NGOs. https://www.oxfam.org/en/research/dont-use-migrants-bargaining-chip.

Jones, S. & Tarp, F. (2016). Does Foreign Aid Harm Political Institutions? *Journal of Development Economics* 118: 266–281. https://doi.org/10.1016/j.jdeveco.2015.09.004.

Joseph, R. & Gillies, A., eds. (2008). *Smart Aid for African Development*. Boulder: Lynne Rienner Publishers.

Kenny, C. (2019). Marginal, Not Transformational: Development Finance Institutions and the Sustainable Development Goals. CGD Policy Paper 156.

Kiratli, O. S. (2021). Politicization of Aiding Others: The Impact of Migration on European Public Opinion of Development Aid. *JCMS: Journal of Common Market Studies* 59: 53–71. https://doi.org/10.1111/jcms.13139.

Lauwers, N., Orbie, J., & Delputte, S. (2021). The Politicization of the Migration–Development Nexus: Parliamentary Discourse on the European Union Trust Fund on Migration. *JCMS: Journal of Common Market Studies* 59: 72–90. https://doi.org/10.1111/jcms.13140.

Lightfoot, S. & Szent-Iványi, B. (2014). Reluctant Donors? The Europeanization of International Development Policies in the New Member State. *Journal of Common Market Studies* 52: 1257–1272. https://doi.org/10.1111/jcms.12141.

Lutz, P. (2019). Variation in Policy Success: Radical Right Populism and Migration Policy. *West European Politics* 42 (3): 517–544. https://doi.org/10.1080/01402382.2018.1504509.

Magombeyi, M. T., & Odhiambo, N. M. (2017). Foreign Direct Investment and Poverty Reduction. *Comparative Economic Research* 20 (2): 73–89. https://do.org/10.1515/cer-2017-0013.

Mah, L. (2018). Promoting Private Sector for Development: The Rise of Blended Finance in EU Aid Architecture. CEsA CSG Working Paper 171/2018.

Marcinkiewicz, K. & Tosun, J. (2015). Contesting Climate Change: Mapping the Political Debate in Poland. *East European Politics* 31 (2): 187–207. https://doi.org/10.1080/21599165.2015.1022648.

Meeks, P. (2018). *Development, Untied. Unleashing the Catalytic Power of Official Development Assistance through Renewed Action on Untying*. Brussels: Eurodad.

Moss, T. J., Pettersson, G. & van de Walle, N. (2006). An Aid-Institutions Paradox? A Review Essay on Aid Dependency and State Building in Sub-Saharan Africa. Center for Global Development Working Paper No. 74.

OECD (2005). Paris Declaration on Aid Effectiveness. Paris: OECD. https://doi.org/10.1787/9789264098084-en.

Oxfam (2016). Good EU Development Plans Must Now Translate Vision into Reality. https://www.oxfam.org/en/pressroom/reactions/good-eu-development-plans-must-now-translate-vision-reality.

Pepermans, Y. & Maeseele, P. (2014). Democratic Debate and Mediated Discourses on Climate Change: From Consensus to De/politicization. *Environmental Communication* 8 (2): 216–232. https://doi.org/10.1080/17524032.2014.906482.

Rajan, R. G. & Subramanian, A. (2011). Aid, Dutch disease, and manufacturing growth. *Journal of Development Economics* 94 (1): 106–118. https://doi.org/10.1016/j.jdeveco.2009.12.004.

Raunio, T. & Wagner, W. (2021). Contestation over Development Policy in the European Parliament. *JCMS: Journal of Common Market Studies* 59: 20–36. https://doi.org/10.1111/jcms.13138.

Rozbicka, P. and Szent-Iványi, B. (2020). European Development NGOs and the Diversion of Aid: Contestation, Fence-sitting, or Adaptation? *Development Policy Review* 38 (2): 161–179. https://doi.org/10.1111/dpr.12417.

Sanchez Salgado, R. (2017). Europeanization of Civil Society Organizations in Times of Crisis? Exploring the Evolution Grant-seeking Strategies in the EU Multi-level System. *European Politics and Society* 18 (4): 511–528. https://doi.org/10.1080/23745118.2017.1286283.

Sky News (2021). UK Aid to Superpower China Hit a Record £70 million in 2019. https://news.sky.com/story/uk-aid-to-superpower-china-hit-a-record-70-million-in-2019-12288997.

Stadelmann, M. J., Roberts, T., & Michaelowa, A. (2011). New and Additional to What? Assessing Options for Baselines to Assess Climate Finance Pledges. *Climate and Development* 3 (3): 175–192. https://doi.org/10.1080/17565529.2011.599550.

Szent-Iványi, B. (2014). The EU's Support for Democratic Governance in the Eastern Neighbourhood: The Role of New Member State Transition Experience. *Europe-Asia Studies* 66 (7): 1102–1121. https://doi.org/10.1080/09668136.2014.927646.

Szent-Iványi, B. (2021). Practising What They Preach? Development NGOs and the EU's Emergency Trust Fund for Africa. *Third World Quarterly* 42 (11): 2552–2571. https://doi.org/10.1080/01436597.2021.1964358.

Szent-Iványi, B. & Lightfoot, S. (2016). Determinants of Civil Society Influence: The Case of International Development and Humanitarian NGOs in the Czech Republic and Hungary. *Comparative European Politics* 14: 761 780. https://doi.org/10.1057/cep.2014.50.

Szent-Iványi, B. & Timofejevs, P. F. (2021). Selective Norm Promotion in International Development Assistance: The Drivers of Naming and Shaming Advocacy among European Non-governmental Development Organisations. *International Relations* 35 (1): 23–46. https://doi.org/10.1177/0047117820954234.

Tétényi, A., Barczikay, T. & Szent-Iványi, B. (2019). Refugees, not Economic Migrants - Why do Asylum-Seekers Register in Hungary? *International Migration* 57: 323–340. https://doi.org/10.1111/imig.12528.

The Local Germany (2009). Germany Plans to Stop Foreign Aid to China. https://www.thelocal.de/20091030/22929/.

The Local Sweden (2007). Sweden Scraps Aid to China. https://www.thelocal.se/20070827/8296/.

Van Waeyenberge, E. (2015). The Private Turn in Development Finance. FESSUD: Working Paper Series 140.

World Bank (2021). World Bank Country and Lending Groups. https://datahelpdesk.worldbank.org/knowledgebase/articles/906519-world-bank-country-and-lending-groups.

List of interviews

All interviews by the author unless otherwise noted.
Interview#1: Hungarian NGDO expert, 5 November 2012.
Interview#2: CONCORD representative 23 January 2013.
Interview#3: Hungarian NGDO expert, 1 February 2013.
Interview#4: Hungarian NGDO expert, 6 February 2013.
Interview#5: Czech NGDO representative, 4 March 2013.
Interview#6: Czech NGDO platform board member, 7 March 2013.

Interview#7: Czech NGDO expert, 7 March 2013.
Interview#8: Czech NGDO expert, 8 March 2013.
Interview#9: Czech NGDO platform representative, 8 March 2013.
Interview#10: Hungarian NGDO expert, 5 August 2013.
Interview#11: Czech NGDO expert, 17 October 2013.
Interview#12: Polish NGDO representative, 5 July 2013.
Interview#13: Representative of CONCORD, 3 March 2017.
Interview#14: UK NGDO platform representative, 3 March 2017.
Interview#15: Belgian NGDO representative 1, 3 March 2017 (by Péteris is Timofejevs).
Interview#16: Austrian NGDO representative 1, 6 March 2017.
Interview#17: Austrian NGDO representative 2, 6 March 2017.
Interview#18: Swedish NGDO representative, 6 March 2017 (by Péteris Timofejevs).
Interview#19: Dutch NGDO representative, 15 March 2017.
Interview#20: Belgian NGDO representative 2, 3 April 2017 (by Péteris Timofejevs).
Interview#21: German NGDO representative, 20 April 2017 (by Péteris Timofejevs).
Interview#22: Save the Children Europe, 22 May 2017 (by Patrycja Rozbicka).
Interview#23: ADRA Europe, 24 May 2017 (by Patrycja Rozbicka).
Interview#24: EuroDAD, 6 June 2017.
Interview#25: CARE International, 6 June 2017.
Interview#26: Act Alliance, 6 June 2017.
Interview#27: Solidar, 7 June 2017.
Interview#28: WWF European Policy Office, 13 June 2017.
Interview#29: Oxfam, 13 June 2017 (by B. Szent-Ivanyi & P. Rozbicka).
Interview#30: World Vision, 29 June 2017.
Interview#31: CONCORD 2, 3 July 2017.

7 Funding versus advocacy

NGDO engagement with the EU Trust Fund for Africa[1]

Introduction

This chapter provides a case study of NGDO advocacy and funding-related decisions, specifically focusing on how NGDOs have engaged with the European Union Emergency Trust Fund for Africa (EUTFA). Set up in 2015 to support the EU's migration management policies by addressing the root causes of migration in Africa, the EUTFA provides an excellent example of a funding instrument where NGDO moral motivations may clash with funding considerations: on the one hand, as discussed in Chapter 6, NGDOs generally view migration as a catalyst for development, and have also been highly vocal about protecting the rights of refugees. They have opposed using aid to manage migration. On the other hand, a new aid instrument provides additional possibilities for NGDOs to access funding. Simply put, NGDOs face the dilemma of practicing what they preach, i.e. standing firmly beside their moral vision and rejecting any funding from the EUTFA. Alternatively, applying for EUTFA funding would send signals to their stakeholders on how funding concerns take primacy over moral vision, which can damage their reputation as morally driven actors.

This chapter provides evidence that the development NGO community has made attempts to have the best of both worlds, and did not eschew EUTFA funding. However, they put actions in place to mitigate potential reputational damage. These actions include (1) very vocal advocacy on the potential problems and shortfalls of the EUTFA, also signalling NGDO moral vision; (2) channelling this advocacy mainly (though not exclusively) through CONCORD; and (3) participating only in EUTFA projects which arguably align with NGDO moral visions. The chapter proceeds by providing some contextual details about the EUTFA, followed by an analysis of NGDO advocacy on it between 2015 and 2020. The final section examines the EUTFA actions NGDOs participated in, using Probit regression analysis on a dataset of EUTFA projects to identify the factors which made NGDO participation more likely.

DOI: 10.4324/9780367861872-7

The EU Emergency Trust Fund for Africa

The European Union Emergency Trust Fund for Stability and Addressing Root Causes of Irregular Migration and Displaced Persons in Africa (to use its full official name) was launched at the Valletta Summit on Migration in November 2015, following the shocks of the European refugee crisis earlier in the year. After a significant increase in arrivals of refugees and irregular migrants to the EU's borders and the reactions of some member states, there was a strong desire for the EU to act in a unified manner to stem the flow of arrivals. The goal of the EUTFA was therefore to 'deliver an integrated and coordinated response to the diverse causes of instability, irregular migration and forced displacement', by achieving 'concrete results in a rapid and effective manner' (European Commission n.d.a). Addressing the 'root causes' of migration, a long list of issues including conflict, poverty, lack of jobs, and low resilience to climate and weather shocks were seen as one aspect of the EUTFA's work, however, it was also set up to contribute to 'better migration management' in countries of origin. This includes support for border management and surveillance, developing regulatory frameworks, data collection, and operating refugee camps in countries of origin and transit. The fund was seen as an addition to existing and other newly announced EU initiatives, including maritime missions (Cusumano 2019), a similar trust fund set up in response to the Syrian crisis in December 2014 (Hauck et al. 2015), and the EU Facility for Refugees in Turkey, a 2016 deal in which Turkey agreed to tighten its border controls in exchange for 6 billion euros in aid (Kirişci 2021). Further initiatives followed, such as the New Partnership Framework, which aimed to create a set of incentives for developing countries to curb outflows of people (European Commission 2016a). Cooperation on migration, especially on returns and readmissions, was increasingly emphasised by the EU as a condition for receiving aid. This gained further prominence in the Neighbourhood, Development and International Cooperation Instrument (NDICI), the EU's main financial instrument for funding development aid in its 2021–2027 budget cycle (Burni et al. 2021).

An important rationale behind the creation of the EUTFA, instead of using the EU's existing financial instruments focused on Africa, most notably the European Development Fund (EDF), was to ensure greater flexibility and the ability to react rapidly to changing realities. The EU's existing processes for programming development aid were seen as 'sluggish', and the EUTFA's more flexible rules would allow quick results, something European publics were keen to see (Castillejo 2016: 19). The creation of a separate aid instrument for tackling migration also sent signals towards the public that the EU is serious on taking action in the wake of refugee crisis.

At its launch, the EUTFA's total amount had reached almost 1.9 billion euros (European Commission 2016a: 4), and this grew to 4.85 billion Euros by the end of 2020 (European Commission 2021: 7). Around 88 per cent of these resources were reallocated from the EU's various existing development budgets, most importantly the 11th EDF, thus representing a diversion of aid from other potential uses. The remaining 12 per cent was made up of new contributions by member states, as well as Norway and Switzerland (European Commission 2020a: 41–44). These additional contributions were rather modest compared to the total amount of the fund, defying early expectations that member states, as well as other developed countries would donate significant amounts.

The EUTFA's actions were divided along three broad geographic regions (North Africa, the Horn of Africa, and the Sahel and Lake Chad; including a total of 26 partner countries),[2] and four thematic priorities:

1 *Greater Economic and Employment Opportunities*, aiming to support skills development and job creation, especially for youth and vulnerable groups.
2 *Strengthening Resilience*, focused on supporting individuals and communities in withstanding and adapting to shocks, by strengthening food security and social protection schemes.
3 *Improved Migration Management*, under which the EUTFA supports the development of government migration policies, including the implementation of regulatory frameworks and strengthening institutions and border controls.
4 *Improved Governance and Conflict Prevention*, aimed at improving the quality of governance, including strengthening the rule of law and promoting conflict prevention.

Table 7.1 shows how the EUTFA's committed resources were distributed along the three geographic regions and the four thematic priorities, as of August 2020. This reveals an interesting observation, namely that while the

Table 7.1 Distribution of the EUTFA's committed resources along geographic and thematic priorities, 2020

	North Africa	*Horn of Africa*	*Sahel and Lake Chad*	*Total*
Greater Economic and Employment Opportunities	0	597.5 (47)	443.4 (28)	1,040.9
Strengthening Resilience	0	642.1 (68)	536.4 (26)	1,178.5
Improved Migration Management	721.8 (30)	145.0 (20)	443.2 (19)	1,310.0
Improved Governance and Conflict Prevention	8 (1)	379.3 (37)	666.9 (32)	1,054.2
Total	742.3	1,763.9	2,089.9	4,596.1

Source: author's calculations, based on European Commission (2020b).

Note: in million euros, action counts in brackets. Data for August 2020. Some actions are coded by the European Commission under more than one theme, in these cases their value is split proportionately between the themes.

four thematic areas were more or less balanced in terms of commitments, improved migration management seems to have been slightly more important than the others. Furthermore, improved migration management was basically the EUTFA's only priority area in North Africa, but it received relatively little emphasis in the Horn of Africa, accounting for only 8% of the commitments to that region. This difference may be due to how countries in North Africa served more as transit countries for migrants than countries of origin, thus actions aimed at addressing root causes were perhaps less relevant there.

As mentioned, the EUTFA's implementation process and rules differed from those in the EU's other aid instruments. While the EDF (and now its successor the NDICI) followed an often long programming process where areas of intervention were planned and agreed jointly by the European Commission (EC) and partner country governments, the EUTFA was planned to be much more flexible. The approach was more 'bottom-up': there was no overarching programme of action, rather individual projects were proposed, in what may seem to have been a slightly ad-hoc manner, by the EU's delegations in the 26 countries covered. The delegations were meant to 'consult widely to ensure strong partnerships with local stakeholders' (European Commission n.d.b), then propose project ideas to the Commission's EUTFA team in Brussels. The decision on whether to fund a proposal was made by the EUTFA's Operational Committee, composed of representatives of the EC, the European External Action Service, and contributing states. There was an aim to operate the Operational Committee by consensus, although each state which had contributed at least 3 million Euros received one vote (European Union 2015). The implementation of the approved actions was carried out by a wide range of partners, which included member state development agencies, United Nations organisations (such as the United Nations High Commissioner for Refugees, the United Nations Development Programme, or the United Nations Children's Fund) other international organisations (especially the International Organisation for Migration, although this became a UN 'related' organisation in 2016), partner country authorities, NGDOs, as well as different consortia of these actors (European Commission n.d.b).

NGDO advocacy on the EUTFA

To map the NGDO community's advocacy regarding the EUTFA, a similar systematic search was performed as in Chapter 4; however, in this case the goal was to locate only NGDO press releases, reports, and any other publications which dealt specifically with the EUTFA. The search was performed on CONCORD's website, as well as the main international websites of its 25 transnational network members. To find texts on the EUTFA, the general search function on each organisation's website was used, as well as the search functions in their publication repositories, with the keywords

'Africa', 'migration' or 'trust fund'. The search was restricted to documents published between 2015 and 2020, and to ones which dealt explicitly with the EUTFA, as opposed to ones which discussed the EU's handling of the development/migration nexus in more general terms.

While there was a very large number of hits on these websites for publications discussing the links between migration and development, showing the high interest the NGDO community had in this topic (see also Chapters 4 and 6), the number of those focusing explicitly on the EUTFA was only 30. Out of this, 21 were short press releases, blog posts, or other statements, the remaining nine were more substantial policy papers or reports which either dealt exclusively with the EUTFA (CONCORD 2015; 2018a; 2018b; Oxfam 2015a; 2017; 2020), or devoted a significant section to it (CONCORD 2016; Islamic Relief 2018; Caritas 2019). Given its nature as a purely advocacy group, CONCORD has been the most active in voicing NGDO criticisms about the EUTFA, but among individual NGDOs, Oxfam was perhaps the most prolific with two detailed reports on the fund. Caritas, Islamic Relief and Solidar have also discussed the EUTFA in their advocacy, although mainly through shorter website posts and press releases. The EUTFA was ignored by all the other large network members of CONCORD. All 30 documents were read in detail and the themes were coded using a qualitative approach.

The analysis revealed that NGDOs were generally highly critical of the EUTFA and the EU's usage of aid to manage migration. One major theme emerged around the EUTFA's underlying narrative, and three smaller ones focused on resources, effectiveness and harm.

The major theme in NGDO criticisms focused on the problems with the EUTFA's underlying narrative, i.e. how it is aimed to reduce migratory pressures on Europe. It thus served the self-interests of the EU, and not those of the poor, whom development aid was generally meant to support. For example, CONCORD (2015: 2) argued that 'the emphasis on border controls and security undermines the achievement of the EU's global development objectives', especially poverty reduction and the respect of human rights. The EUTFA was seen as a tool to stem migratory flows to Europe with 'quick fix' projects, which was at odds not only with the goals of EU development assistance outlined in the Lisbon Treaty (CONCORD 2018b), but more broadly with 'the fundamental values of an open European society, based on respect for human rights and human dignity, promotion of peace and solidarity between and among nations' (van Dillen 2015). Oxfam (2016) argued that the EUTFA blurred the lines between 'development work – which is aimed at lifting people out of poverty – and security projects meant to strengthen border control and stop people on the move'. The EUTFA was branded as a 'political tool that sends a political signal to the European constituency', with actual development objectives side-lined (CONCORD 2018b). NGDOs claimed that the EU has gone so far in looking at its own interests that it was even providing resources to countries known for systematic violations of human rights, all in the name of controlling migration (Oxfam 2016; Caritas 2016). A detailed analysis by Oxfam (2020a) of the projects implemented under the EUTFA showed that more than a quarter of the fund's resources were spent on migration management projects with little development impacts.

According to NGDOs, security and migration management projects of the EUTFA were not the only problematic areas where political self-interests of the EU trumped development objectives. The EU has been increasingly pushing migration related conditionalities on its partner countries in exchange for development aid: security and border cooperation, and agreeing to return and readmission arrangements were heavily emphasised by the EU as conditions for receiving aid, but remained highly unpopular in partner countries. NGDOs have heavily criticised this practice, which was formalised in 2016 with the launch of the EU's New Partnership Framework with third countries (Caritas 2017; CONCORD 2015; Oxfam 2015b). A joint NGDO statement called on the EU to develop safe and open channels for migration, abandon the usage of migration related conditions for receiving aid, and stop the readmission of people to countries that violated fundamental rights (Joint NGO Statement 2016). However, Oxfam later found that only 1.5 per cent of the EUTFA's resources had been spent on developing regular migration schemes between the EU and Africa between 2015 and 2020 (Oxfam 2020a).

The main thrust of NGDO criticism therefore argued that the EUTFA (as well as other EU initiatives linked to it) primarily served the self-interest of the EU, to the detriment of developing country partners. A second theme emerging from the advocacy publications focused on resources, arguing that the amount devoted to the EUTFA was small and did not represent additional development contributions. CONCORD called the Valletta Summit a 'missed opportunity', and argued that the less than 2 billion Euros agreed at the time was insufficient to address the root causes of forced displacement and migration, especially when spread across 26 countries, and compared to the €6 billion granted to Turkey alone (van Dillen 2015; Wirsching and van Dillen 2016). NGDOs also called attention to the fact that much of these resources were basically existing aid commitments that were re-labelled from the EDF and other EU aid instruments (Wirsching and van Dillen 2016).

A third theme focused on the effectiveness of the EUTFA and its specific projects. The EU has been one of the main drivers behind the global aid effectiveness agenda (Carbone 2013; Kim and Lightfoot 2017), and has promoted the implementation of effectiveness enhancing reforms among member states (Lightfoot and Szent-Iványi 2014), although its practice has not always lived up to its ambitions (Delputte and Orbie 2014). NGDOs argued that the EUTFA undermined the EU's commitments to the principles of aid effectiveness. Due to the lack of a robust programming process and the 'flexibility' of the EUTFA, NGDOs questioned just how recipient country ownership and alignment with recipient priorities could be ensured

(CONCORD 2016). The ability of partner countries to feed into the design of projects did not seem to be ensured, with EU delegations formulating the project proposals and decisions being made in Brussels (CONCORD 2018b). It was questionable how such a process could reflect partner country priorities. These criticisms were also echoed by academic research (Castillejo 2016: 20), which found that the EUTFA's operations undermined key aid effectiveness principles, especially recipient ownership: local consultations were short, and aid seemed to be driven much more by EU priorities than recipient needs. NGDOs however did acknowledge that the EUTFA's effectiveness had improved over time, especially in terms of transparency and public communication (Oxfam 2020a).

The fourth theme was around harm caused by the EUTFA, either by providing aid to regimes with questionable human rights records, or through unintended economic consequences emerging from the assistance. For example, NGDOs have called attention to the EU's support to the Libyan authorities, which has fuelled 'human trafficking and the arbitrary detention of refugees in horrific and dangerous conditions' (Oxfam 2020b; see also Islamic Relief 2018). Another widely publicised consequence of the EUTFA was in Niger, where the informal economy in the city of Agadez was built around migrants in transit towards Europe. However, the EU pushed Niger into changing its policies and laws on migration, as well as crack down migrant smuggling networks, which led to a collapse in local incomes, significantly hurting livelihoods in the city (CONCORD 2018b; Oxfam 2020b).

The themes emerging from NGDO advocacy on the EUTFA are fully in-line with the explanations provided in Chapter 6 on migration-focused aid more generally. Most importantly, moral motivations seem to dominate, as NGDOs clearly contest the self-interests of the EU and stand up for people in poor countries, especially vulnerable migrants and refugees. They call for schemes which would increase the welfare of the poor and contest efforts to reduce their rights or harm their livelihoods. In their criticism of the EUTFA, NGDOs have tried to create a positive narrative of migration, focusing on the development benefits it brings to mobile persons, countries which receive migrants, and also sending countries through remittances and other channels. NGDOs have argued that making a clear distinction between mobility and forced displacement is essential, so that the fundamental rights of the latter group, guaranteed in international law, can be protected. There are regular references to the core values of the EU, and how the EU needs to stop undermining these. 'Development aid is meant to fight poverty, inequality, and the growing climate crisis and it should not be politicised' (Oxfam 2020b). While not all NGDOs engaged in direct advocacy relating to the EUTFA, it is clear that through CONCORD or the 2016 Joint Statement, the NGDO community as a whole made its position visible, and this position aligned with the moral motivations driving NGDOs.

NGDO participation in the implementation of the EUTFA

NGDO criticism of the EUTFA has been very strong, and as discussed aligns with NGDO moral motivations. The high degree of politicisation of migration explains why NGDOs needed to expound their moral motivations so visibly. However, NGDOs are also driven by funding concerns, and the EUTFA represented a significant amount of development resources. Given the harshness of their criticism, it may be reasonable to expect NGDOs to fully boycott the EUTFA, or at least be highly cautious when participating in projects funded from it as implementing actors.

This has clearly not been the case however, in fact NGDOs have been heavily involved in the implementation of the EUTFA. Based on data from the EUTFA's website, around 18 per cent of the fund's contracted amount were directly implemented by NGDOs (European Commission n.d.c).[3] This share was actually higher than the amount of EU aid from all aid instruments channelled through NGDOs, which was only 10.5 per cent in 2018 according to OECD.stat (2020; see also Keijzer and Bossuyt 2020 for a broader discussion on the role of NGDOs in EU development assistance). Despite the heavy criticism of the EUTFA, the European NGDO community has left the option open for its members to participate in the EUTFA: as discussed, most of the advocacy was done through CONCORD, which as an advocacy body did not itself bid for EUTFA funding. Relatively few NGDOs have criticised the fund directly, with Oxfam being the most notable exception, and most have opted to contest only more generally the EU's diversion of aid for migration management.

Visibly denouncing the EUTFA allowed NGDOs to signal their moral virtues, and due to the high political salience of the topic, this was visible to their constituents and even beyond. However, taking part in its actual implementation may have carried reputational risks. Large NGDOs may have assumed however that these risks were small: being involved in a small number of EUTFA projects may not have stood out among the many projects that these organisations undertake. In NGDO annual reports, EUTFA projects can be bundled together with funding from other, non-controversial EU aid instruments (such as the EDF or humanitarian aid), under a broad heading of 'EU funding'. There is evidence that many NGDOs regularly do this (see Chapter 5 for more details). Oxfam is perhaps the only large NGDO which drew attention to the fact that it participated in EUTFA projects: in its 2020 report analysing the workings of the EUTFA, it explicitly mentioned that it took part in implementing projects 'in the Sahel and Horn of Africa regions' (Oxfam 2020a: 10).

But is it just about 'sneaking in some funding' in the hopes that it would 'fly under the radar' with stakeholders? The remainder of this section analyses the types of EUTFA projects NGDOs implemented between 2015 and 2020, to get some insights into the factors which may have driven their participation in the fund. An important question is whether these are compatible with their moral standpoints.

The EUTFA's website provides a database of projects implemented under the fund, which is a good source of data for exploring the determinants of NGDO participation (European Commission 2020b). The dataset was downloaded in August 2020, and at the time it included 234 actions. The level of detail varied between actions: most had very detailed documentation, including action fiches, financial details and data on the main implementing actors. A minority of projects however hardly included more than a short description. Out of the 234 actions, reasonably full details could be found for 206. Out of these 206 actions, 34 included an NGDO as the main implementer, or one of the implementers (the rest were implemented by member state development agencies, United Nations organisations, or in some cases partner country authorities). These 34 projects involved a total of 31 NGDOs; their details are provided in Table 7.2., which also includes additional information collected from each group's website and 2018/2019 annual report (cf. Chapter 5).

Table 7.2 shows that the NGDOs participating in the EUTFA's implementation were predominantly large organisations (their median income was 177 million Euros) from Northern/developed countries. Most of them were heavily dependent on funding from official donors, and although exact data was not available for many, they received not insignificant parts of their income from the EU. The financial reports of the 31 NGDOs also confirmed that many have indeed hidden EUTFA funding: most commonly these reports only provided very basic breakdowns of EU funding, only differentiating between humanitarian and development funds.

NGDO participation in EUTFA project implementation may be driven by a number of factors, which can shed light on moral and financial motivations. To examine this further, a Probit regression was performed on the project dataset. The dependent variable was binary, and focused on whether an NGDO was involved in the implementation of a given action or not. If the action involved an NGDO, then the value of the variable was 1, regardless of the exact role the organisation played in the project, which was often difficult to determine from the dataset.

The independent variables aimed to proxy financial and moral motivations, as well as include any other controls which could be reasonably extracted from the project dataset. Financial motivations were proxied by the total budget of the project (in euros, variable 'budget'). To measure moral motivations, the thematic area of the project was used, which was operationalised using a set of dummies. The 'Other' category represented the baseline (these were actions aimed at research and evaluation, and not attributed by the EU to either theme), with dummies for *Greater Economic and Employment Opportunities* (econ_emp), *Strengthening Resilience* (str_res), *Improved Migration Management* (migr_man) and *Improved Governance and Conflict Prevention* (impr_gov). Projects under the theme of *Improved Migration Management* align least with NGDO moral motivations, as they have contested these in their advocacy the most. Taking part in migration

Table 7.2 NGDOs involved in EUTFA projects, 2015–2020

Name	*Origin*	*Income*			*EUTF projects*	
		Total	*From official donors*	*From the EU*	*Number*	*Total value*
Action Contre la Faim	France	424.50	78%	19%	2	50.00
ADRA	USA	NA	NA	NA	1	8.00
ACTED	France	260.00	87%	20%	2	11.10
CARE International UK	USA	74	73.80%	7.70%	1	20.00
Centre pour le dialogue humanitaire - HD	Switzerland	34.1	NA	NA	1	2.20
CESVI	Italy	26.00	80%	27%	1	23.00
Concern Worldwide	Ireland	163.50	57%	14.8%	3	27.00
COOPI	Italy	60.50	93%	31%	1	8.00
Cordoba Foundation	Switzerland	NA	NA	NA	1	2.40
Danish Church Aid	Denmark	90	75%	15%	1	30.00
Danish Refugee Council	Denmark	415.00	84%	NA	4	46.52
Regional Durable Solutions Secretariat	Kenya	NA	100%	NA	1	9.00
GOAL	Ireland	109.7	80%	9%	1	15.00
GRET	France	32	60%	36%	1	40.11
Humanity & Inclusion	France	190.7	65.5%	NA	3	78.00
IMPACT Initiatives	Switzerland	NA	NA	NA	1	10.00
Instituto Marquês de Valle Flôr	Portugal	6.5	100%	89%	1	23.00
International Medical Corps	USA	248.8	98%	NA	1	7.00
International Rescue Committee	USA	711.2	71%	NA	3	56.62
Médecins Du Monde	France	99.2	47.50%	NA	1	9.90
Mercy Corps UK	USA	128.4	83%	22%	1	3.50
Norwegian Refugee Council	Norway	430	90%	16%	2	41.62
Oxfam	UK	493.3	43%	6%	3	82.00
Plan International	UK	895	NA	NA	2	90.00

Name	*Origin*	*Income*			*EUTF projects*	
		Total	*From official donors*	*From the EU*	*Number*	*Total value*
Positive Planet	France	NA	NA	NA	1	40.11
Save the Children	UK	1964.3	55%	2.5%	4	57.90
SNV Netherlands	Netherlands	142	92%	10%	4	90.00
SOS SAHEL	Senegal/ France	19.6	84.80%	NA	1	25.00
Terre des hommes	Switzerland	212	55%	8%	1	30.00
Welthungerhilfe	Germany	249	75.90%	26.50%	2	18.00
World Vision Australia	Australia	362.1	21.40%	NA	1	15.00

Source: collected from individual NGDO websites, annual reports and European Commission (2020b).

Notes: data for 2019, or latest available. Income and project values in million euros. Data provided in currencies other than euro were converted using the average annual exchange rate for 2019 from the European Central Bank. NA denotes data not available.

management projects would contradict rhetoric and pose the strongest reputational risk for NGDOs. This variable is therefore expected to have a negative sign. As discussed on numerous occasions in this book, projects aimed at directly supporting the lives and livelihoods of the poor are the most compatible with NGDO moral motivations, and projects targeting these fall under the *Greater Economic and Employment Opportunities* or *Strengthening Resilience* themes. The latter thematic area is the most likely one to include projects which fit under 'traditional' development cooperation. NGDOs may even have some sort of comparative advantage it this area, given their ability to work with vulnerable communities.

Two further sets of dummies were included as control variables. First, two dummies coded the region in which the EUTFA project was implemented: Sahel and Lake Chad represented the baseline, with dummies for North Africa (n_afr) and the Horn of Africa (horn_afr). Second, the year in which the project was implemented was also coded with a set of dummies, with 2015 serving as the baseline. Summary statistics on the variables are provided in Table 7.3.

The variables listed in Table 7.3 understandably do not cover all the potential determinants of NGDO participation in the EUTFA. However, it was not possible to extract any further, uniformly quantifiable, and comparable data from the project dataset that would have been helpful in the regression analysis. The biggest caveat with the dataset is that it misses data

Table 7.3 Summary statistics

Variable	*Observations*	*Mean*	*Standard deviation*	*Min*	*Max*
Budget	234	19,600,000	22,000,000	1,000,000	144,000,000
NGDO participation	206	0.17	0.37	0	1
North Africa	234	0.13	0.34	0	1
Horn of Africa	234	0.42	0.50	0	1
Improved governance and conflict prevention	234	0.30	0.46	0	1
Improved migration management	234	0.30	0.46	0	1
Strengthening resilience	234	0.40	0.49	0	1
Greater economic and employment opportunities	234	0.32	0.47	0	1

Source: calculations of the author.

relating specifically to the NGDOs themselves, such as on their income and official funding situation, which can clearly be a plausible explanatory factor. However, since NGDOs were only implementers in 34 out of the 206 actions, these variables would not make sense for the majority of the observations which have member state aid agencies, partner country authorities or international organisations as implementers.

The results of the regression analysis are presented in Table 7.4. The table shows two versions of the model: Model 1 does not include the year dummies, treating the entire dataset as a single cross-section, while Model 2 includes these additional dummies. The dummy variable for the managing migration theme is significant in both models (although only at the 10 per cent level) and with a negative sign, implying that NGDOs were indeed less likely to take part in projects aimed at managing migration, as expected. Strengthening resilience is strongly significant, with the expected positive sign. The dummy for projects in the Horn of Africa is significant too. None of the other variables is significant: NGDO participation was not influenced by the size of the project, nor were NGDOs more or less likely to participate in projects in North Africa than in the Sahel, or in those aimed at creating economic opportunities or improving governance. Model 1 was also estimated with the budget variable entered in logarithm, but the results remained practically unchanged (this is not reported in Table 7.4). Adding the year dummies in Model 2 changes little in the results as well. These dummies are not significant individually, and an F-test shows that they are not significant jointly either. This implies that there has been little change in NGDOs' levels of engagement with the EUTFA over time.

Table 7.4 Probit regression results on the determinants of NGDO participation in EUTFA projects

	Model 1	*Model 2*
Budget	1.09E-09 (4.68E-09)	1.99E-09 (5.02E-09)
North Africa	0.8289 (0.5762)	0.7832 (0.5766)
Horn of Africa	-0.6828 (0.2854)**	-0.7118 (0.3288)**
Improved Governance and Conflict Prevention	-0.2582 (0.2992)	-0.2221 (0.2899)
Improved Migration Management	-0.8478 (0.4828)*	-0.8018 (0.4757)*
Strengthening Resilience	0.9150 (0.2906)***	0.9685 (0.2985)***
Greater Economic and Employment Opportunities	0.0677 (0.278659)	0.1956 (0.2719)
2016	–	-0.2963 (0.6543)
2017	–	-0.2095 (0.6902)
2018	–	0.6237 (0.6940)
2019	–	-0.0125 (0.6792
2020	–	-0.5028 (0.7981)
Constant	-1.0733*** (0.2799)	-0.8420 (0.6835)
N	206	205
Pseudo R^2	0.1210	0.1421

Source: author.

Notes: robust standard errors in parentheses. ***, **, and * denote statistical significance at the 0.01, 0.05 and 0.1 levels respectively.

The average marginal effects of migration management and strengthening resilience can give a better picture of the exact impact these have a NGDOs' decisions to participate or not in EUTFA projects. These are provided in Table 7.5., based on Model 1. According to this, on average across all observations, NGDOs are 15.8 per cent less likely to participate in migration management projects, and 21.8 per cent more likely to be included in projects aimed at strengthening resilience, all other factors being constant.

The conclusion emerging from the regression analysis is that NGDO participation in the EUTFA was not that much at odds with their rhetoric as it

Table 7.5 Average marginal effects of *Improved Migration Management* and *Strengthening Resilience* on the probability of NGDO participation in EUTFA projects

	Marginal effect on NGDO participation	*95% confidence interval*
Improved Migration Management	-0.1577** (0.0717)	-0.2983 – -0.0171
Strengthening Resilience	0.2184*** (0.0721)	0.0771–0.3598

Notes: average of marginal effects across all observations. Standard errors in parentheses. ***, **, and * denote statistical significance at the 0.01, 0.05 and 0.1 levels respectively.

first seemed. While fully boycotting the EUTFA would have been the absolutely moral approach to take, it is clearly an unrealistic expectation as well. Nonetheless, the results show that NGDOs were not drawn to larger projects, and they were very unlikely to participate in the kinds of projects most at odds with their moral missions and advocacy positions. NGDO participation in the EUTFA was mostly focused on the projects which fit under the umbrella of traditional development cooperation, which were generally included under the EUTFA's *Strengthening Resilience* theme.

There is one more question left to explore: are there any potential alternative explanations to NGDOs' reluctance to take part in migration management projects? A relatively straightforward explanation would be that they did not take part in these simply because they had no expertise for these projects, as opposed to the argument above about NGDOs making conscious decisions to avoid these for moral and reputational reasons. A common perception, and indeed the general description of the *Improved Migration Management* theme implies that projects under it focused on strengthening government capacities in surveillance, tackling irregular border crossings, building border infrastructure, or managing data on migration. These are areas where NGDOs have little expertise, and indeed it would be difficult to conceive an NGDO implementing these. Getting a better answer on NGDO motivations requires a more careful unpacking of the projects under this theme, however.

Table 7.6 presents a breakdown of the actions under the *Improved Migration Management* theme, along their main activities. According to this, border management and law enforcement projects made up 18 per cent of the total value of actions under the theme, while projects aimed at protecting refugees around 25 per cent. Looking more closely at the refugee protection projects, they included elements like providing basic services (e.g. medical assistance and sanitation), protecting vulnerable groups such as women and children from exploitation and human trafficking, supporting migrants and refugees with legal assistance, providing shelter and generally improving the conditions under which migrants are housed, or sensitising law enforcement and other government officials on the rights of migrants. These are all activities

Table 7.6 Breakdown of *Improved Migration Management* projects according to their main activities

Main activity	*Total project values (in euro)*	*Share of total*
Border control	236,623,927	18.1%
Governance	62,350,000	4.8%
Information campaigns	75,600,000	5.8%
Legal migration routes	40,000,000	3.1%
Refugee protection	329,880,000	25.2%
Return and readmission	439,593,500	33.6%
Other/mixed	125,952,573	9.6%
Total	1,310,000,000	100.0%

Source: author, based on European Commission (2020b).

which many NGDOs have expertise in, especially the larger ones which are active in providing services in refugee camps. NGDOs which take part in migration management projects only did so under these humanitarian refugee protection projects, which fit with their moral missions and expertise. For example, Save the Children was part of a project aimed at protecting migrant children from human trafficking in Mauritania, while the Danish Refugee Council was engaged in one focusing on the provision of basic services to refugees and migrants in Libya (European Commission n.d.d).

There is no evidence of NGDOs participating in projects which aimed at promoting and enhancing return and readmission, nor (with one exception) in information campaigns aimed at deterring would-be migrants, whereas they conceivably could have taken part in these, at least based on their capacities and expertise. These projects generally aimed to incentivise migrants to return to their home communities. Through them, the implementers offered training, implemented various actions to improve local livelihoods and employment opportunities, as well as ran information campaigns about these. These are all things which NGDOs could have conceivably done. However, the philosophy behind these projects was to limit migration, and force or lure migrants to return. This is difficult to harmonise with NGDO moral positions, who have been vocal not only about the benefits of migration, but also about empowering the poor and allowing them to make their own choices. The fact that there were areas under the migration management theme in which NGDOs could have participated, but instead seemed to stay away from, supports the argument that they were wary of migration management projects not because they did not have the expertise for these, but rather because they did not want to harm their reputations by associating themselves with the more controversial aspects of managing migration.

These and further arguments in this chapter show that while NGDOs are partially driven by the need to seek funding, they aim to do this in a way which does not compromise their reputation as morally driven actors, at least in case of a highly politicised area like migration. In the specific case of the EUTFA, NGDOs put forward a strong narrative, signalling their moral vision through advocacy and contestation of the fund's underlying narrative and implementation practice. They were also careful to only participate in actions which aligned with this moral vision.

Notes

1 This chapter is based on, but also expands Szent-Iványi (2021).
2 North Africa includes Algeria, Egypt, Libya, Morocco, and Tunisia; countries in the Horn of Africa are Djibouti, Eritrea, Ethiopia, Kenya, Somalia, South Sudan, Sudan, Tanzania, and Uganda; while the Sahel and Lake Chad region comprises Burkina Faso, Cameroon, Chad, Cote d'Ivoire, the Gambia, Ghana, Guinee, Mali, Mauritania, Niger, Nigeria, and Senegal.
3 This only includes projects where NGDOs were the main implementers. NGDOs may also have been present as indirect subcontractors through contracts signed with member state aid agencies or international organisations acting as the main implementers. The data however is not granular enough to gauge this level of participation. Nonetheless, this means that 18 per cent is most likely a lower bound for NGDO participation, and actual involvement was probably even higher.

References

Burni, A., Erforth, A. & Keijzer, N. (2021). Global Europe? The New EU External Action Instrument and the European Parliament. *Global Affairs* 7 (4): 471–485. https://doi.org/10.1080/23340460.2021.1993081.

Carbone, M. (2013). Between EU Actorness and Aid Effectiveness: The Logics of EU Aid to Sub-Saharan Africa. *International Relations* 27 (3): 341–355. https://doi.org/10.1177/0047117813497300.

Caritas (2016). The EU Agenda Behind the Migration Partnership Framework. https://www.caritas.eu/the-eu-agenda-behind-the-migration-partnership-framework/.

Caritas (2017). Development Aid Cannot Serve as Migration Control. https://www.caritas.eu/development-aid-cannot-serve-the-purpose-of-migration-control/.

Caritas (2019). Caritas Europa's Vision for a Renewed Partnership between the EU and ACP Countries: An Opportunity to Deliver on Agenda 2030. https://www.caritasinternational.be/wp-content/uploads/2019/01/190115-Caritas-Europa-paper-EU-ACP_ENGLISH.pdf.

Castillejo, C. (2016). The European Union Trust Fund for Africa: A Glimpse of the Future for EU Development Cooperation. DIE Discussion Paper 22/2016.

CONCORD (2015). Migration and Development. Spotlight Report 2015 Policy Paper. Brussels: CONCORD.

CONCORD (2016). AidWatch Report 2016. This is Not Enough!Brussels: CONCORD.

CONCORD (2018a). What European Member States and Commission Must Remember While Committing New Funds to the EU Trust Fund for Africa. CONCORD Policy Brief, 22 June.

CONCORD (2018b). Partnership or Conditionality? Monitoring the Migration Compacts and EU Trust Fund for Africa. https://concordeurope.org/wp-content/uploads/2018/01/CONCORD_EUTrustFundReport_2018_online.pdf.

Cusumano, E. (2019). Migrant Rescue as Organized Hypocrisy: EU Maritime Missions Offshore Libya Between Humanitarianism and Border Control. *Cooperation and Conflict* 54 (1): 3–24. https://doi.org/10.1177/0010836718780175.

Delputte, S. & Orbie, J. (2014). The EU and Donor Coordination on the Ground: Perspectives from Tanzania and Zambia. *European Journal of Development Research* 26: 676–691. https://doi.org/10.1057/ejdr.2014.11.

European Commission (2016a). Commission Announces New Migration Partnership Framework: Reinforced Cooperation with Third Countries to Better Manage Migration. Press Release, 7 June.https://ec.europa.eu/commission/presscorner/detail/en/IP_16_2072.

European Commission (2020a). The Emergency Trust Fund for Stability and Addressing Root Causes of Irregular Migration and Displaced Persons in Africa. 2019 Annual Report. Brussels: European Commission.

European Commission (2020b). EU Emergency Trust Fund for Africa – All Projects. https://ec.europa.eu/trustfundforafrica/navigation/all-projects_en.

European Commission (2021). The Emergency Trust Fund for Africa. 2020 Annual Report. Brussels: European Commission.

European Commission (n.d.a). EU Emergency Trust Fund for Africa – About. https://ec.europa.eu/trustfundforafrica/content/about_en.

European Commission (n.d.b). EU Emergency Trust Fund for Africa – How Do We Work. https://ec.europa.eu/trustfundforafrica/content/how-does-it-work_en.

European Commission (n.d.c). EU Emergency Trust Fund for Africa – FAQ. https://ec.europa.eu/trustfundforafrica/content/about/faq_en.

European Commission (n.d.d). EU Emergency Trust Fund for Africa – Strengthening Protection and Resilience of Displaced Populations in Libya. https://ec.europa.eu/trustfundforafrica/region/north-africa/libya/strengthening-protection-and-resilience-displaced-populations-libya_en.

European Union (2015). Agreement Establishing the European Union Emergency Trust Fund Stability and Addressing Root Causes of Irregular Migration and Displaced Persons in Africa. https://ec.europa.eu/trustfundforafrica/sites/euetfa/files/original_constitutive_agreement_en_with_signatures.pdf.

Hauck, V., Knoll, A. & Herrero Cangas, A. (2015). EU Trust Funds – Shaping More Comprehensive External Action? ECDPM Briefing Note 81.

Islamic Relief (2018). Justice and Protection for Refugees: Building on the UN's Global Compact. https://reliefweb.int/sites/reliefweb.int/files/resources/IRW%20GLOBAL%20COMPACT%202018%20v2.pdf.

Joint NGO Statement (2016). Joint NGO Statement Ahead of the European Council of 28–29 June 2016. NGOs Strongly Condemn New EU Policies to Contain Migration. https://oi-files-d8-prod.s3.eu-west-2.amazonaws.com/s3fs-public/file_attachments/jointstatementeumigrationresponse.pdf.

Keijzer, N. & Bossuyt, F. (2020). Partnership on Paper, Pragmatism on the Ground: The European Union's Engagement with Civil Society Organisations. *Development in Practice* 30 (6): 784–794. https://doi.org/10.1080/09614524.2020.1801589.

Kim, S. & Lightfoot, S. (2017). The EU and the Negotiation of Global Development Norms: The Case of Aid Effectiveness. *European Foreign Affairs Review* 22 (2): 159–175.

Kirişci, K. (2021). As EU-Turkey Migration Agreement Reaches the Five-year Mark, Add a Job Creation Element. https://www.brookings.edu/blog/order-from-chaos/2021/03/17/as-eu-turkey-migration-agreement-reaches-the-five-year-mark-add-a-job-creation-element/.

Lightfoot, S. & Szent-Iványi, B. (2014). Reluctant Donors? The Europeanization of International Development Policies in the New Member States. *Journal of Common Market Studies* 52: 1257–1272. https://doi.org/10.1111/jcms.12141.

OECD.stat (2020). DAC Table 1. Total Flows by Donor. https://stats.oecd.org/Index.aspx?datasetcode=TABLE1.

Oxfam (2015a). EU-Africa Cooperation on Mobility, Displacement, and Migration. Oxfam Position Paper for the EU-Africa Summit on Migration, La Valletta, 11–12 November 2015. https://www.oxfam.org/en/research/oxfam-position-paper-eu-africa-migration-summit.

Oxfam (2015b). Valletta: Africa Trust Fund Must Help People, Not Build Barriers. https://www.oxfam.org/en/press-releases/valletta-africa-trust-fund-must-help-people-not-build-barriers.

Oxfam (2016). EU Ministers Must Change Course on Migration Cooperation with Africa. https://www.oxfam.org/en/press-releases/eu-ministers-must-change-course-migration-cooperation-africa.

Oxfam (2017). An Emergency for Whom? The EU Emergency Trust Fund for Africa – Migratory Routes and Development Aid in Africa. https://www.oxfam.org/en/research/emergency-whom-eu-emergency-trust-fund-africa-migratory-routes-and-development-aid-africa.

Oxfam (2020a). The EU Trust Fund for Africa. Trapped Between Aid Policy and Migration Politics. https://oxfamilibrary.openrepository.com/bitstream/handle/10546/620936/bp-eu-trust-fund-africa-migration-politics-300120-en.pdf.

Oxfam (2020b). EU Aid Increasingly Used to Curb Migration. https://oxfamapps.org/media/press_release/eu-aid-increasingly-used-to-curb-migration-oxfam/.

Szent-Iványi, B. (2021). Practising What They Preach? Development NGOs and the EU's Emergency Trust Fund for Africa. *Third World Quarterly* 42 (11): 2552–2571. https://doi.org/10.1080/01436597.2021.1964358.

van Dillen, B. (2015). A Missed Opportunity in Valletta. https://concordeurope.org/2015/11/17/a-missed-opportunity-in-valletta/.

Wirsching, S. & van Dillen, B. (2016). Migration for Development and Human Rights — The Need for EU Policy Coherence. https://concordeurope.org/2016/03/22/migration-development-human-rights-need-eu-policy-coherence/.

8 NGDO advocacy during the COVID-19 pandemic

Introduction

The COVID-19 pandemic has created a global humanitarian emergency with long term development impacts, and has thus had a transformative impact on the global development agenda and the priorities of donor countries. This has understandably also shifted the advocacy of NGDOs, with issues related to the pandemic taking centre stage. This chapter examines this advocacy. It begins with a discussion of the impacts of COVID-19 on developing countries and the policy solutions put forward by academics and think tanks to address these. It then describes the advocacy of three NGDOs: CONCORD, Oxfam, and Save the Children, and compares the policies they called for to the policy solutions identified in the previous section. The goal of this exercise is to determine whether NGDOs really have the best interests of the poor in mind, or whether there is evidence of other motivations at play. The final part of the chapter uses the book's analytical framework to discuss the reasons why NGDO advocacy may have deviated from the 'ideal' policy response.

The impacts of the pandemic in the Global South

Many countries in the Global South were suffering from a number of problems well before the pandemic, which had a negative effect on their resilience and ability to cope. Weak governance and a lack of budgetary resources, as well as lacking healthcare infrastructure and personnel have generally been staple characteristics of countries in the Global South, but many countries were also suffering from high public debt (such as Ghana, Mozambique, Sri Lanka, Zambia, or Zimbabwe), or were experiencing violent conflict (like Afghanistan, Mali, Mozambique, Niger, Nigeria, or Yemen). Disease burdens in many countries were already pressing, with a high prevalence of malaria, HIV/AIDS, tuberculosis. Developing countries however also possessed some characteristics which could have made them more resilient against the pandemic, especially younger populations: for example, the median age in Chad in 2015 was 16.1 years, in Bangladesh 25.6

DOI: 10.4324/9780367861872-8

years, while in most European countries the value was above 40 (Ritchie and Roser 2019). Furthermore, some countries have gained recent experience in managing pandemics, such as the HIV/AIDS pandemic especially in Southern Africa or the Ebola outbreaks in the Congo and Western Africa.

The pandemic hit developing countries especially hard, through at least three channels: the health effects, the effects of local lockdowns and other measures to slow the spread of the virus, and the impacts of decisions made in the developed world, including lockdown measures, but also purchases of equipment, treatments, and vaccines.

In terms of the health effects, many at first argued that given how serious illness and death from infection with SARS-CoV-2 was positively correlated with age, having young populations would mean lower mortality rates in developing countries (Lawal 2021). However, this seems to have been counterbalanced by the numerous weaknesses developing countries faced, and there is evidence that mortality rates in the developing world have in reality actually been higher than those in developed countries. Based on estimates of excess mortality in May 2021, around 86 per cent of global COVID-19-related deaths happened in the developing world (Gill and Schellekens 2021). Modelling by *The Economist* (2021) has found similar results: up to November 2021, the pandemic has led to between 10.6 and 19.9 million excess deaths globally (with 17.1 being the central estimate), and almost 88 per cent of these happened in developing countries. Mortality rates therefore seem to have been positively correlated with a country's level of income, with lacking health infrastructure and resources being the decisive factors.

The excess deaths data also captures the number of people dying not directly because of COVID-19, but due to an inability to access treatment for other illnesses because of the redirection of health system capacities to deal with the pandemic, or an outright collapse of these systems. However, it does not capture long term health impacts, such as the suspension of vaccination campaigns against diseases like measles. The COVID-19 pandemic is clearly undoing years of progress in improving health in developing countries. Since 1990, global health indicators have improved spectacularly. Average life expectancy at birth in low-income countries had increased from 51 years in 1990 to 63.7 in 2019. However, emerging evidence shows that this trend has now reversed (Islam et al. 2021). For example, life expectancy for males in South Africa for example declined from 62.4 years in 2020 to 59.3 in 2021 (Medicalxpress 2021).

The second set of impacts on developing countries are economic, and are consequences of lockdowns, quarantine measures and stay-at-home orders aimed to curb the spread of the disease. Many developing countries were quick to act, and implemented lockdown measures early in the pandemic when infections were still low. These included measures like international and domestic travel controls, work-from-home directives, school closures, the cancelation of public events and restrictions on gatherings (Gurara et al. 2020). These measures were very similar to the ones implemented in most developed countries. However, they had a much more severe impact on livelihoods in the developing world. Stay-at-home orders in the developed world were in many countries accompanied by government support to those unable to work under these rules, such as the UK's furlough scheme, or Germany's *Kurzarbeit* programme. However, developing countries, especially low-income ones, were unable to introduce similar schemes due to a lack of budgetary resources, which meant that people had to rely on their savings (if they had any), or go to work regardless, otherwise they would not have been able to support their families. Poor households have been increasingly likely to go hungry, with problems around accessing food being exacerbated by supply chain problems (University of Oxford 2021). Since large segments of the workforce in developing countries were employed informally, they did not qualify for unemployment benefits even if a country had a meaningful safety net scheme (Khamis et al. 2021). These factors made strict containment measures difficult to achieve in the Global South (Bargain and Aminjonov 2020).

Furthermore, many developing countries closed schools, and reopening has been slow, with the World Bank (2021) calling the situation 'the worst crisis to education and learning in a century'. In South Asia and Latin America, students missed 78 per cent of school in the first year of the pandemic (Evans et al. 2021). Home learning was hampered not only by a lack of technology and internet connectivity, but in many cases, especially in rural areas, even electricity. This has led to permanent learning losses, especially for the poorest children in the poorest countries, and affecting girls disproportionately, which 'translates directly into lower earnings and higher poverty rates' (Evans et al. 2021). Even when schools reopened, many families were not able to afford sending their children back, undoing years of progress in increasing school enrolment.

The third channel, the impacts of decisions made in developed countries, bundles together a number of different effects. There are clear economic knock-on effects from lockdowns in developed countries. These have transformed the structure of market demand, with demand rising for some products and decreasing for others. For example, the start of lockdowns in early 2020 led to contraction in demand for a number of commodities, including oil, minerals and agricultural raw materials. A decrease in their prices led to falling export earnings for commodity exporters, again hitting the poor especially through impacts on government welfare schemes (IMF 2020). A second impact of rich world lockdowns related to remittances, an important source of income in many developing countries. Remittances exceeded 5 per cent of GDP in 30 low-income countries in 2019 and have vital poverty reduction effects (UN DESA 2019). As workers, including those of migrant backgrounds, lost their jobs or were put on furlough schemes in rich countries, their ability to support their families in their home countries diminished. According to the World Bank, remittances to low-and-middle income countries contracted by 7 per cent in 2020 and were likely to contract by a further 7.5 per cent in 2021 (Oxford Economics 2021: 1). The repercussions are likely to be felt widely where remittances are an important source of income for many poor families. A third impact relates to reductions in flows of tourists to the developing world, with most developed countries introducing curbs on foreign travel (Neshat et al. 2021). Finally, developing countries needed to compete with countries of the Global North for purchasing scarce medical resources, including personal protective equipment, ventilators, oxygen, drugs and reagents used for the treatment of patients, and vaccines, which developed countries have been accused of 'hoarding' (Dyer 2020).

Proposed policy responses to the pandemic

Many have argued that the effects of the pandemic, through the three channels discussed above, threaten to undo years of progress in global poverty reduction and human development (Marois et al. 2020). According to some estimates, the number of people living below the 1.90 dollar per day poverty line may have increased by at least 68 million in 2020 (Valensisi 2020). A flurry of academic and think tank publications have put forward policy proposals on how best to support developing countries in this situation and mitigate the impacts that the COVID-19 pandemic has on lives and livelihoods. There is a remarkable degree of consensus among these proposals regarding the policy tools that would be necessary to support the countries of the Global South. Given the focus of this book, only the proposals relating to development aid are discussed. These provide a benchmark for the 'ideal' policy response, against which NGDO advocacy can be compared.

Given how effective lockdowns are difficult, if not impossible in developing countries, saving lives and livelihoods needs to go hand-in-hand. To increase compliance with lockdowns, governments in low-income countries must accompany these measures with some form of consumption support or social safety net (Bargain and Aminjonov 2020). Many analysts agree that cash transfers to the poor are the most effective ways for supporting livelihoods, and if these are not possible, food transfers constitute a second-best option (Khamis et al. 2021; Loayza 2020; Erokhin and Gao 2020; Workie et al. 2020). Cash transfers are more effective than job retention schemes when informality is high (Nonvide 2020). These transfers need to reach the poorest even in remote areas, and be delivered in ways to avoid people crowding in markets to decrease risks of transmission. Since developing countries do not have the resources to fund such schemes, increased aid or concessional loans are necessary. Beyond food aid, ensuring access to food also requires countries not to implement policies which restrict global supply, including export bans (Vasilii and Gao 2020), and also support improving the resilience of food supply chains (Workie et al. 2020), or that of local agricultural producers (Valensisi 2020).

While cash and food transfers as well as supporting food systems are the most frequently mentioned policies which donor countries should fund, the literature puts forward a number of further recommendations as well. Donor funding is also required to support developing country health systems in coping with the pandemic (Rodela et al. 2020; Valensisi 2020), such as through aid aimed at increasing capacities, or funding the purchasing of equipment and medical supplies, including vaccines (Loayza 2020). Support for education is also required, through programmes aimed at up-skilling teachers, making schools COVID-safe, as well as encouraging and supporting the most vulnerable in returning to schools (Evans et al. 2021). Further measures donors can take include actions to ensure liquidity, such as debt standstill arrangements and debt relief for indebted developing countries (Valensisi 2020).

Calling on high income country donors to support these specific areas however presupposes that these countries actually have resources to spare, and a willingness to spend them in developing countries. According to the OECD, developing countries would need around 2 trillion dollars to mitigate the impacts of the pandemic, and this amount does not include the financing needed to reach the Sustainable Development Goals (OECD 2021). The pandemic has hit developed countries hard, with their economics contracting and government budget deficits skyrocketing. Previous economic crises have shown that cutting foreign aid in such situations usually carries little political risk, making governments more likely to seek savings in this policy area. Furthermore, COVID-19 is only defeated if it is defeated everywhere, in the form of high global vaccination rates, preventive measures and widely available treatments. This makes foreign aid aimed at supporting developing countries in combating the pandemic a global public good (Loayza 2020), which may give rich countries incentives to free-ride, and wait for others to increase aid. Therefore, ensuring that developed countries at the very least do not decrease their assistance to the Global South is an important policy goal. Monitoring whether increases in funding by donors to specific programmes, such as cash transfers or food aid are actually additional, and not just a redirection of resources already committed to developing countries, is also essential.

Summing up, the main policies through which donors can most effectively support developing countries during the pandemic are providing *additional* aid to programmes on cash transfers, food aid, healthcare (including equipment and vaccines), education for the most vulnerable, and actions related to debt.

NGDO advocacy during the pandemic

This section analyses the degree to which actual European NGDO advocacy during the outbreak and early months of the COVID-19 pandemic was in line with the academic and think tank recommendations discussed above on the 'ideal' policy responses.

Methods

To collect data on NGDO advocacy during the pandemic, a similar approach was used as in Chapter 4, focusing on advocacy-related publications of CONCORD and Oxfam, but with the addition of a third NGDO, Save the Children (STC). In all three cases, a search was performed in the publication repositories of the main global websites of the three organisations, using 'COVID-19', 'coronavirus' and 'pandemic' as search terms. The focus was only on advocacy publications, especially policy briefs, longer reports and open letters, which had a clear foreign aid dimension with specific recommendations for donor countries and international organisations. Other publications, such as ones reporting on the on-the-ground activities of the three organisations, or where there was no link to foreign aid, were excluded. Additionally, the search was restricted to publications from 2020 only. The analysis thus focused on the initial advocacy during the pandemic, and certain topics which emerged later during course of the pandemic, especially the issues around the fairness of global vaccine distribution, were not included.

The search yielded six documents for CONCORD, eight for Oxfam and eight for Save the Children (see Table 8.1 for a full list). The documents were read in detail, and the specific advocacy demands and recommendations were coded in each. There was a strong degree of repetition among these publications: the key advocacy points for each organisation were usually repeated in each of these publications, which gives confidence that no important demand from these three NGDOs was missed.

* Joint paper with CAFOD, Jubilee, AVAAZ, and Global Justice Now.

CONCORD

CONCORD's COVID-19 related advocacy included a wide range of topics, some of which linked directly to the pandemic and were very closely associated with the issues identified in the previous section as needing an urgent donor response. However, CONCORD's publications also included a number of much broader topics, which's links to the pandemic were more tenuous.

The main message in CONDORD's advocacy was that solidarity needed to come first, and that donors must focus on the lives, livelihoods and rights of people, especially the most marginalised. CONCORD's advocacy included all the topics that have been identified above as parts of the 'ideal' policy response to COVID-19. Most importantly, CONCORD called on donors to increase their aid spending, which was not surprising given how this was traditionally the strongest element in the group's advocacy before the pandemic as well (see Chapter 4). CONCORD emphasised that these resources must be additional, and donors must make efforts to target the most vulnerable, both in terms of selecting countries and selecting target groups

Table 8.1 Main COVID-19 related advocacy publications of CONCORD, Oxfam, and Save the Children in 2020

Organisation	*Publication title*
CONCORD	EU global response to COVID-19: Forging a path to an equitable future
	Open letter to Josep Borrell and Jutta Urpalainen
	It's not the end, it's just the beginning: With COVID-19, now is the time to boost aid
	CONCORD recommendations – EU response to the COVID-19 pandemic around the globe
	Responding to COVID-19: Key advocacy messages
	CONCORD analysis of the Communication on the Global EU response to COVID-19
Oxfam	Whatever it takes
	G20 must cancel debt to stop coronavirus 'third wave' devastating developing countries*
	Shelter from the storm. The global need for universal social protection in times of COVID-19
	From catastrophe to catalyst. Can the World Bank make COVID-19 a turning point for building universal and fair public healthcare systems?
	How the coronavirus pandemic exploits the worst aspects of extreme inequality
	How the EU's coronavirus response can work for people
	Oxfam's response to coronavirus
	No one is safe from coronavirus until everyone is. Oxfam coronavirus response report
Save the Children	The hidden impact of COVID-19 on child poverty.
	Beyond the shadow pandemic. Protecting a generation of girls from gender-based violence through COVID-19 to recovery
	Save our education. Protect every child's right to learn in the COVID-19 response and recovery
	Three things to know about Integrated Cash and Voucher Assistance
	COVID-19: Gender equality matters
	Global response plan to COVID 19
	Protect a generation. The impact of COVID-19 on children's lives
	The global girlhood report 2020. How COVID-19 is putting progress in peril

Source: compiled by the author.

within countries. Social protection programmes also featured heavily in CONCORD's publications, including cash transfers and food support. CONCORD also emphasised food and nutrition security, and called on the strengthening of developing country health systems and universal free access to care. Education however received more marginal treatment, although there were some sporadic calls to ensure that children had the possibilities to continue their learning. CONCORD also called for action related to debt, which included not only a suspension of debt payments during the pandemic, but a complete cancellation of these payments, coupled with more systematic debt relief efforts for the poorest countries. Finally, CONCORD emphasised the importance of reaching the most vulnerable and specifically focusing on the protection of their rights. The largest weight in this regard was placed on women and girls, who were seen as disproportionately impacted by the pandemic. This included calling for more gender-based analysis in planning support, and focusing especially on protecting women and girls from gender-based violence.

CONCORD's COVID-19-related advocacy publications however also included a plethora of further calls, demands and recommendations for donors, some of which were not strictly related to the pandemic and recovery from it. The main such topic was the environment. CONCORD made a link between environmental degradation and the origins of COVID-19, and argued that the 'drivers of nature loss and climate change should be prioritised and fully integrated into recovery packages' to build resilience against future pandemics (CONCORD 2020a: 4). In a more radical sense, some CONCORD publications even called for countries to 'steer away from [GDP] growth as the main objective for the economy' (CONCORD 2020b).

CONCORD, as in its pre-pandemic advocacy, also devoted significant space in its COVID-19-related publications to calling for more support for civil society organisations, and also ensuring their greater involvement in decision making. CONCORD argued that the EU needed to ensure that civil society groups could access funds from donors. The EU was also called on to promote the development of frameworks in partner countries which would enable the better functioning of civil society. A further long-standing CONCORD topic which came up in COVID-19 advocacy was domestic taxation. While resource mobilisation was undoubtedly important for addressing the consequences of the pandemic, CONCORD called for a wide variety of broad systemic reforms, including promoting progressive tax systems, addressing tax avoidance, fighting illicit financial flows and lowering the costs of remittances. Another CONCORD demand related to human rights. CONCORD argued that the pandemic may have provided a pretext for authoritarian governments to curb political freedoms and human rights more broadly, and called on donors to ensure that recipient countries respected human rights, civic space, the rule of law and the principles of participatory democracy. Given how these had been problematic areas in most of the developing world even before the pandemic, CONCORD was again calling for systemic change under the guise of pandemic response. A number of further, less frequently mentioned issues in CONCORD's advocacy included calls to promote labour rights and environmental standards, invest in economic sectors or industries contributing to sustainable development and equality, focus support for the private sector on local micro, small and medium-sized enterprises as well as mission-driven enterprises, demanding more from companies both in social and environmental terms, respecting principles of development effectiveness and ensuring policy coherence for development.

CONCORD clearly had too many messages in its COVID-19 related advocacy, and some of these were very broad demands and recommendations calling for systemic global change, linked only indirectly to the pandemic. The potential reasons for this are discussed in the following section, but one impression that emerges is that the vast number of demands dilutes the overall message of how exactly donors need to react to save lives and livelihoods in the developing world.

Oxfam

'Whatever it takes', published in May 2020, was Oxfam's main COVID-19-related advocacy publication (Oxfam 2020a). The title echoes then European Central Bank President Mario Draghi's famous speech in 2012, when he vowed to do 'whatever it takes' to save the common currency, marking a turnaround in the Eurozone crisis. The fact that the EU was able to mobilise hundreds of billions of euros (especially raising 500 billion Euros for the European Stability Mechanism) to save its own economy and the common currency during the crisis, yet has been unable to raise relatively smaller amounts for developing countries, or to address the growing climate crisis, has been a point of reference for NGDOs ever since.

'Whatever it takes' follows a similar vein as CONCORD's advocacy did, i.e. it is more comprehensive and goes well beyond what the recommendations from the literature on the ideal policy response say. The publications has a strong focus on the post-pandemic world and how the international community should use the pandemic to 'build back better'. There is a strong call in the paper for an urgent and massive increase in aid, which must be additional to existing aid budgets. The increase in aid must be used to support health systems, social protection (including funding cash transfers), food security, water, and sanitation. These demands clearly align with the recommendations in the literature. Furthermore, Oxfam argued that aid should be composed of grants instead of loans, and debt problems also need to be addressed. Finally, the increase in aid needs to respect the principles of 'quality' aid.

Going beyond the recommendations in the literature however, 'Whatever it takes' also called for reshaping 'the future of aid to help build more equal and resilient societies, so that humanity is better prepared for future crises' (Oxfam 2020a: 2). Or, as stated in another publication, 'there can be no return to normal' (Oxfam 2020b: 17). This means more aid spending on universal public services is needed, including universal social safety nets and free, quality healthcare – both of these clearly highly ambitious asks for developing countries. Aid should also help 'build a human and planet-centred economy that will keep the chance of limiting global heating to 1.5°C alive' (Oxfam 2020a: 4). Oxfam also called for more support to civil society, to ensure that they can hold governments to account, and that aid should become explicitly feminist with women's rights at its core. As with CONCORD, these recommendations went beyond what was strictly needed to save lives and livelihoods in the pandemic, and pointed to Oxfam re-packaging its long standing advocacy concerns into demands linked to COVID-19.

Further publications by Oxfam during the first year of the pandemic were more thematic, and elaborated on specific areas mentioned in 'Whatever it takes' in more detail. Oxfam, jointly with other organisations, called for the cancellation of all external debt payments by developing countries for 2020 (Oxfam 2020c). In terms of scaling up international funding for social protection, Oxfam put forward ideas about creating a Global Fund for Social Protection that supports low- and middle-income countries in realising social protection for all, funded by aid from the North and the international financial institutions (Oxfam 2020d). Debt cancellation was meant to play an important role here, leaving more resources in developing countries to fund social protection. A specific publication dealt with inequalities, a key topic in Oxfam's pre-pandemic advocacy (see Chapter 4), and how COVID-19 has exacerbated these, with a focus on the poorest, women, and those in refugee camps. Oxfam called for the largest ever economic stimulus in history to help these people and their families through this crisis (Oxfam (2020e). Interestingly, education was relatively missing from Oxfam's advocacy, even though it was an area where Oxfam had significant project activities.

Finally, Oxfam also published a COVID-19-related paper specifically about the EU's global response to the pandemic (Oxfam 2020f). This publication went very much beyond COVID-19 recovery, and called for the EU to reshape its aid to tackle inequality, and also the climate crisis through increased support for the reduction of greenhouse gas emissions and to those affected by the climate crisis. EU support for economic recovery in developing countries (and in member states) needed to focus on building a greener world. The publication also dealt with the EU's track record in migration management, calling attention to the horrific conditions in Greek and other refugee camps, where there was a lack of basic necessities and healthcare. Oxfam also called on the EU to take a lead in creating greater tax justice, by supporting taxes on wealth, speculative financial transactions, and corporate profits. As seen in Chapter 4, these have been long standing demands of Oxfam, and while it is an exaggeration to say that they have nothing to do with the pandemic, demanding reforms in these areas clearly goes beyond pandemic recovery.

The messages sent in Oxfam's advocacy are therefore very similar to those in CONCORD's. They include a similarly wide range of topics, and generally use pandemic-related advocacy to campaign for the same issues around the need for global systemic change which Oxfam advocated for before the pandemic as well.

Save the Children

As opposed to Oxfam's more generalist and broad activities, STC is a specialised development NGO, focusing on supporting child welfare and rights. STC's advocacy priorities for the pandemic were most comprehensively listed in its paper entitled 'Global Response Plan to COVID 19. Protecting a Generation of Children', published in May 2020 (Save the Children 2020a). In this report, STC highlighted four pillars of action during the pandemic, which related both to its own programmes and activities, but also to advocacy towards donors. The first pillar focused on mitigating the impact of COVID-19 on child survival, where STC called on donors to increase their funding for public health and nutrition systems, which should be free at the point of use, especially for vulnerable children. The second pillar was about ensuring that children learned and were able to return to school. Here donors needed to increase aid for education, and support developing country governments in ensuring the continuity of learning during lockdowns. The third pillar was about supporting family survival and food security through safety nets. Developing countries were called upon to create (or expand) universal child benefits, the most effective form of which were cash transfers. To fund these, similarly to Oxfam, STC also promoted the idea of donors 'coming together' to finance a Global Fund for Social Protection. Governments should also ensure adequate access to affordable food. The final pillar was about protecting children from exploitation and abuse. While all four pillars placed a strong emphasis on children from more vulnerable backgrounds (including girls, those from the poorest families, those living in remote rural areas, children living in conflict zones, non-binary and transgender children, migrant and refugee children, and children with disabilities; see also Loperfido and Burgess 2020), the fourth focused explicitly on protecting their lives and rights. Among others, STC called on donors to ensure that their COVID-19 responses prioritised and funded child protection. The focus was especially on protecting girls from various forms of gender-based violence, including early and forced marriage. Social services and humanitarian workers also required funding and protective equipment to continue their work in protecting children, and donors needed to fund the scale-up of emergency family-based care. Finally, STC called for warring parties in conflict zones to de-escalate conflicts and agree to cease fires.

As with Oxfam, STC also elaborated each of these advocacy priorities in more detail in specialised reports. These did not really add new priorities, but rather developed specific recommendations for donor countries and organisations, as well as partner country governments. STC's flagship advocacy report on education during the pandemic, 'Save our Education. Protect every child's right to learn in the COVID-19 response and recovery' (Warren and Wagner 2020) for example illustrated the immense impact the pandemic had on children's possibilities to learn, and how it required a 'coordinated global education response that was well planned, adequately monitored and accountable' (Warren and Wagner 2020: v). Calls for donors to increase funding were central in this report: donors should provide supplementary funding to the World Bank's International Development Association (IDA), cancel all debt service payments for 2020 and ensure that the resources this freed up were spent on education. Donor governments should also support developing countries in raising funds by tackling illicit financial flows and tax avoidance, and by strengthening international tax cooperation.

An emerging picture from STC's advocacy, especially when compared with that of CONCORD and Oxfam, is that it was much more focused on the pandemic, and did not bring in calls for broad systemic change to the same degree. While there were calls to 'build back better' or for tax justice as mentioned above, these were fairly specific, and not as broad ranging as the ones seen with the other organisations. Environmental sustainability was hardly mentioned, and while global financial and tax justice did appear, it was not a central call and was linked very closely to raising resources for education. Similarly, all calls for greater aid flows were tied to specific purposes, unlike CONCORD's calls which seemed to imply that reaching the 0.7 per cent aid target was a good thing in itself, with only general level discussions on how to spend the increases. STC also emphasised the need to fund civil society (Save the Children 2020b), but these calls were again more marginal than in the case of CONCORD and Oxfam, and focused on specific types of organisations, especially girls' grassroots groups.

A key observation therefore is that STC did not really bundle long-standing NGDO advocacy demands with its COVID-19 advocacy, unlike CONCORD and Oxfam. It is possible to argue that this may have made its advocacy more targeted and effective, as it was very specific to the given situation and not diluted by longer term messages.

Explaining COVID-19 advocacy

The different natures of the three organisations shed some light on their different approaches to advocacy. CONCORD is an advocacy body which needs to cater to all of its members, which may lead to 'common denominator' type advocacy and the need to include a wide number of topics. Oxfam works on wide number of topics and may have felt the need to reflect all of these in its advocacy, while STC's more narrow approach may be a consequence of its more specialised focus. Further insights can be derived by applying the book's analytical framework to make sense of NGDO advocacy priorities during the pandemic. As introduced in Chapter 2, the framework in this book uses the topic's politicisation, its potential impact on NGDO funding, and its relationship with NGDO moral vision as explanatory variables of Northern NGDO advocacy.

The politicisation of the pandemic has obviously been greater than that of any other issue in past decades. It has been at the centre of political debates in all European countries. Positions on issues associated with the pandemic, such as quarantines and lockdowns, compulsory mask wearing, or attitudes towards vaccination seem to have been driven much more strongly by politics than the actual scientific evidence behind them (Ward et al. 2020; Wong and Claypool 2021). No actor with a role in politics, including advocacy stakeholders like NGDOs, could avoid dealing with the topic, as especially during the first months of the pandemic, it was practically 'the only' issue.

The overwhelmingly strong politicisation of the pandemic means that NGDOs needed to deal with the issue, as neglecting it could have led to criticisms of playing down the pandemic or ignoring it. In fact, if one looks at the publications of the three groups during the first months of the pandemic, there is hardly anything that does not deal with the COVID-19. While this picture gradually changed, and the relative political salience of the pandemic waned as people realised that other aspects of life needed to continue, it has nonetheless remained highly politicised throughout 2020 and 2021.

This means that to get the attention of their policy audiences, and also the broader public, NGDOs needed to focus on the pandemic in their advocacy, otherwise they risked becoming irrelevant or out of touch. However, they may not have wanted to drop everything they have been working for previously, and aimed to maintain a consistent message about the longer term issues they had been campaigning for. This may further explain why CONCORD and Oxfam decided to link their previous advocacy and calls for systemic global change to their COVID-19 advocacy. They may have even seen an opportunity to amplify those messages through the pandemic, and ensure that it reaches broader audiences. Both organisations portrayed the pandemic as proof that the global economic order is environmentally and socially unsustainable, which strengthened their earlier messages. Oxfam's paper 'How the EU's coronavirus response can work for people' (Oxfam 2020f) is evidence of how the pandemic was used instrumentally to call attention to long lasting problems and pre-COVID advocacy topics. Linking previous and broader advocacy messages to COVID-19 thus makes sense from this perspective, even if it leads to too many (and too broad) demands.

Access to funding may have been an important consideration for all three organisations. Calls for increasing aid were prominent with all three organisations, and mostly these calls focused on increasing aid to sectors where NGDOs were active, especially education, health and social protection. There were also calls in case of all three organisations for greater involvement of the civil sector in planning and allocating aid, and while in many cases this referred to local, Southern groups, large Northern NGDOs were often the mediators between official donors and these groups (see Chapter 3). Clearly, NGDOs were interested in ensuring that their pre-COVID funding did not get crowded out or diverted by donors, and hence the importance of additional funding was emphasised.

Can differences in funding structures explain differences between the three groups, but especially between Oxfam and STC, given how CONCORD is a purely advocacy-focused association? As shown in Chapter 5, official (government and multilateral) sources of funding are much more important for STC than they are for Oxfam: between 2015 and 2019, close to 60 per cent of STC's funding came from bilateral and multilateral donors, whereas this share for Oxfam was only 38 per cent (see Figure 5.1 in Chapter 5). Thus, STC may have greater interests in ensuring that it does not demand actions which may undermine its access to official resources, including funding from the EU.

STC's advocacy demands are potentially more compatible with the EU's world view as those of Oxfam. Oxfam's advocacy makes a very clear link between the pandemic and what it views as an economically, socially and environmentally dysfunctional global order. Oxfam calls on the EU and other actors to spearhead the transformation of global capitalism into a more equitable and sustainable system, with much higher taxes on the wealthy and broader global tax justice, as well as drastic reductions in carbon emissions (Oxfam 2020f). STC's advocacy on the other hand, as discussed, does not put forward such radical demands, and instead articulates very specific actions donors should implement. Holden (2019), focusing on trade policy and sustainability, showed the clear differences between NGOs' interventionist, radically anti-capitalist views and the EU's 'nuanced, but essentially neoliberal approach to trade and development' (Holden 2019: 958; see also Young and Peterson 2013; Siles-Brügge 2014). As argued by Holden, the EU, while adapting some NGO rhetoric on moral/human imperatives in development, has been highly resistive of the more radical demands. Further research has shown that the EU is more likely to fund NGOs that have similar world views to it and promote its values (Mahoney and Beckstrand 2011). Too radical demands therefore may be counterproductive for NGDOs, not only in terms of getting their voice heard and their ability to influence policy, but also potentially for their access to funding. This may explain STC's more cautious position.

Different moral visions can also explain differences between the three groups. STC is a specialised organisation, and its moral vision focuses on children, championing 'the rights and interests of children worldwide, putting the most vulnerable children first' (Save the Children n.d.). Oxfam however has a much broader mandate, 'fighting inequality to end poverty and injustice' (Oxfam n.d.), and so does CONCORD, which needs to amalgamate the positions of all its members. This means that STC's advocacy messages, focusing on children, can be packaged much more succinctly and clearly (such as around four pillars, compared to CONCORD's long lists and Oxfam's very diverse messaging). CONCORD focuses only on advocacy, and it needs to inclusively accommodate the diverse views and moral visions of all its members, which include organisations campaigning for a number of issues linked to development and poverty reduction, including tax justice or nature conservation. Oxfam's activities also cover a wide range of areas: water, women's rights, climate change, ending hunger, health, education and humanitarian response. This may create a need for the organisation to ensure that all of the priorities it worked on pre-COVID appear in its COVID advocacy as well, to accurately reflect its moral vision.

The analytical framework therefore provides some explanation for the differences in the COVID-19 related advocacy of the three groups. The broad messages of Oxfam and CONCORD can best be explained by the nature and moral visions of the organisations. STC's moral vision is focused more narrowly on (vulnerable) children, which allows for more focused advocacy messages. The other two variables in the framework provide further nuance to this. The extremely high politicisation and political salience of the COVID-19 pandemic have given incentives for organisations to package their pre-existing advocacy messages into their COVID-related advocacy. Oxfam, which was less dependent on official and EU funding for its programmes than STC, seemed to have been keener to do this, while STC may have been more cautious not to include messages and demands that were less compatible with the EU's world view, and thus could have jeopardised its potential influence and access to funds.

These three cases of course do not provide a comprehensive picture of NGDO advocacy during the pandemic, even if CONCORD claims to speak for the entire sector. They do however show that there is variation in COVID-19-relataed advocacy among NGDOs, and that not all of this advocacy was (strictly speaking) about saving lives and livelihoods during the pandemic. These cases again provide evidence of how strategically development NGOs behave in their advocacy, for example by packaging less politically salient topics together with demands directly linked to the pandemic.

References

Bargain, O. & Aminjonov, U. (2020). Between a Rock and a Hard Place: Poverty and Covid-19 in Developing Countries. IZA Discussion Paper 13297.

Dyer, O. (2020). Covid-19: Many Poor Countries Will See Almost no Vaccine Next Year, Aid Groups Warn. *BMJ: British Medical Journal* 371: m4809. https://doi.org/10.1136/bmj.m4809.

CONCORD (2020a). Recommendations for EU Response to the COVID-19 Pandemic Around the Globe. https://concordeurope.org/resource/recommendations-to-the-covid-19-pandemic-around-the-globe/.

CONCORD (2020b). COVID-19 Key Advocacy Messages. https://concordeurope.org/resource/covid-19-key-advocacy-messages/.

Erokhin, V. & Gao, T. (2020). Impacts of COVID-19 on Trade and Economic Aspects of Food Security: Evidence from 45 Developing Countries. *International Journal of Environmental Research and Public Health* 17 (16): 5775. https://doi.org/10.3390/ijerph17165775.

Evans, D., Hares, S., Mendez Acosta, A. & Saintis, C. (2021). It's Been a Year Since Schools Started to Close Due to COVID-19. Centre for Global Development. https://www.cgdev.org/blog/its-been-year-schools-started-close-due-covid-19.

Gill, I. & Schellekens, P. (2021). COVID-19 is a Developing Country Pandemic. Brookings Institute. https://www.brookings.edu/blog/future-development/2021/05/27/covid-19-is-a-developing-country-pandemic/.

Gurara, D., Fabrizio, S. & Wiegand, J. (2020). COVID-19: Without Help, Low-income Developing Countries Risk a Lost Decade. IMF. https://blogs.imf.org/2020/08/27/covid-19-without-help-low-income-developing-countries-risk-a-lost-decade/.

Holden, P. (2019) Finding Common Ground? European Union and European Civil Society Framing of the Role of Trade in the Sustainable Development Goals, *JCMS: Journal of Common Market Studies* 57: 956–976. https://doi.org/10.1111/jcms.12862.

IMF (2020). World Economic Outlook, Commodity Special Feature. https://www.imf.org/-/media/Files/Research/CommodityPrices/WEOSpecialFeature/CSFApril2020.ashx.

Islam, N., Jdanov, D. A., Shkolnikov, V. M., Khunti, K., Kawachi, I. & White, M. (2021). Effects of Covid-19 Pandemic on Life Expectancy and Premature Mortality in 2020: Time Series Analysis in 37 Countries. *BMJ: British Medical Journal* 375: e066768. https://doi.org/10.1136/bmj-2021-066768.

Khamis, M., Prinz, D., Newhouse, D., Palacios-Lopez, A., Pape, U. & Weber, M., (2021). The Early Labor Market Impacts of COVID-19 in Developing Countries: Evidence from High-Frequency Phone Surveys. World Bank Jobs Working Paper 58.

Lawal, Y. (2021). Africa's Low COVID-19 Mortality Rate: A Paradox? *International Journal of Infectious Diseases* 102: 118–122. https://doi.org/10.1016/j.ijid.2020.10.038.

Loayza, N. (2020). Costs and Trade-offs in the Fight Against the Covid-19 Pandemic: A Developing Country Perspective. World Bank Research and Policy Briefs 148535.

Loperfido, L. & Burgess, M. (2020). *The Hidden Impact of COVID-19 on Child Poverty*. London: Save the Children International.

Mahoney, C. & Beckstrand, M. J. (2011). Following the Money: European Union Funding of Civil Society Organizations. *JCMS: Journal of Common Market Studies* 49: 1339–1361. https://doi.org/10.1111/j.1468-5965.2011.02197.x.

Marois, G., Muttarak, R. & Scherbov, S. (2020). Assessing the Potential Impact of COVID-19 on Life Expectancy. *PLoS ONE* 15 (9): e0238678. https://doi.org/10.1371/journal.pone.0238678.

Medicalxpress (2021). COVID Slashes Life Expectancy in South Africa. https://medicalxpress.com/news/2021-07-covid-slashes-life-south-africa.html.

Neshat, N., Moayedfar, S., Rezaee, K. & Biuki, N. A. (2021). Sustainable Planning of Developing Tourism Destinations after COVID-19 Outbreak: A Deep Learning Approach. *Journal of Policy Research in Tourism, Leisure and Events*. https://doi.org/10.1080/19407963.2021.1970578.

Nonvide, G. M. A. (2020). Policy for Limiting the Poverty Impact of COVID-19 in Africa. In: Djankov, S. & Panizza, U. (eds) *COVID-19 in Developing Economies*. London: CEPR Press, pp. 214–219.

OECD (2021). *Development Co-operation Report 2020: Learning from Crises, Building Resilience*. Paris: OECD.

Oxfam (2020a). Whatever It Takes: Aid and the Coronavirus Pandemic. https://www.oxfam.org/en/research/whatever-it-takes-aid-and-coronavirus-pandemic.

Oxfam (2020b). No One is Safe from Coronavirus until Everyone is. Oxfam Coronavirus Response Report. https://www.oxfam.org/en/research/no-one-safe-coronavirus-until-everyone.

Oxfam (2020c). G20 Must Cancel Debt to Stop Coronavirus "Third Wave" Devastating Developing Countries. https://www.oxfam.org/fr/node/12401.

Oxfam (2020d). Shelter from the Storm. The Global Need for Universal Social Protection in Times of COVID-19. https://www.oxfam.org/en/research/shelter-storm-global-need-universal-social-protection-times-covid-19.

Oxfam (2020e). How the Coronavirus Pandemic Exploits the Worst Aspects of Extreme Inequality. https://www.oxfam.org/en/how-coronavirus-pandemic-exploits-worst-aspects-extreme-inequality.

Oxfam (2020f). How the EU's Coronavirus Response Can Work for People. https://www.oxfam.org/en/eu/how-eus-coronavirus-response-can-work-people.

Oxfam (n.d.). About Us. https://www.oxfam.org/en/what-we-do/about.

Oxford Economics (2021). The Remittance Effect: A Lifeline for Developing Economies through the Pandemic and into Recovery. https://www.oxfordeconomics.com/recent-releases/The-remittance-effect-A-lifeline-for-developing-economies-through-the-pandemic-and-into-recovery.

Ritchie, H. & Roser, M. (2019). Age Structure. Our World in Data. https://ourworldindata.org/age-structure.

Rodela, T. T., Tasnim, S., Mazumber, H., Faizah, F., Sultana, A. & Hossain, M. (2020). Economic Impacts of Coronavirus Disease (COVID-19) in Developing Countries. Economic Impacts of COVID-19: Working Paper Series. https://doi.org/10.31235/osf.io/wygpk.

Save the Children (2020a). Global Response Plan to COVID 19. Protecting a Generation of Children. https://resourcecentre.savethechildren.net/pdf/stc_protect_a_generation_aw_final.pdf/.

Save the Children (2020b). The Global Girlhood Report 2020. How COVID-19 is Putting Progress in Peril. https://www.savethechildren.org/content/dam/usa/reports/ed-cp/global-girlhood-report-2020.pdf.

Save the Children (n.d.) Who We Are. https://www.savethechildren.net/about-us/who-we-are.

Siles-Brügge, G. (2014). *Constructing European Union Trade Policy*. London: Palgrave Macmillan.

The Economist (2021). Covid-19 Data. The Pandemic's True Death Toll. https://www.economist.com/graphic-detail/coronavirus-excess-deaths-estimates.

UN DESA (2019). Remittances Matter: 8 Facts You Don't Know About the Money Migrants Send Back Home. https://www.un.org/development/desa/en/news/population/remittances-matter.html.

University of Oxford (2021). COVID-19: Inequalities Widen for Poorest Young People in Developing Countries. https://www.ox.ac.uk/news/2021-03-04-covid-19-inequalities-widen-poorest-young-people-developing-countries.

Valensisi, G. (2020). COVID-19 and Global Poverty: A Preliminary Assessment. In: Djankov, S. & Panizza, U. (eds) *COVID-19 in Developing Economies*. London: CEPR Press, pp. 188–199.

Ward, J. K., Alleaume, C., Peretti-Watel, P., Seror, V., Cortaredona, S., Launay, O., Raude, J., Verger, P., Beck, F., Legleye, S., L'Haridon, O. & Ward, J. (2020). The French Public's Attitudes to a Future COVID-19 Vaccine: The Politicization of a Public Health Issue. *Social Science & Medicine* 265: 113414. https://doi.org/10.1016/j.socscimed.2020.113414.

Warren, H. & Wagner, E. (2020). Save our Education. Protect Every Child's Right to Learn in the COVID-19 Response and Recovery. https://resourcecentre.savethechildren.net/pdf/save_our_education_0.pdf/.

Wong, J. & Claypool, E. (2021). Narratives, Masks and COVID-19: A Qualitative Reflection. *Qualitative Social Work* 20 (1–2): 206–213. https://doi.org/10.1177/1473325020973330.

Workie, E., Mackolil, J., Nyika, J. & Ramadas, S. (2020). Deciphering the Impact of COVID-19 Pandemic on Food Security, Agriculture, and Livelihoods: A Review of the Evidence from Developing Countries. *Current Research in Environmental Sustainability* 2: 100014. https://doi.org/10.1016/j.crsust.2020.100014.

World Bank (2021). Urgent, Effective Action Required to Quell the Impact of COVID-19 on Education Worldwide. https://www.worldbank.org/en/news/immersive-story/2021/01/22/urgent-effective-action-required-to-quell-the-impact-of-covid-19-on-education-worldwide.

Young, A. & Peterson, J. (2013). 'We Care About You, But …': The Politics of EU Trade Policy and Development. *Cambridge Review of International Affairs* 26 (3): 497–518. https://doi.org/10.1080/09557571.2012.734782.

9 Concluding thoughts

This book has provided a comprehensive picture about the European development NGO sector's advocacy, and the incentives which drive this advocacy and shape its contents. The introductory chapter gave a detailed overview of the book's arguments and findings, so these are not repeated here in detail. It does make sense however to summarise the main findings along the book's five research aims.

The book's first aim was to map the European development NGO community and its advocacy behaviour. A detailed overview of the sector's history and population ecology has revealed a highly diverse and heterogeneous set of organisations, ranging from large multinational networks to essentially single person NGDOs. Although exact numbers are difficult to come by, it is clear that there is a high degree of concentration in the sector, with about two dozen large networks accounting for most of the activities and advocacy undertaken by European NGDOs. Advocacy towards the EU is coordinated by CONCORD, the sector's pan-European umbrella group, which represents both member state level umbrella groups, as well as the largest multinational networks.

Second, the book aimed to analyse the contents of NGDO advocacy. The empirical analysis provided a detailed topic map for the advocacy of CONCORD between 2006 and 2018 and Oxfam, one of the most visible multinational networks, between 2008 and 2018. A number of interesting and novel findings emerged from this mapping. The European NGDO community has been both reactive and proactive in its advocacy, although it was the more reactive elements which dominated: much of the advocacy reacted to the policy discussions and topics on the agendas of the EU institutions. Examples of this included the contestation of using aid to leverage private sector investments and diverting development funding to manage migration. However, there were instances of proactive advocacy as well, where NGDOs put forward creative ideas on how to increase European support for poverty reduction in the Global South. Most notably, these included calls for more 'genuine' aid: this refers to aid that actually reaches the partner countries, and is not 'inflated' with expenditures which are spent in the donor country.

As its third aim, the book examined the funding structure of the European NGDO community, and that of individual NGDOs. The analysis

DOI: 10.4324/9780367861872-9

confirmed previous findings on how Western European NGDOs were much more successful in obtaining EU funding than their counterparts in the Eastern member states, and it also painted a picture about the relative differences in (financial) strength between the various national NGDO sectors. The data supported the idea of how NGDOs engaged in 'venue shopping' to ensure an optimal funding mix. However, there was also evidence of 'winner takes all' situations, referring to countries with robust national funding systems which strengthen local NGDOs to perform well in winning EU funding as well (Ireland was the most notable example of this). For the largest NGDOs, the EU was generally not an important source of funding, as they had highly diversified funding structures. Grassroots funding however accounted for only a relatively small portion of total incomes for most of these large groups, which reinforced notions on how they have become professionalised 'grant-seeking machines'.

The fourth aim was to analyse how the various motivations which push NGDOs to engage in advocacy (moral vision, funding concerns, and the need to build/maintain a 'good' reputation) shape the contents of their advocacy behaviour, especially towards the EU. Using the book's theoretical framework, the advocacy topic map mentioned above, as well as a number of qualitative interviews with NGDO staff, the analysis revealed that a significant part of NGDO advocacy behaviour was consistent with behaviour one could expect based on their need to ensure access to funding. Calls for more aid, greater NGDO involvement in development policy making, or contesting changes that would increase competition for aid were all examples of this. Direct evidence for the role of funding concerns however was relatively scarce. Moral motivations, and the need to uphold a reputation as being morally driven were also present, especially in cases where a topic was highly politicised. The EU's diversion of aid to manage migration following the 2015 refugee crisis was the most visible example of this, where NGDOs took a moral position despite the fact that this position did not have much public support across most EU member states. A key finding therefore is that the motivations driving NGDO advocacy need to be looked at within the specific policy context, and generalisations about single factors which drive NGDO behaviour can be overly simplistic. A case study of NGDO reactions to, and engagement with, the EU's Emergency Trust Fund for Africa nuanced this even further, showing that even if NGDOs gave in to financial temptations, they put in place strategies to mitigate any negative fallout this may have on their reputation as morally driven actors.

The book's final aim was to examine NGDO advocacy specifically during the COVID-19 pandemic. The chapter mapped the contents of European NGDO advocacy during the first year of the pandemic, and compared the topics promoted by NGDOs to a benchmark set of 'ideal' COVID-19 support and recovery policies, as put forward by the academic literature and various policy-oriented think tank papers. The key finding was that NGDOs, specifically CONCORD and Oxfam, used the pandemic to call for broad systemic global change, and to draw attention to their long-standing demands, regardless of whether these were necessary for saving lives and livelihoods during the pandemic or not. Another NGDO, Save the Children however had advocacy rather tightly focused around supporting children during the pandemic. The book's theoretical framework proved useful in explaining these differences: the different moral visions of the three organisations, as well as the extremely high degree of the COVID-19 pandemic's politicisation, which potentially gave higher visibility to advocacy demands, proved useful in shedding light on potential drivers of NGDO choices. Funding concerns may have also played a role: Save the Children, far more dependent on EU funding than Oxfam, may have been more cautious and refrained from including advocacy messages that were seen as less compatible with the EU's world view.

The main, overarching message of the book is a call to embrace complexity when analysing the motivations of NGDOs. Painting them as 'saintly' or 'money hungry' are both unrealistic simplifications. Their drivers, at least in the case of advocacy and lobbying, are complex, and interact with each other in different ways, depending on the policy in question, and also the characteristics of the NGDO itself. While financial interests matter, the book showed that the need to ensure their credibility and uphold their reputation as morally driven actors and as champions of the global poor is equally important for NGDOs. This limits how much their financial interest can impact their actions.

The remainder of this brief concluding chapter reflects on two further topics, and how these can provide fruitful areas for future research: the impact of NGDO advocacy and the actual influence these groups have on the making of international development policy in the EU, and the relationship between NGDOs and their grassroots.

In the grand scheme of things, NGDOs do not look to be strongly influential. With the exception of some member states, levels of official aid by European donors have not increased visibly between 2006 and 2020, hovering between 0.27 per cent and 0.32 per cent of GNI (OECD 2021). The definition of official development assistance (ODA) has not been changed to reflect NGDO concerns around inflated aid. Aid continues to be diverted to manage migration: even though the EU Trust Fund for Africa is now being wound down, its approach has been mainstreamed into the EU's main development financing instrument for the 2021–2027 financial cycle, the Neighbourhood, Development and International Cooperation Instrument (NDICI). European donors are increasingly focusing on leveraging funds from the private sector for development, despite NGDO concerns about the effectiveness of this in terms of poverty reduction. The EU's Global Gateway initiative, announced in 2021, aims to raise 300 billion Euros by 2027 for investments in developing countries, and relies heavily on private sector blending and guarantees to reach this goal. While a more sophisticated analysis could reveal some finer details, the lack of correlation between NGDO positions and EU policies on these and other issues hints at limited influence at best. NGDO concerns have clearly not changed the EU's direction of travel. NGDOs may of course have had some less visible impacts on EU development policy, and there is no counter-factual data available to determine how EU development policy would have evolved in the absence of NGDOs. There is some evidence in the literature of NGDOs having an impact on EU-level development policy discourses (see e.g. Holden 2019), but this literature is rather thin, with a very small number of contributions focused on specific case studies.

Examining the impact of NGDO advocacy was not a goal of this book, but it is clearly an area that needs more attention. Nonetheless, the insights derived in this book regarding the contents of NGDO advocacy do provide at least two pointers regarding potential effectiveness, and how it should be understood and examined.

First, driven by moral vision and the need to visibly signal this to maintain reputation, NGDOs often put forward unrealistic or utopian advocacy demands. While donors have committed to providing 0.7 per cent ODA, most have never reached this target in the past, and deadlines to achieve it have been repeatedly missed. One needs to wonder how realistic it is to expect rich countries to actually increase ODA, not to mention 'genuine' ODA, given the vast number of competing budgetary priorities, especially following the massive expenditures many European countries incurred during the COVID-19 pandemic. NGDO calls for systematic global transformation are potentially even more unrealistic. NGDOs are also mostly reactive in their advocacy, and very often aim to block proposals and changes, most recently in the cases of diverting aid to manage migration or to leverage private sector funding. Utopistic demands and not being constructive on other topics are useful for signalling moral vision, and potentially for attracting funding from some sources, especially grassroots, but less so for building pragmatic cooperation with policy makers and achieving influence.

Second, NGDOs are also competing with other actors for influence over EU development policy. Corporate lobbyists are also present in this policy area (see e.g. Koff and Maganda 2016), and potentially wield much greater resources for influencing donors than NGDOs do. NGOs from other sectors, most notably environmental groups, are also possible competitors, and they are again potentially better endowed than development NGOs. More broadly and as briefly alluded to above, NGDOs compete for taxpayer resources, and so also have to compete with numerous other societal interests and spending priorities, many of which have direct impacts on the daily lives of taxpayers. The literature looking at NGDO influence in most cases fails to account for this competitive environment. Policy makers are bombarded with different messages coming from different groups, and while NGDOs usually have relatively distinct (and as mentioned above, often utopian) positions, they need to work towards ensuring that these are communicated and argued as strongly as possible. Societal resonance is important here: NGDOs need to show to policy makers not only how efficient and credible they are, but also that their positions have societal support.

This takes us to the question of how representative Northern NGDOs really are of the societies from which they originate and raise their resources in, and specifically what relationships they have with their grassroots. It is often mentioned that Northern NGDOs need to 'reconnect' with their grassroots. The argument is usually centred around how, through an excessive focus on obtaining funds from official donors, NGDOs prioritise accountability towards donors, and not towards the civil society they are meant to represent. Professionalisation has meant that many aid workers have close understandings of the international development system, but perhaps weaker ones of societal preferences in their home countries. In this sense, so the argument goes, lower levels of official funding would actually have positive impacts on the European NGDO community. They would need to raise more of their funding from Western citizens, and thus potentially become more representative of the societies from where they originate. It would also allow them to focus more on the needs of their beneficiary communities in the Global South, and be less pressured to follow the interests and priorities of official or other large donors. There would also be less need for their advocacy to serve organisational and financial interests, making it more genuinely aligned with moral visions. And finally, as discussed above, it could make their advocacy more effective by allowing them to claim that they represent the preferences of citizens.

One side effect however is that it is unlikely that NGDOs would be able to make up for all lost official funding and their activities in developing countries would suffer. If we assume that financial interests drive at least some NGDO advocacy, then the lack of official funding would mean fewer incentives to engage in advocacy. Little official funding, or none at all, means that NGDOs would have a lower stake in donor policies, and may choose to concentrate their efforts elsewhere. The result may not be more morally driven and potentially more effective advocacy, but less advocacy overall towards donors. This may not be desirable. As shown in this book, NGDO advocacy is vibrant and diverse, and although not discussed in detail, it surely puts at least some reputational pressure on the EU institutions and member state governments. Less advocacy in the form of fewer publication, less joint NGDO action and fewer contacts between NGDOs and policymakers would result in international development policies which are less reflective of the needs of the poor. Funding from donors therefore, even if it does distort the topics which NGDOs prioritise and the policies they call for in their advocacy, gives them a material stake in development policy and thus an additional incentive to attempt to shape it. This can be an interesting avenue for further research. While counter-factual data does not exist on 'what would happen if European governments stopped funding NGDOs', official NGDO funding levels between European countries do differ. Exploiting this natural variation can allow for cross-national comparison to determine whether NGDOs engage in lower degrees of advocacy in countries which provide less official funding to them.

References

Koff, H. & Maganda, C. (2016). The EU and The Human Right to Water and Sanitation: Normative Coherence as the Key to Transformative Development. *European Journal of Development Research* 28: 91–110. https://doi.org/10.1057/ejdr.2015.77.

Holden, P. (2019). Finding Common Ground? European Union and European Civil Society Framing of the Role of Trade in the Sustainable Development Goals. *JCMS: Journal of Common Market Studies* 57: 956–976. https://doi.org/10.1111/jcms.12862.

OECD (2021). Development Finance Data. https://www.oecd.org/dac/financing-sustainable-development/development-finance-data/.

Index